The Grammar Dimension in Instructed Second Language Learning

Advances in Instructed Second Language Acquisition Research Series

Series Editor Alessandro Benati, University of Greenwich, UK.

The mission of this series is to publish new theoretical insights in Instructed Second Language Acquisition (SLA) research that advance our understanding of how languages are learnt and should be taught. Research in Instructed SLA has addressed questions related to the degree to which any form of external manipulation (e.g. grammar instruction, input manipulation, etc.) can affect language development. The main purpose of research in instructed SLA is to establish how classroom language learning takes place and how an understanding of SLA contributes to language teaching.

Despite the clear relationship between theory and research in SLA, and language practice, there are still very few cross-references between these areas. This series will publish research in instructed SLA that bridges this gap and provide academics with a set of theoretical principles for language teaching and acquisition. The calibre of research will inspire scholars and practitioners to learn more about acquisition and to reflect on their language teaching practices more generally.

Task Sequencing and Instructed Second Language Learning
Edited by Melissa Baralt, Roger Gilabert and Peter Robinson

The Developmental Dimension in Instructed Second Language Learning
The L2 Acquisition of Object Pronouns in Spanish
Paul A. Malovrh

The Interactional Feedback Dimension in Instructed Second Language Learning
Linking Theory, Research, and Practice
Hossein Nassaji

The Metalinguistic Dimension in Instructed Second Language Learning
Edited by Karen Roehr

The Grammar Dimension in Instructed Second Language Learning

Edited by Alessandro Benati,
Cécile Laval and María J. Arche

Advances in Instructed Second Language
Acquisition Research

BLOOMSBURY
LONDON · NEW DELHI · NEW YORK · SYDNEY

Bloomsbury Academic

An imprint of Bloomsbury Publishing Plc

50 Bedford Square	1385 Broadway
London	New York
WC1B 3DP	NY 10018
UK	USA

www.bloomsbury.com

Bloomsbury is a registered trade mark of Bloomsbury Publishing Plc

First published 2014

© Alessandro Benati, Cécile Laval, María J. Arche and contributors 2014

Alessandro Benati, Cécile Laval and María J. Arche have asserted their right under the
Copyright, Designs and Patents Act, 1988, to be identified as Editors of this work.

British Library Cataloguing-in-Publication Data
A catalogue record for this book is available from the British Library.

ISBN: HB: 978-1-4411-6204-5
ePDF: 978-1-4411-4865-0
ePub: 978-1-4411-1501-0

Library of Congress Cataloging-in-Publication Data
The grammar dimension in instructed second language learning/Edited by Alessandro Benati,
Cécile Laval and María J. Arche.
pages cm. – (Advances in Instructed Second Language Acquisition Research)
Includes bibliographical references and index.
ISBN 978-1-4411-6204-5 (hardcover) – ISBN 978-1-4411-1501-0 (epub) –
ISBN 978-1-4411-4865-0 (epdf) 1. Language and languages–Study and teaching.
2. Grammar, Comparative and general–Study and teaching. 3.
Language and languages–Grammars. I. Benati, Alessandro G. editor of compilation.
II. Laval, Cécile. editor of compilation. III. Arche, María J.
editor of compilation.
P53.412.G73 2013
418.0071–dc23
2013033650

Typeset by Deanta Global Publishing Services, Chennai, India
Printed and bound in Great Britain

Contents

List of Contributors

María J. Arche is a senior lecturer in Spanish and Linguistics at the University of Greenwich in London. Her research falls within the syntax-semantics interface in both adult and second language learners' grammars, with a special interest in tense, aspect and argument structure. She has published a monograph entitled *Individuals in Time: Tense, Aspect and the Individual/Stage Level Distinction* (John Benjamins Publishing, 2006). She is currently editing a special issue on aspect across languages for *Natural Language and Linguistic Theory* and another one for *Lingua* entitled *Aspect and Argument Structure of Adjectives and Participles*.

Tanja Angelovska holds a PhD in English Linguistics and Language Teaching from University of Munich (LMU), Germany. She has taught courses in second language acquisition, applied linguistics, psycholinguistics and multilingualism. Her research focuses on language processing in second and additional language acquisition. In 2012, she has been involved in a Leverhulme Trust post-doc research project on individual differences in SLA at the University of Greenwich, United Kingdom, within the research group 'Applied Linguistics'.

Alessandro Benati is a professor of Applied Linguistics and Second Language Studies at the University of Greenwich. He is the author and co-author of a number of books on second language learning and language teaching (*Issues in Second Language Teaching, Key Terms in Second Language Acquisition*). His research focuses on input processing and processing instruction.

Angela Hahn is a professor of Applied Linguistics at the Department of English and American Studies of the University of Munich and Head of the University Language Centre. Her main research interests include SLA, applied linguistics, phonology and pronunciation, contrastive linguistics and multilingualism. Her current research interests focus on the acquisition processes of learners who acquire their second or third foreign language (L3) supported by various means of data-driven learning. She teaches a wide range of courses in applied linguistics.

Cécile Laval is a senior lecturer in French at the University of Greenwich where she obtained a doctorate in applied linguistics (2008). She has researched and published in the area of SLA and processing instruction.

James F. Lee is deputy head of the School of Humanities and Languages at the University of New South Wales, Sydney, Australia. He teaches courses on Hispanic linguistics and SLA. His primary research interests include the relationship between L2 comprehension and input processing as an integral part of how L2 learners make form-meaning connections. He has recently published a book with Paul A. Malovrh, *The Developmental Dimension in Instructed Second Language Learning: The L2 Acquisition of Object Pronouns in Spanish* with Bloomsbury. He has recently edited a volume of research with Alessandro G. Benati, *Individual Differences and Processing Instruction* with Equinox.

Hossein Nassaji is a professor of applied linguistics in the Department of Linguistics, University of Victoria, Victoria, BC, Canada. His recent books are *Teaching Grammar in Second Language Classrooms*, 2010, Routledge (with Sandra Fotos) and *Form-Focused Instruction and Teacher Education*: Studies in Honour of Rod Ellis, 2007, OUP (with Sandra Fotos). He is the winner of the twenty-first annual Kenneth W. Mildenberger Prize of Modern Language Association of America for an article he co-authored with Gordon Wells.

María del Pilar García Mayo is full professor of English Language and Linguistics (University of the Basque Country UPV/EHU). Her major research interests include the acquisition of L2/L3 English morphosyntax (generative perspective), the analysis of cognitive factors in L2 learning (interactionist approach), language processing and bilingual/multilingual education. She has published widely in those areas.

Jason Rothman is a professor of Multilingualism and Clinical Language Sciences at the University of Reading. His research interests include the acquisition of morphosyntactic and semantic properties, linguistic processing and the relationship between cognition and linguistic development in children and adults.

Mike Sharwood Smith has worked in various countries including France, Sweden, Poland, South Africa and the Netherlands. He has taught applied linguistics, SLA, TESOL and advanced EFL for many years and has over a hundred publications in one or the other of these areas, among other things, introducing into the field the terms grammatical consciousness-raising, cross-linguistic influence and input enhancement (IE).

Jun Tian received her doctorate degree in linguistics. She is an assistant teaching professor at the University of Victoria, Victoria, BC. Her research interests are in the areas of applied linguistics, SLA, second language writing, collaborative learning, teaching Chinese as a second language, teaching English as a second language and Chinese linguistics.

Megan Smith is a PhD student in Second Language Studies at Michigan State University. Her research interests include sentence processing, the L2 acquisition of Japanese and the development of linguistic representations in language learners.

Bill VanPatten is a professor of Spanish and Second Language Studies at Michigan State University where he is also affiliate faculty in the Cognitive Science department. His research interests include input processing and sentence processing, the acquisition of morphosyntactic properties and instructed SLA.

Foreword

To understand that the sentence *Bees make honey* means 'bees make honey' and not 'bears eat honey' requires a speaker to have mental representations that link the arbitrary strings of sounds /biː/, /z/, /meik/, etc., with their specific meanings 'insect with a rounded hairy body', 'plural', 'cause to come into being' and so on. To know that *Bees make honey* is a well-formed sentence of English, while **Bees honey make* is not, requires a speaker to have mental representations for possible combinations of the morphemes involved. Such representations constitute a person's 'mental grammar' for the language they know. Young children learning their first language(s) establish mental grammars almost entirely on the basis of encounters with samples of language spoken by the people around them. Most classroom second-language learners do not have the benefit of such intensive contact with the target language and, as a result, language teachers and researchers have for decades sought the best ways of managing the encounters that they do have, with the aim of providing the optimal conditions for the acquisition of mental grammars.

The present collection of articles, brought together by Alessandro Benati, Cecile Laval and María J. Arche, offers a number of perspectives on the form that instruction might take to optimize the development of 'grammatical knowledge' (in the sense of mental representations of sound-meaning correspondences). The editors set the scene by providing an overview of the history of thinking on this topic from, at one extreme, the traditional grammar-translation approach of de-contextualized explicit statements about the target language accompanied by drills and translation exercises, to Krashen's natural approach (encounters with comprehensible input) at the other. Their survey covers communicative language teaching (CLT), task-based learning, focus on form, processing instruction, interaction-oriented learning and others.

Following the introduction, the book is divided into two sections. The articles in Part 1 – 'Theoretical and pedagogical developments' – are reflective assessments of the problem. VanPatten and Rothman suggest that the notion of 'rule' used by many practitioners and researchers interested in instructed SLA misunderstands the nature of mental grammars. They argue that instructed SLA should focus on enhancing the learning of form-meaning mappings. Innately determined knowledge of linguistic features, categories and computations ensure that mental grammars will develop. Sharwood Smith considers whether a better understanding of how learners process and store language might help in determining the kind of IE that will 'speed up learning'. Lee describes the language teaching approach known as 'processing instruction' that gets learners interacting with form through focus on meaning and discusses how it can be used in the classroom. García Mayo reflects on how collaborative tasks can lead learners to pay attention to formal aspects of language. Nassaji discusses what is meant by 'interactional feedback' and the factors that may influence its effectiveness in drawing learners' attention to form in the context of communication.

In Part 2 of the book – 'Empirical research' – four studies on the effects of instruction on the development of second language grammars are reported. Smith and VanPatten use evidence from a study of the first 30 minutes in the classroom learning of Japanese by English speakers to argue that mental grammars develop from the interaction between input and innate 'language-making mechanisms'. The representations created 'project' beyond the data available in the input. Lee applies 'processing instruction' to the learning of the Spanish passive voice. Nassaji and Tian compare the effects of task-based production activity following input-based instruction versus the absence of such activity on the learning of English phrasal verbs and find improved knowledge in learners who engaged in the production tasks. Angelovska and Hahn report a study where L3 learners come to identify cross-linguistic similarities and differences using 'intelligent guessing'.

The collection is a useful addition to the growing body of evidence we have about the relationship between the kinds of input that second language learners encounter in the classroom and the kinds of grammatical knowledge they develop. It should stimulate fruitful debate between teachers and researchers.

Roger Hawkins
University of Essex, United Kingdom

Acknowledgements

We would like to express our gratitude to all the contributors of this volume. The content of some of the chapters in this edited book were presented at the Conference on *The Role of Grammar Instruction in Second Language Acquisition: Theoretical and Practical Considerations*, held at the University of Greenwich in April 2012.

A special thank you to the anonymous reviewers who provided valuable feedback to the contributors and the editors. We are also very grateful to Roger Hawkins for kindly agreeing to write the foreword.

The editors also gratefully acknowledge the support from the University of Greenwich.

We wish to thank Patricia Vazquez Lopez, who prepared the index and Grishma Fredric, who assisted us in the production of this book. Last but not least, we wish to thank Bloomsbury for publishing this volume.

Introduction: Grammar Dimension in Instructed Second Language Learning

Alessandro Benati, Cécile Laval, María J. Arche
University of Greenwich, United Kingdom

What is the role of grammar instruction in instructed second language learning? Is there an effective approach to grammar instruction? These are key issues in understanding the possible effects of grammar instruction on the acquisition of a second language (L2). In this introductory chapter, it is our intention to examine how the role of grammar in instructed second language learning has been addressed from a variety of perspectives and theoretical frameworks.

Theoretical developments

What is the role of grammar instruction in instructed second language learning? This has been a key question and a central issue in this field of research. It was addressed by Long (1983) in a well-known paper (does instruction make a difference?) in which he presented the results of a number of classroom-based empirical studies, all addressing the question as to whether instruction can be beneficial for second language learners. Long (1983) considered eleven studies which examined whether the learners receiving grammar instruction achieve a higher level of proficiency than those learners who do not. The main findings from his review were ambiguous and did not provide a clear answer.

Long's paper identified the need for further classroom research investigating more systematically the possible effects of grammar instruction in SLA. Empirical research (Ellis 1997, 2008) conducted in the last 30 years has focused on measuring the role of instruction in affecting the route (learning of various features in a specific order), the rate (learning of features at a specific speed) and the ultimate level of second language attainment (reaching higher or lower proficiency levels). VanPatten and Benati (2010) have provided a succinct review of the role of instruction in SLA. Overall, they have identified two main views around the role of instruction. The first view is that instruction has a limited and constrained role. The second view asserts that instruction might have a beneficial role under certain conditions (cf. DeKeyser 2005).

In Krashen's theoretical framework called *The Monitor Theory* (Krashen 1982), Krashen argued that instruction plays a limited role in SLA.

According to Krashen (1982), acquisition is an unconscious and implicit process, and learners acquire a second language through exposure to comprehensible and meaning-bearing input rather than learning grammar consciously through explicit grammatical rules (Krashen 2009). In addition to the limited role assigned to grammar instruction, Krashen also argued that L2 learners acquired grammatical features (e.g. morphemes) of a target language in a predictable order, and this is regardless of their first language or the context in which they acquire them. In the English language, for example, progressive *-ing* is acquired before regular past tense *-ed*, which is acquired before third-person *-s*. Krashen concludes that instruction might be unable to alter the route of acquisition as L2 learners follow specific orders of acquisition.

In the *Processability Theory*, Pienemann (1998) sustains the view that L2 learners acquire single structures through predictable stages. According to the *Processability Theory*, instruction is constrained by these developmental stages, and L2 learners follow a very rigid route in the acquisition of grammatical features which cannot be skipped. If instruction is targeted at grammatical features for which L2 learners are developmentally ready, then instruction can be beneficial in helping them to move faster along their natural route of development.

Ellis (1997) has suggested that there is some evidence to support the thesis that instruction helps L2 learners to develop a good level of attainment particularly if opportunities to natural exposure are given. He also argued that instruction has a facilitative role when it is used for linguistic features, which are not too distant from the learner's current level of language development.

Gass (1997) has affirmed that instruction might have a facilitative role in helping learners to pay selective attention to form and form-meaning connections in the input. Learners make form-meaning connections from the input they receive as they connect particular meanings to particular forms (grammatical or lexical). For example, they tend to connect a form with its meaning in the input they receive (the morpheme *–ed–* on the end of the verb in English refers to an event in the past). VanPatten (1996, 2002, 2004) has indicated that L2 learners find it difficult to attend to form and meaning simultaneously with the input they receive. Therefore, learners must be trained on how to process input more effectively and efficiently so that they are in a better position to process grammatical forms and connect them with their meanings.

These theoretical views are based on the assumption that the route of acquisition cannot be altered; however, instruction might in certain conditions speed up the rate of acquisition and develop greater language proficiency. What are the conditions that might facilitate the speed in which languages are learnt? A first condition is that L2 learners must be exposed to sufficient input. A second condition is that L2 learners must be psycho linguistically ready for instruction to be effective as indicated by Pienemman. A third condition is that instruction must take into consideration how L2 learners process the input.

Pedagogical developments

Is there an effective approach to grammar instruction? Over the years, we have witnessed to a number of 'shifts' on the role and practice of grammar instruction. In the Grammar-translation Method, an explicit approach to grammar instruction was proposed. One of the main assumptions of this method was that a second language is learnt through the deduction of the grammatical properties of L2, and this process would allow learners to develop a conscious and explicit representation of that language in their internal system. Therefore, grammar instruction consisted mainly in studying and memorizing forms and structures. The Direct Method proposed a more inductive view of the role of grammar instruction. According to this method, L2 learners should learn grammar by interpreting contextual and situational cues rather than receiving explicit information about the grammatical rules of the new language. The Audio-lingual Method suggested that grammar is learnt through the process of repetition, imitation and reinforcement. Grammatical structures were presented in a linear manner with no attention to meaning. This method emphasized the use of memorization and pattern drills as grammar teaching tasks.

A very common approach to grammar instruction is the so-called PPP method (presentation-practice-production). This approach proposes a three-stage model. The first stage consists in the internalization of a new form or structure, which is usually presented through a text. The second stage implies the practice of the new form of structure through its systematic use. In the final stage, activities are organized involving personal use of the target form or structure. The PPP suggests the use of tasks which allow the learner to move from systematic to appropriate use of the language in contexts. It is only when the learner has mastered the form that he/she will be able to use it in the context where the message becomes more important than the medium.

Grammar instruction was relegated to a fragile and peripheral role in the Natural Approach and in the CLT approach. In CLT, it was assumed that grammar instruction does not help learners develop any kind of communicative ability in the L2. It was believed that the process of learning a second language is just like learning a first language.

In the CLT and task-based learning approach, learners are asked to perform tasks with large quantities of meaning-focused language input which contains target forms and vocabulary. The main focus of these approaches is the purpose to develop learners' ability to interpret and use meaning in real-life communication and not focus on the learning of forms and structures. However, both the approaches have attempted to incorporate a component of grammar instruction within an overall focus on meaning and communication. This is the understanding that drawing L2 learners' attention to form in the input within a meaningful context seemed to have beneficial effects for L2 learning.

Long (1991) and Long and Robinson (1998) distinguished between two types of grammar instruction options: 'focus on form' and 'focus on forms'. Focus on forms refers to a type of instruction that isolates specific linguistic forms and teaches them one at the time. In this traditional approach, grammar instruction is often characterized by paradigmatic explanations of specific linguistic forms or structures. The paradigmatic explanation is followed by pattern practice and substitution drills. In this type of mechanical practice, real-life situations are completely ignored and practice is implemented in a completely decontextualized way. The idea that acquiring grammar can be simply achieved by learning about the grammatical rules of a target language and practice those rules through production tasks (very often mechanical and traditional) has been challenged by many scholars in the field of instructed SLA research (Wong and VanPatten 2003).

The term 'focus on form', instead, is characterized by grammar instruction approaches, which provide a focus on meaning and a focus on form. L2 learners' attention is being focused on specific linguistic properties in the course of a communicative task. Spada (1997: 73) has defined more broadly 'focus on form' as 'any pedagogical effort that is used to drawn learners' attention to language form either implicitly or explicitly'. In recent years, findings from instructed SLA research (Nassaji and Fotos 2011) have demonstrated that a component of focus on grammar ('focus on form') might facilitate acquisition if it is provided in combination with a focus on meaning.

One of the key conditions for L2 learners to acquire the grammatical properties of a second language is that they are exposed to sufficient input. The centrality of input in L2 learning has been emphasized by many theories (e.g. *Universal Grammar*; *Interaction Hypothesis*; *Input Processing*) and scholars (White 2003; Gass 1997; VanPatten 1996). Gass (1997: 1) has defined input as 'the single most important concept in second language acquisition'. Considering the limited role for instruction, and the importance of incorporating grammar in a more meaningful approach to instruction, we should look at devising grammar tasks that, on one hand, enhance the grammatical features in the input, and on the other hand, provide L2 learners with opportunities to focus on meaning.

How grammar can be focused in the language classroom has been proposed through a number of approaches: input-oriented, interactional-oriented and output-oriented.

Input-oriented approaches

Considering the limited role for instruction, researchers have investigated the effects of a number of input-based options to grammar instruction which might help L2 learners to internalize the grammatical features of a target language. Processing instruction (VanPatten 1996; Lee and VanPatten 2003; Benati and Lee 2008) is an instructional approach that through the manipulation and restructuring of the input facilitates the acquisition of grammatical and syntactic features of a target language. Empirical research (Lee and Benati 2009) into the relative effects of processing instruction has demonstrated that it is an effective approach (online and in the classroom) to grammar instruction in helping L2 learners to make appropriate form-meaning connections and parse syntactic structures correctly (at sentence and discourse levels and for both interpretation and production tasks) and efficiently in different languages (Romance and Asian languages) and linguistic features. The effects of processing instruction have been proved to be both durative and longitudinal.

Schmidt (1990, 2001) has suggested that L2 learners require attention in order to successfully process the forms in the input. Learners must first notice a form in the input for that form to be processed. Given the importance of 'noticing' a form in the input, the question is: How can we best facilitate the noticing of a certain form in the input? IE has been defined by Sharwood Smith (1991) as a process by which linguistic data will become more salient for L2 learners. This approach (enhancing the input to allow learners to notice some specific forms) should effect changes in learners' linguistic competence. Sharwood Smith (1991) has proposed various techniques to enhance the input which varies in terms of explicitness and elaboration. A practical example would be to underline or to capitalize a specific grammatical item in a text to help learners notice that particular grammatical feature (textual enhancement). A different one would require a modification of the text so that a particular target item would appear over and over again so that the text would contain many more exemplars of the same feature (input flood).

IE is an approach to grammar instruction through which the input is made more noticeable with the understanding that making certain features salient in the input might help drawing learner's attention to that specific feature. Empirical research has measured the effectiveness of input flood and textual enhancement using a variety of assessment tasks (e.g. grammatical judgement, form production, form recognition). Despite the mixed results obtained in classroom-based research (Lee and Benati 2007), textual enhancement seems overall to be an effective input manipulation technique depending on two factors: target form and assessment task (Wong 2005).

Interactional-oriented approaches

In SLA research, interaction refers to conversations between learners and other interlocutors (e.g. native speakers and non-native speakers, learner-teacher interactions). Very often the input of one speaker is modified by another speaker, and this is normally due to lack of comprehension and breakdown in communication (e.g. What did you say? Do you mean *tonight*? Sorry?). Corrective feedback refers to utterances from a language instructor or another speaker which indicates that the learner's output in not correct. This term is often interchanged with the term 'negative evidence' which relates to different techniques used to alert L2 learners about what is not possible in a second language.

Nassaji and Fotos (2011) have distinguished between two types of interactional feedback: reformulation and elicitation. Reformulations are those corrective feedback techniques such as recasts. Recast refers to an implicit technique to corrective feedback in which L2 learners are provided with the correct form immediately after their erroneous utterance. Elicitation refers to other corrective feedback techniques which do not provide L2 learners with the correct form (e.g. clarification requests), but with an opportunity for the learners to repair their own errors. Empirical research on corrective feedback has attempted to establish whether or not it is a necessary and/or beneficial factor for language development. Cross-sectional and longitudinal studies have been conducted to establish the effectiveness of implicit corrective feedback techniques (particularly recasts, Long 2007). One line of research (Lyster and Ranta 1997) has argued that recast is not effective in eliciting immediate revision by the learners of their output. Corrective feedback is more effective when L2 learners are actively engaged in negotiating a form or when they have to think about and respond to the language instructor's feedback. The opportunity of negotiating the forms is better achieved when the language instructor does not provide the correct form but instead provides cues to help the learner consider how to reformulate his or her incorrect language.

A second line is, instead, more positive about the role of recast (see Doughty and Williams 1998). Scholars in support of recast techniques suggest that it might enable learners to be exposed to target forms and elicit repetition, and this repetition may in turn enhance salience. Recast has a facilitative role and provides learners with a focus on form without interrupting the flow of conversation, and at the same time, learners focus on message content.

Output-oriented approaches

Swain (2005) has argued that comprehensible input is not sufficient for developing native-like grammatical competence. L2 learners need opportunities for *pushed output* (speech or writing that demands learners to produce language correctly and appropriately). Swain has proposed that output contributes to L2 acquisition in three ways: L2 learners have the opportunity to test out their hypotheses about how they express their meaning in a second language, L2 learners have the opportunity to notice a gap in their linguistic ability, L2 learners have the opportunity to reflect consciously on the target language. Considering the various roles that output can have in second language learning, scholars have proposed a number of collaborative output tasks (e.g. dictogloss, jigsaw tasks, problem-solving tasks, structured output activities) that might help L2 learners in acquiring the grammatical properties of the target language.

Dictogloss is a type of task-based collaborative output which aims at helping learners to use their grammar resources to reconstruct a text and become aware of their own shortcomings and needs. In a jigsaw collaborative output task, L2 learners can work in pairs or in small groups. Each pair or group has different information, and they have to exchange their information to complete the task.

Structured output tasks are an effective alternative to mechanical output practice. As stated by Lee and VanPatten (1995: 121), structured output activities have two main characteristics: '(1) They involve the exchange of previously unknown information; and (2) They require learners to access a particular form or structure in order to process meaning'.

Empirical research on the role of different output-based options to grammar instruction has indicated that these types of tasks can make a number of contributions (Nassaji and Fotos 2011): generating better input for the development of learners' competence, trying out hypotheses about grammar, developing discourse skills.

Conclusive remarks

The role of instruction in SLA is limited and constrained by a number of factors. However, despite the fact that instruction is, for instance, not able to alter the route of acquisition, it might have some beneficial effects in terms of speeding up the rate of acquisition. Traditional grammar instruction is not an appropriate way to approach the teaching of grammatical forms and the structure of a second language (Wong and VanPatten 2003). However, there are types of 'focus on form' approaches to grammar instruction that can in certain cases and conditions enhance and speed up the way languages are learnt and are an effective way to incorporate grammar instruction in second language teaching. IE techniques provide L2 learners with access to comprehensible input, positive evidence and help them to pay attention to grammatical forms in the input. Processing instruction through structure input practice helps learners to process the input correctly and efficiently, and as a result of this, the learner's intake of language input is increased. Classroom research has also indicated that it is desirable and helpful to provide corrective feedback without interrupting the flow of communication. Interactional feedback techniques can be a useful tool to promote acquisition. Output options in grammar instruction might also play an important role in SLA. Collaborative output tasks generate better input and should be used to promote language production and the development of grammatical skills.

According to Nassaji and Fotos (2011: 139), 'teachers should be eclectic in their pedagogical approach. That is, they should choose and synthesize the best elements, principles and activities of different approaches to grammar teaching to attain success. Thus, not only do teachers have to maximize opportunities for the students to encounter important target forms in communicative contexts, they also need to be flexible and use a variety of means to do so'.

Here are some overall principles (cf. Benati 2013) language instructors should take into account when developing grammar tasks and providing effective grammar instruction in the language classroom:

- given that acquisition can be effectively influenced by manipulating input, grammar tasks should be developed to ensure that (at least initially) learners process the input correctly and efficiently;
- grammar tasks should be designed for learners to notice and process the forms in the input and eventually make correct form-mapping connections;
- language teaching should include a variety of grammar tasks (input, output and interactional options) that invite both a focus on form and a focus on meaning.

Although it is not clear from current empirical research whether there is particular approach to grammar instruction better than another, 'it is clear that the field has slightly shifted from the more global question "Does instruction make a difference?" (Long 1983) to more specific question "Does manipulating input make a difference"' (VanPatten and Benati 2010: 52).

References

Benati, A. (2013), *Issues in Second Language Teaching*. London: Equinox.

Benati, A. and Lee, J. F. (2008), *Grammar Acquisition and Processing Instruction*. Clevedon: Multilingual Matters.

DeKeyser, R. (2005), 'What Makes Learning Second-Language Grammar Difficult? A Review of Issues'. *Language Learning*, 55, 1–25.

Doughty, C. and Williams, J. (eds). (1998), *Focus on Form in Classroom Second Language Acquisition*. Cambridge: Cambridge University Press.

Ellis, R. (1997), *SLA Research and Language Teaching*. Oxford: Oxford University Press.

— (2008), *The Study of Second Language Acquisition (2nd edn)*. Oxford: Oxford University Press.

Gass, S. (1997), *Input, Interaction, and the Second Language Learner*. Mahwah, NJ: Lawrence Erlbaum.

Krashen, S. (1982), *Principles and Practice in Second Language Acquisition*. London: Pergamon.

— (2009), 'The comprehension hypothesis extended', in T. Piske and M. Young-Scholten (eds), *Input Matters*. Bristol: Multilingual Matters, pp. 81–94.

Lee, J. F. and VanPatten, B. (1995), *Making Communicative Classroom*. New York: McGraw-Hill.

— (2003), *Making Communicative Classroom*. New York: McGraw-Hill.

Lee, J. F. and Benati, A. (2007), *Second Language Processing*. London: Continuum.

— (2009), *Research and Perspectives on Processing Instruction*. New York: Mouton de Gruyter.

Long, M. (1983), 'Does second language instruction make a difference?' *TESOL Quarterly*, 17, 359–82.

— (1991), 'Focus on form: a design feature in language teaching methodology', in K. De Bot (ed.), *Foreign Language Research in Cross-Cultural Perspectives*. Amsterdam: John Benjamins, pp. 39–52.

— (2007), *Problems in SLA*. Mahwah, NJ: Lawrence Erlbaum Associates.

Long, M. and Robinson, P. (1998), 'Focus on form: theory, research and practice', in C. Doughty and J. Williams (eds), *Focus on Form in Classroom Second Language Acquisition*. Cambridge, UK: Cambridge University Press, pp. 15–41.

Lyster, R. and Ranta, L. (1997), 'Corrective feedback and learner uptake: negotiation of form in communicative classrooms'. *Studies in Second Language Acquisition*, 19, 37–66.

Nassaji, H. and Fotos, S. (2011), *Teaching Grammar in Second Language Classrooms*. New York: Routledge.

Pienemann, M. (1998), *Language Processing and L2 Development*. New York: Benjamins.

Schmidt, R. (1990), 'The role of consciousness in second language learning'. *Applied Linguistics*, 11, 129–58.

— (2001), 'Attention', in P. Robinson (ed.), *Cognition and Second Language Instruction*. Cambridge: Cambridge University Press, pp. 3–32.

Sharwood Smith, M. (1991), 'Speaking to many minds: on the relevance of different types of language information for the L2 learner'. *Second Language Research* 7, 118–32.

Spada, N. (1997), 'Form-focused instruction and Second Language acquisition: a Review of classroom and laboratory research'. *LanguageTeaching*, 30, 73–87.

Swain, M. (2005), 'The output hypothesis. Theory and research', in E. Heikel (ed.), *Handbook on Research in Second Language Teaching and Learning*. Mahwah, NJ: Lawrence Erlbaum Associates, pp. 471–83.

VanPatten, B. (1996), *Input Processing and Grammar Instruction: Theory and Research.* Norwood, NJ: Ablex.

— (2002), 'Processing instruction: an update'. *Language Learning,* 52, 755–803.

— (ed.). (2004), *Processing Instruction: Theory, Research, and Commentary.* Mahwah, NJ: Erlbaum.

VanPatten, B. and Benati, A. (2010), *Key Terms in Second Language Acquisition.* London: Continuum.

White, L. (2003), *Second Language Acquisition and Universal Grammar.* Cambridge: Cambridge University Press.

Wong, W. (2005), *Input Enhancement: From Theory and Research to the Classroom.* New York: McGraw-Hill.

Wong, W. and VanPatten, B. (2003), 'The evidence is IN: Drills are OUT'. *Foreign Language Annals,* 36, 403–23.

Part One

Theoretical and Pedagogical Developments

1

Against 'Rules'

Bill VanPatten and Jason Rothman
Michigan State University, United States, and
University of Reading, United Kingdom

How does the field of instructed SLA define the construct of language? Is there consensus on what language is and what is acquired? These are not trivial questions as the entire enterprise of instructed SLA (indeed, the premise of the present volume) rests on the idea that pedagogical intervention can cause change in something. What is that something, and for that matter, what is the change?

The purpose of this chapter is to describe certain aspects of current generative theory as they apply to the notion of 'grammar', and in so doing to argue against the vague concept of 'learning rules' that is prevalent in instructed SLA research. Although we understand that not everyone in SLA takes a generative approach to the nature of language (e.g. emergentism and sociocultural theory, to name two widely distributed frameworks), many of us do (as in the case of UG-based approaches, the Acquisition by Processing Theory, Autonomous Induction and others). A generative approach to understanding language acquisition has been fruitful not only in child L1 acquisition (e.g. Guasti 2004; Snyder 2007) but also adult SLA (e.g. Herschensohn 2000; White 2003). In the broader field of more general SLA, the application of generative theory has been useful in understanding language transfer, ultimate attainment and developmental stages of acquisition as well as providing testable hypotheses about the nature of specific error types and variability in L2 production: for example, prosodic L1 transfer effects on morphological suppliance (Goad and White 2006), form-to-function mapping induced problem for morphology (Lardiere 1998) and integration problems at interfaces (Sorace 2011), to name a few. One of the reasons for this successful application to understanding adult SLA centres on the fact that generative theory offers a well-articulated framework for talking about language itself, especially its formal aspects (e.g. Gregg 2003). In short, although we begin this chapter acknowledging alternative approaches, we take the position that a generative approach should add insight into the focus of the present volume, namely, the nature of instructed SLA. We also acknowledge that this point is not original to us, to be sure, and has its roots elsewhere (Bruhn de Garavito 1995; Schwartz 1993; among others).

Some definitions

We begin with two definitions that are relevant to this chapter: *mental representation* and *learning*. We take mental representation to mean the abstract, implicit and underlying linguistic system in a speaker's mind/brain. By *abstract* we mean that the linguistic system is not something akin to a set of textbook or prescriptive rules, but instead is a collection of abstract properties from which rule-like behaviour is derived (e.g. Harley and Noyer 1999; Jackendoff 2002; Radford 2001; Rothman 2010; White 2003). As an example, let's look at auxiliary *do* in *yes/no* questions in English.[1] Typical *yes/no* question are formed using *do*, while other options, such as subject-verb inversion, are prohibited as in (1) and (2) below. The reverse is true in a language such as Spanish that has subject-verb inversion and lacks so-called auxiliary *do*-support as in (3).

1. Does John live near the university?
2. *Lives John near the university?
3. ¿Vive Juan cerca de la universidad?

While we can describe the use of *do* in questions with a statement like 'insert *do* for *yes/no* questions and invert with the subject', in a mental grammar of English, *do* is the result of a series of interactions between abstract features of the grammar. Comp, which is the head of the complementizer phrase (CP), contains some feature that is able to enter into what is called an 'AGREE relationship' with the features enumerated in auxiliary verbs in English that probe movement. This feature-based Agree relationship forces movement of *do* out of the Inflectional Phrase (Infl), where it is generated to carry Tense features. These kinds of syntactic operations occur when relevant lexical units have functional features that must be checked in the course of a syntactic derivation. What we describe as varying syntactic word orders are thus surface reflexes of functional feature checking resulting in observable lexical insertion or movement of a constituent into a phrase to fulfil the AGREE relationship. Thus, our textbook-type rule of 'insert *do* and invert subject and auxiliary verb' is not what actually exists in the grammar or in people's minds; it is a specific shorthand way to describe a particular consequence of more abstract principles and underlying features of the grammar. We will see more examples later as we delve into the nature of language and what can be learnt.

Distinct from mental representation is skill.[2] We use skill as it is normally used in the literature on cognitive psychology; that is, the speed and accuracy with which people can perform certain actions or behaviours (Anderson 2000; Schmidt 1992; Segalowitz 2003). Skills can be general (e.g. problem-solving, learning), or they can be domain- or context-specific (e.g. cooking omelettes at a restaurant, mixing margaritas in a bar, delivering a speech). Regardless of generality or specificity of domain, that skill involves both speed and accuracy is important – and the measurement of skill considers how quickly someone can do something in addition to how well (the 'how well' being contextually defined). It is important to note that some kind of skill implies some kind of mental representation, but mental representation does not necessarily imply any kind of skill. That is, if someone is producing language or comprehending language, the implication is that at some level there is mental representation that underlies that language use. However, one can have mental representation that is not manifested in production, for example. In this chapter, we will focus our attention on mental representation and not on the ability to use language for communicative purposes.

Another concept meriting a definition is *learning*. We take the following to be a general definition of learning: the internalization of 'something' from the environment that leads to changes in underlying mental representation (or cognitive structures, more generally speaking). For example, we have just completed reading a book arguing for the existence of extraterrestrials on Earth thousands of years ago. Regardless of whether or not we agree with the central thesis, there are certain facts we picked up in the reading that for some reason we had not picked up before. One, for example, is the nature of the distance of planets from the Sun. It is a fact that planets occur in predictable orbits, with each planet twice as far from the Sun as the planet before it (e.g. Venus is twice as far from the Sun as Mercury, and the Earth is twice as far from the Sun as Venus). This is known as the Titius-Bode law. What is curious is that Jupiter is not twice as far from the Sun as Mars is if indeed Jupiter is the next planet out from the Sun after Mars. Curiously, Jupiter is twice as far from the Sun as the asteroid belt, which is twice as far from the Sun as Mars is. One of the conclusions of the author is that the asteroid belt represents some of the remains of a once extent planet, that for some reason exploded. (We are omitting lots of details here, including that there is some discrepancy with the law when we get to the outer planets, although the Kuiper belt – asteroids beyond Pluto – do fit well into the law.) Additional evidence is found in the makeup of the asteroids (and meteors that 'fall' to Earth from this belt). They are not made up of primitive pre-solar system material but instead contain material that is only found in planets themselves (e.g. certain heavy metals). And the case of comets is even more peculiar, as they contain ice – and water is only found on planets. Interesting stuff, to be sure, but the point here is that in reading this book, we extracted 'something' from the input (e.g. the nature of the Titius-Bode law, who both Titius and Bode were and when they lived, how long the law has been around, the nature of asteroids). Our cognitive construct about the solar system has changed.

When applied to language, learning means extracting 'something' from the linguistic input we are exposed to and somehow internalizing it so that our mental representation of language is somehow changed. To be sure, we are not talking about facts such as 'each planet is twice as far from the sun as the planet before it'. Instead, that 'something' is raw linguistic data (more on that to come later). What is more, with this definition of learning, we are not making any claims about explicitness or implicitness of learning itself, especially when it comes to language (but see VanPatten and Rothman, in press, for a discussion of the explicit-implicit issue). For now, it is sufficient to be neutral on the nature of the learning itself. What this all means, then, is that adult learners of an L2 'extract' data from the input by (at this point in this chapter) unspecified means. Where we will differ from others later in this essay is that we will maintain that what are extracted are not rules at all. In fact, we will argue that 'rules' aren't even learnt, at least by any reasonable definition of what learning entails.

Aspects of language that cannot be learnt

Throughout the history of generative theory, a central claim has been that humans possess innate language-specific mechanisms responsible for constraining the shape of languages (see Chomsky 2007, for a review of the theory and its tenets). In the current minimalist instantiation of generative theory, as in previous ones, one such mechanism is Universal Grammar (UG), which is now envisioned to consist of an inventory of linguistic primitives or functional features (e.g. case, number, person), operations (e.g. Merge/Move, Agree) and universal constraints on linguistic computation (e.g. Structure Dependency, Recursion, conditions on the application of operations, such as Last Resort). As part of UG, these aspects of language are 'owned' by everyone and need not be learnt. That is, they are not dependent on external stimuli for them to exist in the mental representation. In our example (1) earlier, we would say that a number of aspects of UG come to bare on a *yes/no* question such as *Does John live near the university?* From the universal feature inventory, as one example, Comp as a functional feature is selected. And because all languages consist of phrases (XPs), we know that Comp must be a head and occupied by a head (as opposed to something that normally occupies a Spec position). The Extended Projection Principle also comes to bear as this *yes/no* question must have something that fills the subject slot (Spec, TP) part of the sentence for it to be licit. And as we will see later, the feature AGR (agreement) is important in determining word order in English, as is the feature T (Tense) which triggers the need for an auxiliary such as *do*. We will not belabour the workings of UG here. Our intent at this point is to argue that any learner of English has automatic access to Comp, the EPP, AGR, T, structure forming and other aspects of language as part of UG and does not need to learn these from the input. Instead, what UG does is to impose its internal content onto the processed input data; input doesn't impose itself onto UG.

The reader may be familiar with the concept of the Poverty of the Stimulus (POS) argument. What the POS argument refers to is that all speakers of any language come to know more about their language, albeit unconsciously, than what is available in the input. That is, their grammars (whether L1 or L2) project beyond the input data. One aspect of the POS is manifested by the operation of the content of UG. For example, all speakers of Spanish implicitly know (whether L1 or L2) that clitics move and that (4a) and (4b) are fine but that (4c) is not.

4a. Juan dice que quiere hacerlo.
    'John says that he wants to do it'
4b. Juan dice que lo quiere hacer.
4c. *Juan lo dice que quiere hacer.

While the input may provide someone with samples to conclude that the 'a' and 'b' versions are possible, nothing in the input prohibits someone (or more specifically, someone's grammar) from concluding that 'c' is also possible; yet this never happens. Why not? Because the constraints imposed by UG (in this case, those related to case checking and binding) do not permit the movement of something marked by accusative case out of its clause. In short, the application of universals (in the UG sense) results in knowledge about the way a language behaves that is not learnt from the input.

Aspects of language that are derived and not learnt

In addition to universal aspects of language that aren't learnt in the traditional sense, there are other derived aspects of language that evolve from the interaction of universals with particular input information. These derivations have traditionally been referred to as parameters, although the status of parameters has changed since 1985 (and the change is not really relevant to the current discussion, so we will omit it here – see Gallego 2011, for discussion). An example of a derivation/parameter involves verb movement.

Verb movement is a shorthand way of talking about the consequences of certain underlying features in the syntax of languages. For instance, a prediction is that the verb raising contrast between English and Spanish, as in (5–10) below, is determined by variation in the feature specification of the inflectional head which attracts or probes the verb overtly in Spanish (as well as in other Romance languages like French, Italian and European Portuguese) but not in English. This inflectional head is the one that carries tense and or agreement (see, e.g. Pollock 1989, Chomsky 1995). In this theory, a syntactic functional head – the locus of inflection (tense and/or agreement) – displays the feature specification which forces the verb to raise overtly to the inflectional head in Spanish, but not in English. In other words, English lacks the feature specification that Spanish apparently has, resulting in verbs (generally) remaining in their based-generated location, which is why we get such things as pre-verbal negation with *not*, insertion of *do* with *yes/no* questions and the inability to invert subject-verb to make such questions, the impossibility of verb-adverb-object word order, all illustrated in (5)–(7) below.

5. Bill does not drink sugared colas/*Bill drinks not sugared colas.
6. Does Bill drink vodka?/*Drinks Bill vodka?
7. Bill often drinks martinis/*Bill drinks often martinis.

On the other hand, in a language like Spanish, the functional head of TP has a feature specification that probes movement obligatorily. Thus, there is no *do* insertion in Spanish, and the other things that are impossible in English are possible in Spanish, as illustrated by the translations of the above sentences in (8)–(10). For ease of references, *toma* is the equivalent of the verb 'drinks'. (Note that the *no* of Spanish is not equivalent to the 'not' of English; in French, *pas* would be the functional equivalent of 'not'.)

8. Bill no toma refrescos con azúcar.
9. Toma Bill vodka?
10. Bill toma a menudo vodka (pero Jason, no).

What we see, then, is that the specification of one feature, AGR, results in a series of derived aspects of the grammar. These derived aspects (consequences of what we call or called *parametric variation*) are not learnt in the classic sense. They 'happen' to the learner once the internal grammar selects the feature inventory of the target language. Thus, once the proper set of features is selected, learners' grammars 'automatically' entertain verb movement with the surface manifestations shown in (8)–(10), for example. (For more detailed description and for research on this phenomenon in the L2 setting, see VanPatten et al. 2012.)

Very often, parametric variation (like universal constraints) results in POS situations, and not necessarily at the advanced or native-like stages, but at almost every stage of acquisition. We won't illustrate this here, as a good example can be found in Smith and VanPatten (this volume) with beginning learners of Japanese as L2. But to preview their contribution, they found that after only 30 minutes of treatment (consisting of 100 input sentences), naïve learners of Japanese with English as L1 demonstrated projection of head directionality beyond the types of sentences contained in the input they received. Thus, at the earliest stages of acquiring Japanese, these learners demonstrated a POS situation.

To conclude this section, learners' internal mechanisms can project beyond the input data during parameter resetting (or whatever one wishes to call this in more modern terms). The result is derived aspects of grammar not encountered in the environment. Such aspects of the grammar are not learnt, then, in the classic sense. They are the result of processing other data in the input.

Aspects of language that have to be learnt

So far, we have briefly examined two aspects of language that are not learnt in the classical sense of 'learning': (1) universals and universal constraints within UG and (2) derived aspects of the grammar because of UG options (i.e. feature specifications and their consequences). What is learnt in the classic sense? In short, all of those things that reside in the lexicon, namely, lexical and morphological form. We underscore here 'form' for as we will argue later, learners do not get rules from the input but forms that are used by the internal devices to create a particular language grammatical system.

Let's look at two of the examples we have seen so far. What is learnt from the input when it comes to *yes/no* questions? The answer is the auxiliary *do*, in all of its allomorphic realizations: *do, does* and *did*. The learner must tag this lexical unit in the input, and during sentence computation (comprehension), the processor must assign it some kind of status. If the processing is successful, it will get tagged with the Q feature described earlier in this chapter (along with other relevant features). What gets internalized from the input, then, is *do* with at least these features:

do: $<+Q>$, $<\text{-past}>$
does: $<+Q>$, $<\text{-past}>$, $<\text{3rd person}>$, $<\text{sing}>$
did: $<+Q>$, $<+\text{past}>$

Once the auxiliary is tagged in this way, it can participate in the constraints and/or parametric variations on the grammar that yield *yes/no* questions (e.g. verb movement or not). Of course, nothing guarantees that *do* gets tagged correctly at the outset, but that is irrelevant to the discussion here. The point is that learners do not learn a rule about *yes/no* question formation from the input; they process *do* and from this, *yes/no* question formation evolves in the grammar. (See VanPatten 1996, for some discussion of how the acquisition of *do* blocks verb movement in English L2 when the L1 has verb movement.)

Our second example relates to verb movement in Spanish. The reader will recall that verb movement is the result of feature specification that probes for movement in Spanish. According to current generative theory, uninterpretable or syntactic features trigger what is called 'movement' so that features that are interpretable can get 'erased'. What this means in a language like Spanish is that in the sentence *Bill toma a menudo vodka*, the AGR feature of the tense phrase (TP) is uninterpretable and contains the specifications $<\text{3rd}>$, $<\text{sing}>$. It searches for something in the sentence that also contains those specifications with an interpretable feature counterpart. In this case, it is the verb form *toma*. Spanish has unique person-number endings for verbs and in the present example, this verb form is specified for $<\text{3rd}>$, $<\text{sing}>$. The consequence of T having an uninterpretable feature, then, is that the verb in the underlying sentence, *Bill a menudo toma vodka*, moves out of its position in the verb phrase (VP) so that AGR can get its features checked. In fact, the verb is required to move. If we sketched out the result, it would look something like the following sentence (some details left out). ('toma' stands for an empty space, the copy of the moved element and the spot vacated during the course of its movement, while the letters 'i' and 'j' are used to indicate co-indexing between an element and where it originated.)

$[_{TP} \, [_{VP} \, \text{Bill a menudo toma vodka}] \rightarrow [_{TP} \, \text{Bill}_i \, \text{toma}_j \, [_{VP} \, \text{Bill}_i \, \text{a menudo toma}_j \, \text{vodka}]$

What do learners have to get from the input for verb movement to happen? As VanPatten et al. (2012) have argued, the answer is that verb movement is evident in the input from the very beginning with *wh*-questions. Unlike English, standard Spanish requires subject-verb inversion with such questions, as is clear in (11) and (12).

11. What does Bill drink?/*What drinks Bill?
12. ¿Qué toma Bill?/*¿Qué Bill toma?

Learners hear these types of questions from the get-go when exposed to Spanish so the processors get immediate data that verbs have moved, and thus the internal grammar posits that Spanish T has a feature specification that will probe obligatory verb movement. But what must also be learnt are the morpho-phonological forms of verbs that contain the information also specified in AGR. Thus, learners must learn the lexical forms and their specifications, which are, of course, unique to Spanish. Examples:

tomo: <drink>, <1st>, <sing>
toman: <drink>, <3rd>, <pl>
tomamos: <drink>, <1st>, <pl>
tomas: <drink>, <2nd>, <sing>
and so on.

The learner of Spanish, then, must extract from the input these morpho-phonological forms along with their meanings and features and store them in the lexicon so that they can be 'accessed' or 'inserted' into the syntax during sentence comprehension and production, respectively. Again, the learner is not learning something like verb movement from the input. What the learner is getting are pieces and parts of surface properties of language that, when incorporated into the lexicon and also computed by the mechanisms responsible for grammar, allow syntax to grow over time.

Does instruction on these surface elements aid in their acquisition, and by acquisition, we mean the creation of an implicit mental representation? The jury is out on this question more generally, but let us briefly describe a recent study relevant to this topic. In VanPatten et al. (2012), we tested native speakers and intermediate-level (third-year university students beginning their formal study of literature and culture) on three structures in Spanish. All were related to verb movement in some way: (1) *wh*-question formation (see 12 above), (2) adverb placement with *no más* ('no longer') and (3) person-number endings on simple present tense verbs. All participants were tested for sensitivity to grammaticality via self-paced reading. In self-paced reading, participants read a sentence fragment by fragment, controlling what they see and how long they read by pressing a button. All reading is for meaning, for after each sentence they read they answer a content question about what they just read. A non-cumulative reading test was used in which the sentence fragments did not stay on the screen once a button is pressed to move on to the next fragment, so readers are required to keep what they just read in working memory as they move from fragment to fragment. Comprehension questions appear on a separate screen after reading a sentence. What is measured are reading times of target fragments and the spillover region right after the targets (other reading times can be measured as well, but for the present purpose, this is all that is required). Because the sentences are paired so that there are grammatical and ungrammatical versions of each (randomized, counterbalanced, blocked, surrounded by distractors and fillers and so on), we are interested in how long it takes them to read the target and spillover regions of the same grammatical and ungrammatical sentences. Even though participants are reading for meaning, the expectation is that they will slow down slightly on ungrammatical segments in one of the two regions examined as their internal processors detect something wrong. For the *wh*-questions, grammaticality had to do with subject-verb inversion (grammatical sentences had the inversion, ungrammatical sentences did not). For the placement of the adverb *no más*, grammaticality had to do with whether the verb had moved out of its VP or not (e.g. *Juan no viaja más a Francia porque no tiene dinero/*Juan no más viaja a Francia porque no tiene dinero* 'John no longer travels to France because he doesn't have the money'). For person-number, the grammaticality had to do with subject-verb morphological agreement (e.g. *Ahora yo tomo un refresco en la cafetería/*Ahora yo toma un refresco en la cafetería* 'Right now I'm drinking a soda in the cafeteria').

The data revealed that the native speakers showed significant reading time differences on all sentences. That is, on the ungrammatical sentences for all three structures, they slowed down. They clearly demonstrated sensitivity to grammaticality on all structures. The L2 learners slowed down on the ungrammatical *wh*-questions and the adverb sentences. They did not slow down on the person-number sentences. In short, they demonstrated grammatical sensitivity on two structures but not on the third. What is interesting about these results and why they are relevant to the present discussion is that *wh*-question formation is not taught in most Spanish classes and we know that adverb placement never is. These structures are consequences of the feature specification we have been discussing throughout. Clearly, the L2 participants were demonstrating some kind of underlying representation for this feature and for the parameterized consequences of it in Spanish (the things that in our model do not have to be learnt). However, the L2 participants did not show underlying representation for the morpho-phonological units related to person-number on verbs. These are precisely the things related to verb movement that need to be learnt from the input and are a particular aspect of Spanish 'grammar' taught and practised from day one. Yet, these non-beginners did not show evidence of any mental representation for the very thing that has been present in their formal instruction from the first day of Spanish classes. What VanPatten, Keating and Leeser concluded was that things like person-number endings on verbs must be learnt from the input like anything else; they can't be taught and practised in order to build a mental representation of them. When they examined the input of typical classrooms and textbook materials, they discovered how relatively poor the input is in terms of providing lots of samples of the various person-number endings. Third-person singular (and plural) tend to dominate the input, and overwhelmingly so.

Although this particular study was not a study about instructed SLA, the reader can see that it has consequences for thinking about instructed SLA. A singular question comes to mind from the viewpoint of the current volume, 'What happened to all that instruction, practice, feedback, and so on related to person-number endings in Spanish? Where did it go?'

Against the notion of 'rules'

We are now in the position to formally state the central thesis of this chapter:

- Learners do not acquire rules from the input. Instead, learners process surface morpho-phonological units (e.g. lexical form, morphological form) and internalize these units along with underlying features or specifications. These units interact with information provided by UG and the language-making mechanisms of the human language faculty such that anything that resembles rules (from an outside perspective) evolves over time.[3]

Why is this thesis important and germane to the focus of the present volume? The reason is that too much – if not all – of instructed SLA research has been concerned with learning rules (presumably) from the input. For example, in his discussion of the issues surrounding the debate on explicit and implicit learning in adult SLA, Hulstijn (2005) says, 'Explicit learning is input processing with the conscious intention to find out whether the input information contains regularities and, if so, *to work out the concepts and rules* with which these regularities can be captured' (p. 131, emphasis added). Robinson (1995) researches training on 'easy and hard rules' (p. 303). Other researchers are less direct about what is learnt, referring to 'knowledge' or 'structures'. However, a careful reading suggests they are interested in rules in the traditional sense. For example, Ellis's (2005) study on testing explicit and implicit 'knowledge' is clearly about rules that are the focus of English-language teaching as exemplified in his Table 3 (e.g. third person *–s*, question tags, *yes/no* questions, use of modals with bare verbs). For additional examples, the reader is invited to examine De Jong (2005), Henshaw (2011) and Leow et al. (2011).

Sometimes scholars hedge on the focus of instructed SLA. In the case of Spada and Tomita (2010), the authors refer to 'features' of language as the object of research, while in the same paragraph switching to easy and hard 'rules' (see p. 264). Such hedging and confusion about the object of acquisition are, in our estimation, reflective of the field's having not grappled with the most fundamental question underlying instructed SLA: *What* is acquired? A related unasked question, and one that falls out of the previous discussion, is this: *What* is there in the input for the learner to grasp? Our thesis is that it is not rules but surface properties of language, namely (again) lexical and morphological form.

Why is this thesis important? First, a more principled account of the nature of language will help us to understand and make better predictions about instructed SLA. For example, there are aspects of language that cannot and need not be taught, while there are candidates for explicit learning (ignoring the question for now as to whether those candidates indeed can be learnt via some kind of intervention). Once we separate out these properties of language, rules disappear. The object of instructed SLA now becomes surface forms, but particular kinds of surface forms specifically chosen because they become apparent to us for formal linguistic reasons.

A second consequence of adopting this thesis is that it invites a re-examination of some of instructed SLA's most cherished notions, such as individual differences in 'rule learning'. VanPatten and colleagues recently completed a major four-part study with four languages (Spanish, French, Russian and German) using processing instruction as the framework (VanPatten et al. in press). Processing instruction, if the reader is familiar with its underlying theory, is not about rule learning but about processing behaviours and their relationship to particular kinds of surface forms. In that study, the focus was word order (the first-noun strategy) and its effects on four different structures across the four languages (clitic object pronoun interpretation in Spanish, case interpretation in German and Russian and interpretation of causative structures in French). One of the variables examined was the most studied aspect of language aptitude – grammatical sensitivity (as measured by the Modern Language Aptitude Test). Using trials-to-criterion as the measure of correct processing (i.e. when learners began to process/interpret sentences correctly), no correlations or relationships between grammatical sensitivity and when learners began to process correctly were found. No relationships between grammatical sensitivity and final outcome were found either (i.e. a post-test). This finding stands in stark contrast to the widely accepted results of aptitude research in which a relationship between aptitude and learning is taken to be a 'fact' (see, e.g. the discussion in Sawyer and Ranta 2001). What VanPatten et al. have argued in this study was that because they were (1) focused on processing and not learning, and (2) they were focused on surface elements and not rules, one would not expect something like grammatical sensitivity to be an important variable in processing instruction (in contrast to the claim by Robinson 2002, who says grammatical sensitivity should be important to processing instruction). Aptitude and grammatical sensitivity in particular relate to explicit rule learning, not to processing of surface forms of language. Once we get away from the concept of rule learning, something like aptitude makes less sense than it did previously. This argument, however, does not mean that other individual differences don't come into play. But those individual differences need to be reasoned out and researched within the idea that learning from the input is about processing surface elements of language as described in the previous section of this chapter.

To be sure, not all scholars in instructed SLA are concerned with rules in the traditional sense of rules. Some constructs and hypotheses are neutral on the issue, such as the noticing hypothesis (e.g. Schmidt 1990) and the interaction hypothesis (e.g. Gass 2003). However, some problems have arisen because these hypotheses have been applied to rules as these hypotheses get adopted and used by others. One reads or hears of not just noticing form but also 'noticing rules' or of interactional feedback focusing learner attention on rules (but see the conclusion in Gass 2003, for some careful and thoughtful remarks on what interaction can actually affect and what learners focus on).[4]

A third consequence of adopting this thesis is that it directs the field of instructed SLA research away from the classical notion of learning and instead nudges it towards issues in processing. In SLA theory more generally, processing and its relationship to acquisition are now widely accepted and incorporated into a number of models and theories, such as the Acquisition by Processing framework (Truscott and Sharwood Smith 2004), Autonomous Induction (Carroll 2001), various emergentist accounts (e.g. Ellis 2007; O'Grady 2010), the Shallow Structure Hypothesis (Clahsen and Felser 2006) and, to be sure, VanPatten's Input Processing model (VanPatten 2004, 2007, and elsewhere). Although not all of the theories and models listed here adopt a generative position as this chapter does, all of these theories and models are clear that what gets processed in the input are forms (morpho lexical in nature) and that underlying grammars are built over time as a result of the processed data being stored and organized either by language-special mechanisms (under generative accounts) or by general learning mechanisms (under emergentist accounts). None of them claims that rules are learnt from the input. The point to be made here is that instructed SLA (with the exception of work on input processing) had tended to ignore the concept of processing as the fundamental bridge between 'data out there' and 'mechanisms inside the head'. What the central thesis of this chapter does then, as a third consequence, is to further imply that instructed SLA should be concerned with *models of processing* and the extent to which external intervention results in changes in processed data (and/or how data are processed from the input).

One of the questions we sometimes hear from non-generativists when discussing the 'no rules' issue is 'What are learners building in their heads then if they are not learning rules?' To be clear, there is a difference between rules and rule-like behaviour. Rules, as normally understood by applied linguists, are (again) shorthand ways of talking about things that are often too complex and/ or too abstract to describe easily. If we return to *yes/no* questions in English, we can easily illustrate this. What we hear and see as a *yes/no* question in English is the surface reflex of a variety of underlying aspects of the grammar interacting. We list them briefly here:

- weak AGR (keeps lexical verbs in VP)
- T features (trigger *do* to carry T features since verbs can't move out of VP)
- Q features (force *do* out of the TP and into the CP)
- Non-null-subject parameter requires an overt subject

So to answer the question of what learners are internalizing or getting, our answer for the example from *yes/no* questions is that they are creating a grammar with the characteristics above along with the computational system that derives the surface word order seen in *Does Bill drink vodka?* Of course, teachers and applied linguists generally don't talk about *yes/no* questions referring to the above list. Instead, they shorthand it with 'insert do and invert subject and auxiliary' which clearly describes the surface phenomena, but not what causes the surface phenomena. The problem is, from a pedagogical viewpoint, if one teaches surface rules, then one is not getting at the underlying issue, and that is mental representation. And, as we have argued, mental representation only comes about from interaction with input. What is perhaps more problematic is that many teachers think that the rules they teach are indeed the ones that learners 'internalize'. The result is a perpetuation of the myth of 'teach rules and practice rules, and that's how you get language'.[5]

A few comments about non-linguistic factors

The field of SLA (and by implication, instructed SLA) has witnessed a multiplicity of approaches emerge since the earliest days of contemporary theorizing (e.g. Corder 1967; Selinker 1972). In particular, we have seen the emergence of social perspectives on adult language acquisition that have included constructs such as the Zone of Proximal Development, scaffolding, dialogic learning, the social turn, among others. While some scholars taking a social perspective are neutral or agnostic on the nature of underlying mental representation and the role of generative theory in describing this representation (and how it might get there), others have vociferously decried the merits of what they term 'mentalist' approaches. Some researchers deny the existence of a mental representation as described here and have denied the idea of innate structures such as UG and linguistic processors. We do not intend to argue why decrying a generative approach is either right or wrong (obviously, we think it's wrong). Instead, we would like to say that taking a generative approach does not deny the existence of social aspects of language acquisition.

Because the object of generative (and by extension, processing) accounts of acquisition is the underlying mental representation, the theory by definition is narrowly construed. By the same token, *every* theory about adult SLA is narrowly construed, even the social ones. Our point here is that a generative perspective does not imply that social context and such things as the social turn are irrelevant to language acquisition. In one sense, a generative perspective *assumes* that such things are part of acquisition if for nothing more than the social environment delimits the availability of and the ability to uptake input, the raw material of grammar formation. But the social aspects of acquisition are just not the objects of study in generative circles. By contrast, much of the work on the social nature of language acquisition does not assume a generative grammar as the underlying representation. (It's not clear to us how socially based research constructs language as an object.)

In making these points, we are explicitly stating that by taking the position we take in this chapter does not obviate the need for those working in other frameworks to continue their work. In fact, in other work, we have argued that multiplicity of perspectives on adult SLA is both expected and needed (Rothman and VanPatten 2013). Our hope is that the reader of this chapter, then, does not walk away assuming that because we have taken a generative-cum-processing perspective on language acquisition means that all else is either irrelevant or not worth looking at. Quite the contrary. We are asking, however, that various perspectives on the nature of grammar in instructed SLA (the focus of this volume) consider to what extent they can be informed by a generative theory about mental representation. For instance, is interaction incompatible with a generative perspective? We see no reason for it not to be, because believing in the role of interaction assumes a role for input, which in turn begs the question of how learners engage that input during interactions and what is actually processed and 'learned'. These comments include, for example, feedback and its role during interaction (see Gass 2003, for some discussion). Is generative theory incompatible with sociocultural theory? Again, we see no reason why they are not complementary. For example, there is nothing incompatible with constructs such as zones of proximal development and mediation (to name two constructs within the theory) and the growth of mental representation in the mind/brain of the learner. One assumes learner control over the environment (which ultimately affects the quality and quantity of input) while the other assumes that internal mechanisms control how the data from the environment are processed and how a grammar evolves.

To summarize, there is no a priori reason that a generative approach cannot work with other approaches to give a fuller account of adult SLA and by extension, no reason why a generative account cannot work with other approaches to better inform research on instructed SLA. The title of the present volume is *The Grammar Dimension in Instructed SLA: Theory, Research, and Practice*. Echoing what Kevin Gregg said in 1989, our point is that we should approach the 'grammar dimension' with rigour and clarity, regardless of our frameworks.

Concluding remarks

Before concluding, we offer a list that summarizes our main points.

- From a generative perspective, there are aspects of language that need not be – indeed cannot be – learnt because they are innate and are available from the start in language acquisition. These include the inventory of universal features as well as universal constraints that all languages must obey. Examples: The Extended Projection Principle, Tense.
- There are other aspects of language that are not necessarily innate but fall out from or are automatically derived from universal properties. These, too, are not learnt in the classic sense. Example: Verb Movement.
- A third category contains those of aspects of language that are individual to languages and must be learnt from exposure. Example: the morpho-phonological manifestations of auxiliary *do* in English and the morpho-phonological manifestations of verbs in Spanish.

Because of these three main points, we have argued for the thesis that learners do not learn rules from the input. Instead, they process particular forms (morpho-phonological units) that are used by internal mechanisms to create a grammar. Rules – if they exist, and they surely don't exist in the classic sense used in instructed SLA research – are by-products of the growth of language in the learner's mind/brain. We have also argued that there are a serious of implications for instructed SLA in taking the position we take here; namely, (1) a more principled account of the nature of language, (2) a re-examination of various notions within instructed SLA (we offered aptitude as one) and (3) a move away from learning rules to processing surface properties in the input.

To be sure, instructed SLA as a research field is complex and involves a multitude of variables and constructs that need to be considered when one puts together a research project – or wants to make theoretical claims about the effects of instruction. But too often research on instructed SLA takes a simplistic and reductionist approach to some of those variables and constructs. This is understandable for a variety of reasons (which would take us more time and space to explore here than we have). Our hope is that this chapter takes at least one construct – the nature of language – and demonstrates how having a richer and more complete statement about what it is can inform research on instructed SLA. This chapter is neither definitive and will not be the last word on this one topic. We hope it initiates discussion not just on the nature of language and 'learning' in instructed SLA, but also serves as a model for discussions about other variables and constructs as well.

Notes

1   Here, we acknowledge and put aside so-called auxiliary-subject inversion in English, as in (i) and (ii) below given its syntax is different from what we are discussing and is thus peripheral to our point (see Radford 2004). Indeed, this entails that English does avail itself syntactically of subject-verb inversion in a restricted set of *yes/no* question environments in addition to so-called *do*-support, but never with lexical verbs (iii) or in embedded contexts (iv) as in Spanish.

    i   Have you lived in Spain?
    ii   Is she coming to the party?
    iii   *Buy she the book?
    iv   *John asked Mary if had she bought the book?

2   We are being necessarily brief here, perhaps too brief. But VanPatten has dealt with the differences between mental representation and skill in detail in other publications, and we refer the reader to those: VanPatten (2010, in press).

3   We are leaving out actual phonological processing and other steps for ease of illustration here. For detailed discussion of all the modules of processing and how they provide input to each other, see Carroll (2001).

4   See Truscott (1998) for a critical overview of how noticing is problematic from a generative viewpoint.

5   Returning to the issue of aptitude for a moment, we note here that almost all tests on aptitude (e.g. the Modern Language Aptitude Test, LLAMA, Canal-F) include some kind of section on grammatical sensitivity or 'rule learning'. We point out to the reader that the LLAMA and Canal-F tests were developed in the 2000s as opposed to the MLAT developed in the 1950s, yet these tests still conceptualize language acquisition as (conscious) rule learning. The reader is referred to VanPatten (forthcoming) for some discussion on this matter.

References

Anderson, J. (2000), *Learning and Memory* (2nd edn). New York: John Wiley & Sons.

Bruhn de Garavito, J. (1995), 'L2 acquisition of verb complementation and binding principle B', in F. Eckman, D. Highland, P. W. Lee, J. Mileham, and R. Rutkowski Weber (eds), *Second Language Acquisition Theory and Pedagogy*. Mahwah, NJ: Lawrence Erlbaum Associates, pp. 79–100.

Carroll, S. E. (2001), *Input and Evidence: The Raw Material of Second Language Acquisition*. Amsterdam: Benjamins.

Chomsky, N. (1995), *The Minimalist Program*. Cambridge, MA: MIT Press.

— (2007), 'Of minds and language'. *Biolinguistics*, 1, 9–27.

Clahsen, H., and Felser, C. (2006), 'Grammatical processing in language learners'. *Applied Psycholinguistics*, 27, 3–42.

Corder, S. P. (1967), 'The significance of learners' errors'. *International Review of Applied Linguistics in Language Teaching*, 4, 161–70.

De Jong, N. (2005), 'Can second language grammar be learned through listening? An experimental study'. *Studies in Second Language Acquisition*, 27, 205–34.

Ellis, N. C. (2007), 'Dynamic systems theory and SLA: the wood and the trees'. *Bilingualism: Language and Cognition*, 10, 23–25.

Ellis, R. (2005), 'Measuring implicit and explicit knowledge of a second language: a psychometric study'. *Studies in Second Language Acquisition*, 27, 141–72.

Gallego, A. J. (2011), 'Parameters', in C. Boeckx (ed.), *The Oxford Handbook of Linguistic Minimalism*. Oxford: Oxford University Press, pp. 523–50.

Gass, S. M. (2003), 'Input and interaction', in C. Doughty and M. H. Long (eds), *The Handbook of Second Language Acquisition*. Oxford: Blackwell, pp. 224–55.

Goad, H. and White, L. (2006), 'Ultimate attainment in interlanguage grammars: a prosodic approach'. *Second Language Research*, 22, 243–68.

Gregg, K. R. (1989), 'Second language acquisition theory: the case for a generative perspective', in S. M. Gass and J. Schachter (eds), *Linguistic Perspectives on Second Language Acquisition*. Cambridge: Cambridge University Press, pp.15–40.

— (2003), 'SLA theory: construction and assessment', in C. Doughty and M. Long (eds), *The Handbook of Second Language Acquisition*. Oxford: Blackwell, pp. 831–65.

Guasti, M. T. (2004), *Language Acquisition: The Growth of Grammar*. Cambridge, MA: MIT Press.

Harley, H. and Noyer, R. (1999), 'Distributed morphology'. *Glot International*, 4(4), 3–9.

Henshaw, F. (2011), 'Effects of feedback timing in SLA: a computer assisted study on the Spanish subjunctive', in C. Sanz and R. P. Leow (eds), *Implicit and Explicit Language Learning: Conditions, Processes, and Knowledge in SLA and Bilingualism*. Washington, D.C.: Georgetown University Press, pp. 85–99.

Herschensohn, J. (2000), *The Second Time Around: Minimalism and L2 Acquisition*. Amsterdam: John Benjamins.

Hulstijn, J. (2005), 'Theoretical and empirical issues in the study of implicit and explicit second language learning'. *Studies in Second Language Acquisition,* 27, 129–40.

Jackendoff, R. (2002), *Foundations of Language.* Oxford: Oxford University Press.

Lardiere, D. (1998), 'Case and Tense in the 'fossilized' steady state'. *Second Language Research,* 14, 1–26.

Leow, R. P., Johnson, E., and Zárate-Sández, G. (2011), 'Getting a grip on the slippery construct of awareness: toward a finer grained methodological perspective', in C. Sanz and R. P. Leow (eds), *Implicit and Explicit Language Learning: Conditions, Processes, and Knowledge in SLA and Bilingualism.* Washington, D.C.: Georgetown University Press, pp. 61–72.

O'Grady, W. (2010), 'Emergentism', in P. Hogan (ed.), *The Cambridge Encyclopedia of the Language Sciences.* Cambridge, UK: Cambridge University Press, pp. 274–76.

Pollack, J. Y. (1989), 'Verb movement, universal grammar and the structure of IP'. *Linguistic Inquiry,* 20, 365–424.

Radford, A. (2001), *Syntax: A Minimalist Introduction.* Cambridge: Cambridge University Press.

— (2004), *English Syntax: An Introduction.* Cambridge, UK: Cambridge University Press.

Robinson, P. (1995), 'Aptitude, awareness and the fundamental similarity of implicit and explicit second language learning', in R. Schmidt (ed.), *Attention and Awareness in Foreign Language Learning.* Honolulu: University of Hawai'i at Manoa, pp. 303–58.

— (2002), 'Learning conditions, aptitude complexes, and SLA: a framework for research and pedagogy', in P. Robinson (ed.), *Individual Differences in Instructed Language Learning.* Amsterdam: John Benjamins, pp. 113–33.

Rothman, J. (2010), 'Theoretical linguistics meets pedagogical practice: pronominal subject use in Spanish as a second language (L2) as an example'. *Hispania,* 93, 52–65.

Rothman, J. and VanPatten, B. (2013), 'On multiplicity and mutual exclusivity: the case for different SLA theories', in M. P. García-Mayo, M. J. Gutiérrez-Mangado, and M. Martínez Adrián (eds), *Contemporary Approaches to Second Language Acquisition.* Amsterdam: John Benjamins, pp. 243–56.

Sawyer, M. and Ranta, L. (2001), 'Aptitude, individual differences, and instructional design', in P. Robinson (ed.), *Cognition and Second Language Instruction.* Cambridge: Cambridge University Press, pp. 319–53.

Schmidt, R. W. (1990), 'The role of consciousness in second language learning'. *Applied Linguistics,* 11, 129–58.

— (1992), 'Psychological mechanisms underlying second language fluency'. *Studies in Second Language Acquisition,* 14, 357–85.

Schwartz, B. (1993), 'On explicit and negative evidence effecting and affecting competence and linguistic behavior. *Studies in Second Language Acquisition,* 15, 147–64.

Segalowitz, N. (2003), 'Automaticity and second languages', in C. Doughty and M. H. Long (eds), *The Handbook of Second Language Acquisition.* Oxford: Blackwell, pp. 382–408.

Selinker, L. (1972), 'Interlanguage'. *International Review of Applied Linguistics in Language Teaching,* 10, 209–31.

Snyder, W. (2007), *Child Language: The Parametric Approach.* Oxford: Oxford University Press.

Sorace, A. (2011), 'Pinning down the concept of "interface" in bilingualism'. *Linguistic Approaches to Bilingualism,* 1, 1–33.

Spada, N. and Tomita, Y. (2010), 'Interactions between type of instruction and type of language feature: a meta-analysis'. *Language Learning,* 60, 263–308.

Truscott, J. (1998), 'Noticing in second language acquisition: a critical review'. *Second Language Research,* 14, 103–35.

Truscott, J., and Sharwood Smith, M. (2004), 'Acquisition by processing: a modular perspective on language development'. *Bilingualism: Language and Cognition,* 7, 1–20.

VanPatten, B. (1996), *Input Processing and Grammar Instruction.* Norwood, NJ: Ablex.

— (2004), 'Input processing in second language acquisition', in B. VanPatten (ed.), *Processing Instruction: Theory, Research, and Commentary.* Mahwah, NJ: Lawrence Erlbaum & Associates, pp. 5–31.

— (2007), 'Input processing in adult second language acquisition', in B. VanPatten and J. Williams (eds), *Theories in Second Language Acquisition.* Mahwah, NJ: Lawrence Erlbaum Associates, pp. 115–35.

— (2010), 'The two faces of SLA: Mental representation and skill'. *International Journal of English Language Studies,* 10, 1–18.

— (in press), 'Mental representation and skill in instructed SLA', in J. Schwieter (ed.), *Innovations in SLA, Bilingualism, and Cognition: Research and Practice.* Amsterdam: John Benjamins.

— (in press), 'Aptitude as grammatical sensitivity: recent research on processing instruction', in C. Sanz and B. Lado (eds), *Individual Differences, L2 Development & Language Program Administration: From Theory to Application.*

VanPatten, B. and Rothman, J. (in press), 'What does current generative theory have to say about the explicit-implicit debate?' in P. Rebuschat (ed.), *Implicit and Explicit Learning of Languages.* Amsterdam: John Benjamins.

VanPatten, B., Borst, S., Collopy, E., Qualin, A., and Price, J. (2013), 'Explicit information, grammatical sensitivity, and the first-noun principle: a cross-linguistic study in processing instruction'. *The Modern Language Journal,* 506–27.

VanPatten, B., Keating, G. D., and Leeser, M. J. (2012), 'Missing verbal inflections as a representational problem: Evidence from self-paced reading'. *Linguistic Approaches to Bilingualism,* 2, 109–40.

White, L. (2003), *Second Language Acquisition and Universal Grammar.* Cambridge: Cambridge University Press.

2

Possibilities and Limitations of Enhancing Language Input: A MOGUL Perspective

Mike Sharwood Smith
*Heriot-Watt University, United Kingdom, Edinburgh University,
United Kingdom and the Social Academy of Sciences, Poland*

Once it became clear to SLA researchers that learners do not simply learn what is put in front of them, what is explained to them and what they then practise reproducing, it was understood that the processes underlying language learning are much more subtle and elusive than many supposed, especially with regard to grammatical systems. Some researchers have been investigating the idea that various systematic characteristics of a target language can, in various subtle or less subtle ways, be made more salient, that is, noticeable to the learner with the aim of speeding up learning. Acquisition research to date has generally fought shy of going too deeply into questions of how language is processed and stored although this would seem to be vital for a scientific account of how new knowledge and ability are acquired. There are nevertheless clear advantages in pursuing this line. One particular approach that does this, Modular On-line Growth and Use of Language (MOGUL), will be outlined and its relevance for explaining different types of IE will be explained.

Overview

In this chapter, the concept of 'L2 input' in the SLA literature will be reconsidered. The main conclusion to be drawn will be that research into how L2 input is processed by the learner to create mental grammars still suffers from a relatively undeveloped theoretical foundation despite all the valuable pioneering research into the fleshing out the various concepts involved. The lack of a widely accepted foundation continues to be a major stumbling block for research into IE which has still not yielded any convincing results despite more than a decade of experimental research. One big problem lies in the fact that the processing-based accounts that we do have focus on the principles behind what L2 learners at one given point in time subconsciously select for processing (Pienemann 1998). The *developmental* dimension still needs to be explored, that is, what, in processing terms, happens *next* when currently processed input leads to, or fails to lead to, stable new knowledge states. The discussion will address the basic requirements for any respectable theory of language processing before examining just one of a small number of recent proposals that hold out promise for a more rigorous analysis of the effect of pedagogical interventions of various types (Whong 2011; Sharwood Smith et al. 2013; Sharwood Smith and Truscott forthcoming).

L2 input: The basics

The notion 'L2 input' is generally interpreted as referring to language utterances to which a learner is exposed and which are assumed to form the basis of what is learnt. It is sometimes referred to, especially by those espousing a generative linguistic perspective, as 'primary linguistic data' (PLD). Not all of the current input will be processed. Following Corder's terminology, the subset of L2 input that is actually processed is referred to as L2 'intake' (Corder 1967). This is the point where things become complicated. Processing does not necessarily lead to any form of change in the learner's L2 system. It can simply be processed for communication, and any potentially useful information for promoting further development of the L2 grammar or lexicon may be ignored (Sharwood Smith 1985). Nevertheless, intake is often understood as that part of input that is processed sufficiently to cause a change in the learner's current L2 system.

Input and the teacher

If we take 'the teacher' to stand for the complete set of resources intervening in the learning process, that is, the teacher plus all other learning resources, then the teacher has two basic roles. The first one is as input provider. The second is as enhancer of input. Although the two roles are sometimes hard to distinguish since provision involves selection and by selecting what the learner is exposed to, the teacher has already started the process of intervention. However, the term 'enhancement' is normally used to refer to more focused kinds of intervention by attempting to make specific aspects of the input more salient. In point of fact, the original use of the term covered indicated many different ways of making the learner attend to the input. These ranged from traditional grammatical explanation to visually or acoustically highlighting certain linguistic features or making certain aspects of the L2 much more frequent than they would be in normal everyday speech and writing in order to attract the learner's attention and make them more memorable (Sharwood Smith 1981, 1991, 1993). Research in recent years has focused more on a restricted range of techniques such as highlighting (e.g. italicizing or marking in boldface) specific grammatical or morphological forms without necessarily explaining to the learner why these forms are marked in these ways. The basic definition adopted for present purposes of this discussion is the original one, although, as the discussions develop, it will clear that an even broader definition might be needed especially where the issue of affect is concerned. The basic definition runs as follows:

Input Enhancement: A definition
The manipulation of selected (usually linguistic) features of the input deemed important by language teachers or teaching materials creators with the specific aim of speeding up development.

Three basic types of IE
according to teacher intention

There are three broad types of IE that fall under the above definition. This categorization is based on the teacher's *intended focus* and not on the *actual effects* of the. By default, IE simply refers to what happens *outside* the learner. The very natural but nonetheless misleading teacher-based perspective of the earlier term 'consciousness-raising' was dropped since it seemed to assume, in advance, a specific learner response (conscious awareness) when the effects on the learner of given techniques were actually the objects of research (Sharwood Smith 1981). Here, no such assumption is made although it is important to know what the intended effects are, and this gives us the three subcategories listed below. At least we can have some confidence in knowing what the teacher's intended target. We can have much less confidence in knowing whether the required mental processing by the learner, conscious or otherwise, together with any intended outcomes has actually been achieved. Our lack of detailed knowledge about processing prevents from knowing what the effects of this or that teacher intervention may be. Also, if a desired outcome is ultimately achieved, we cannot be sure of whether this was because of the intervention or despite it. At any rate, the three basic subcategories are as follows:

1. Perceptual IE
2. Conceptual IE
3. Affective IE

Perceptual IE:
Getting past the front door

The prime target of perceptual enhancement is the learner's perception. The goal is to get the learner to perceptually process some piece of linguistic input to a greater degree than they might otherwise have processed it, that is, to make the perceptual processing of some relevant visual or auditory stimulus more intense. The hope here clearly is that once you get the input repeatedly, as it were, through the front door, further internal processing will take place and eventually lead to stable changes in the learner's L2 system. This hope relates to the vexed question of what noticing entails which has been much discussed in the literature (see, e.g. Gass 1997; Schmidt 2001; Schmidt and Frota 1986; Truscott and Sharwood Smith 2011).

Conceptual IE

The prime target of conceptual enhancement is the learner's understanding. It takes perceptual processing for granted and targets the learner's comprehension of linguistic input. This comprehension can take two forms. First, such enhancement can aim to facilitate the interpretation of something in an utterance, say a word or phrase such as 'queasy', 'industrial quality' or 'high five'. Second, it may be analytic in nature. The aim here is to promote an understanding of how the linguistic system works. For example, it could explain some L2 property or rule, or it could explain what the learner got wrong and why. This last type of conceptual IE could also be called 'metacognitive' enhancement, although the first type might just happen to trigger some accompanying conscious, and hence metacognitive (or 'metalinguistic') reflection about the meaning of a word or phrase although it certainly does not have to.

Affective IE

The prime target of affective enhancement is the attitude, the emotions or values of the learner with regard to the L2. This can mean attributing positive value to particular linguistic items or it can enhance the input in more indirect, contextual ways by making the experience of using the L2 in and outside the classroom more positive. In the case of strictly linguistic input, as opposed to accompanying contextual input, this would what Burt et al. would call lowering the 'affective filter' and allowing the learner to process the L2 input more effectively (Burt et al. 1982; Sharwood Smith (forthcoming)). According to whether negative or positive value is attached, various types of emotion may be experienced by the learner with consequences that still need to be properly explored.

Again continuing to see IE from the perspective of the teacher's intentions, these three basic types are often *combined* in various ways. Here is one example related to grammar:

Example

The teacher 'explains' [attempted conceptual IE], in, an 'exciting and stimulating' manner [attempted affective IE], the way YES/NO questions are formed in English, 'highlighting' [attempted perceptual IE] the **DO** form wherever it occurs, pointing out that in sentences like 'They *do*[attempted perceptual IE] not know' 'do' is meaningless and bears no relation to the 'doing' as in 'they do a lot work'[attempted conceptual IE].

Experimental work on IE

The most widely investigated type of enhancement in recent years seems to have been **perceptual IE**, especially the visual enhancement of text (typographical enhancement). This is probably because of its greater amenability to controlled experimental research (Leow et al. 2003; Han et al. 2007, 2008; Lee et al. 2008;

Overstreet 1998; Park and Han 2008; White 1998). Some studies have included other types on enhancement such as explicit instruction now included under 'conceptual enhancement' (e.g. White et al. 1991; Alanen 1995; Gascoigne 2006; Berent et al. 2009).

There have been conflicting results as regards the perceptual IE of morphosyntactic features. White et al. reported positive effects for the acquisition of question formation (White et al. 1991). Izumi found that visual IE had no significant effect. Furthermore, 17 years after the White et al. study, Lee and Huang did a meta-analysis of visual IE and grammar learning and concluded that the results of research to date were inconclusive and nothing to date has altered that impression (Izumi 2002; Lee and Huang 2008). In fact, the general picture as far as more rigorous testing of instructional techniques in general is concerned seems to be disappointing for those who hoped for easy access to learner's acquisitional mechanisms, whatever they might be (see Trenkic and Sharwood Smith 2001). In 2003, Doughty looked at research on the effectiveness of language instruction as a whole finding only very tentative (Doughty 2005):

> After reviewing the cases for and against L2 instruction, we will conclude that instruction is potentially effective, provided it is relevant to learners' needs. However, we will be forced to acknowledge that the evidence to date for either absolute or relative effectiveness of L2 instruction is tenuous at best, owing to improving, but still woefully inadequate, research methodology

The conclusion for IE of whatever type is that, so far, there is no strong evidence that it helps, although this of course does not preclude further research into the issue. This is most obviously the case for what was referred to above as perceptual enhancement. Part of the explanation for this tentativeness about the effectiveness of techniques to improve the noticing of linguistic features in the L2 input may indeed be methodological weakness. This does not have to be a blanket criticism of all research that has been done thus far. Controlling all the variables in investigations into teaching techniques is extremely difficult: it is just tough doing this kind of research.

There is, however, another major problem other than methodology that bedevils such research, and this is the focus of this particular chapter. It is also related to methodology since experimental techniques, however sophisticated, have to be guided by good thinking. Since data do not come ready labelled, collecting more and more facts is not much good unless we have a rationale for their collection and an insightful way of interpreting them. For this we need theory. In other words, the other major weakness is the explanatory framework. We need to have a more precisely outlined account of how learners process the L2 to which they are exposed and the connection between this processing and the development of new knowledge and new skill.

At the outset of SLA research as an independent field, we had a choice between Selinker's interlanguage proposals and the creative construction model as developed by Burt et al. (Selinker 1972; Burt et al. 1982; Krashen 1982). At the time, these approaches were enormously exciting and stimulated a great deal of research. They also upset a lot of common-sense assumptions about language instruction, and rightly so. But that was then. Since that time, the field has seen great leaps in the linguistic sophistication of research into L2 grammars at particular stages of development and some advances in our understanding of the principles behind development through time, that is, the psycholinguistic aspects (see, e.g. Pienemann 1998; VanPatten 2004). What we have not had is a coherent account of the longer-term impact of online processing. In other words, we need answers to the question 'how does this millisecond-by-millisecond activity as the learner processes chunks of the L2 relate to the growth of that L2 in the learner's mind?'. Put another way, we need psycholinguistic accounts which have a *developmental* dimension, that is, developmental processing theories as opposed to just an account of how learners process language at on particular occasion and at one particular stage of their development (Sharwood Smith forthcoming.)

Explaining development

In the last few years, some interesting proposals for explaining online developmental mechanisms have been made. They are:

1. Carroll's Autonomous Induction Theory (AIT) (Carroll 2001)
2. O'Grady's Radical Nativism Theory (O'Grady 2005)
3. Sharwood Smith and Truscott's Modular Online Growth and Use of Language (MOGUL)

In this chapter, the third option will be used, for the most part, to demonstrate how processing and development can be related within an explanatory framework with some references to the other two approaches (for a somewhat more detailed comparison of all three approaches, see Sharwood Smith et al. in press).

Modular On-line Growth and Use of Language framework

As with Carroll's approach (and many others), MOGUL makes a clear distinction between *language* processing and other kinds of cognitive processing Truscott and Sharwood Smith 2004). Like O'Grady, Truscott and Sharwood Smith see online processing as the driver of growth. No special acquisition mechanisms are needed. Very briefly, the basic components of the mind according to MOGUL (the perpetual system, the linguistic system, etc.) are responsible for the following different types of representation, all relevant for understanding language use and language development:

> PERCEPTUAL REPRESENTATIONS (including the visual and auditory systems)
>
> LINGUISTIC REPRESENTATIONS (phonological and syntactic systems]
>
> CONCEPTUAL REPRESENATIONS (the meaning system including semantic/pragmatic meaning)
>
> AFFECTIVE REPRESENTATIONS (the value assignment and emotional system)

The basic areas depicted above involve perception, affect (emotion, value), conceptualization (meaning) and the core language system. Articulation (the motor systems) is not mentioned here. Note in any case that spoken and written utterance comprehension and utterance production involve all these areas and not just linguistic representations. In other words, 'language' processing involves much more than 'linguistic' processing in the narrow sense. Semantics, pragmatics and discourse considerations are handled in the conceptual system (Jackendoff 1987, 2002). Phonetics is handled by (auditory) perceptual system. Somehow these different representations have to be linked up to achieve a full, rich interpretation in either the hearer (in utterance comprehension) or the listener (in utterance production). This will be discussed more fully later in the sections directly related to IE.

The questions for those interested in developing much more comprehensive explanations of acquisitional mechanisms have been as follows. Does there exist current research in cognitive science that can inform us about how these might operate singly and together during linguistic processing. Are there any theoretical frameworks that capitalize on such research? Specifically, in the context of this discussion, is there anything that can help us explain input enhancement in a manner that can be claimed to have some degree of broad scientific backing?

Any comprehensive account that provides this service to second-language researchers and ultimately to practitioners such as teachers should have something to say about:

1. Specialized (expert) subsystems
2. How these subsystems collaborate (freely or not?)
3. Storage (temporary and in the longer term)
4. How items in memory are activated
5. How items compete for selection
6. The explicit/implicit distinction.

Specialized subsystems

A quite respectable assumption in current cognitive science is that the totality of language activity in the mind/brain at any given moment, that is, in the system as a whole, is the outcome of a number of specialized mental subsystems that 'talk' to each other in various ways. Any modular system is dysfunctional if there are no ways for the subsystems to collaborate. How they are constructed is of course still a hotly debated topic. People disagree about whether all the basics pre-exist at birth but are later configured in different ways by experience, during life or whether they are essentially developed from scratch during a person's lifetime and as a result of experience.

These subsystems collaborate online in the production and comprehension of utterances. By so doing, they also collaborate in development over time, whether the resulting changes are regarded as moving *towards* more advanced knowledge states or whether development is seen as regressive, moving *away from* some more advanced state as is the case in language attrition. Although the totality of a person's behaviour can certainly be viewed in holistic terms, each new state in some sense unique, each subsystem provides its own special, independent contribution to this whole. Each subsystem is an expert system and works according to its own principles. The visual and auditory systems are cases in point and, for those who accept the need to posit a domain-specific component to human natural language, the 'language module' is another example of an expert system that obeys principles of its own, not shared with any other one.

Communication possibilities vary, that is to say, collaboration between subsystems in the mind is not a free-for-all. The effect on one subsystem will not always have an automatic knock-on effect (or the *same* knock-on effect) on other subsystems. An effect on one system may not get passed on to the neighbour next door. This is crucial difference between this kind of constrained architecture and classical connectionist architecture which has no such internal constraints. A relevant question with regard to the present discussion is which system or systems in the mind will be affected by particular enhancement techniques. Answers to this question may help to explain why certain enhancement techniques appear *not* to produce the desired result.

Perception and input

From a strictly processing point of view, all input processing begins as perceptual processing. It is also important to remember that there is not just one kind of input, the kind referred to in Krashen's '$i + 1$' but many kinds (Carroll 2001). Language information is hidden in a whole crowd of sensory signals many of which will not be relevant at all for linguistic processing and some of which do not carry any specifically linguistic properties but do carry contextual information that will be useful for decoding utterances. This why different expert systems are required to collaborate to optimize utterance comprehension. After that first perceptual processing step comes an internal, complex set of steps, none of which are a foregone conclusion. Teachers seem best able to directly influence only the first step, the immediate impact of the perceptual input to the learner. The rest involves influencing the deeper internal processes about which we still know relatively little.

Memory (storage) and 'acquisition'

In the mental architecture sketched above, memory is also partitioned out among the various expert systems. It is uncontroversial nowadays to view memory as modular in character: that is why we commonly talk of visual memory, semantic memory, etc. MOGUL adheres to one particular view of memory, and particularly of *working* memory, which is a temporary buffer holding items temporarily during the act of processing. Memory is viewed in terms of single stores with working memory as those items in the stores which are currently activated

(Cowan 2005). In other words, working memories are not separate from 'long term memory' stores, or indeed are not merged into some common pool into which the individual stores feed into. This may be illustrated by imagining how we process a vaguely familiar visual image by trying to make sense of something we have just seen in the form of light waves hitting the retina of each eye. In extremely simplistic terms, the millisecond-by-millisecond sequence of events will go something like this:

i.   A pattern of light waves on the retina triggers the visual system [the perceptual stage].
ii. A representation in *visual* memory is located to match this sensory input.
iii. The matching visual representation is now activated and held in visual working memory.
iv. If the environmental signal is deficient and the first overall match is not perfect, events i-ii may be repeated until the best match is found.
v.   The currently activated visual representation triggers an interface between the visual and *conceptual* system which then activates a match (created by prior experience) and calls up the appropriate conceptual representation (the meaning).
vi. The matching conceptual representation, now activated, is held in conceptual working memory [the interpretation stage].
vii. Events i-vii may be repeated until the best match is found.

Step vi shows that it is not actually just a one-way sequential process but an incremental and parallel process. The outcome is the best fit between the chain of activated items, each member of the chain sitting in its own memory store and not merged into a single unit. The message as far as IE is concerned is that by making features in the input perceptually salient and thereby succeeding in influencing the first stages of processing is just the beginning of a chain of events involving different mental systems. The above example assumed that provided the visual information was perceptible enough, it could be automatically matched to a meaning because there had already been prior learning to establish this match. In the case of there not being any conceptual match yet for the visual input, initial processing, however successful, provides no guarantee of later processing since various new matching processes have to take place. In the classic morpheme studies, the third-person singular -s is presumably robustly present in the input almost from the point of earliest exposure and certainly perceptually processed by readers if not L2 listeners, yet it seems always to be acquired very late compared to the other grammatical morphemes in the list. This and examples like this suggest that robust input, made robust simply by repeated exposure if not by other means as well, has only been processed shallowly, and nothing has proceeded far enough to knock on the door of the linguistic system and be admitted. Note that 'acquired' in this context means that a novel combination of features in the appropriate memory store(s) has been created in the appropriate memory store(s) during online processing. Alternatively, acquisition can be simply the result of an item in memory, an inherent but hitherto unused property of the system, being used for the first time to cope with unfamiliar input. One example would be an L2 sentence which requires a particular syntactic feature to trigger its word order but which is a feature not needed for the L1 and which, therefore, the system has never needed to process. Acquisition in this minimal sense may be very transitory indeed and may quickly fade from memory: repeated processing will be necessary to ensure its survival in the longer term. Language attrition is explained in exactly the same way.

Resting levels, competition and co-activation

In the MOGUL framework, items (structural units/representations) residing in a memory store will have a current 'resting level'. A well-established item that is regularly used in online processing will have a high resting level (see structures '3' and '4' in Fig 2.1). This means that, when activated, it has rapid access to working memory, which, in the metaphor being used here, means rising temporarily to the upper level of the memory store (see structure '3' in Fig 2.1). A freshly acquired structure, however, or one that has long fallen into disuse, will have a relatively low resting level which hinders easy access up into working memory (see structures '1' and '2' in Fig 2.1). In reality, any item's resting level is never really completely stable, of course but only relatively so. During online processing, items in memory stores compete. Competition is an important feature of mental processing in general. Where language is concerned, it is accepted by many, not necessarily of the same persuasion in the other respects, that whatever language is being used at a particular moment, items belonging to other languages known to the user will be also (always) co-activated to some extent (Dijkstra and van Heuven 2002; Grosjean 1998, 2001). In other words, there is constant competition going on all the time.

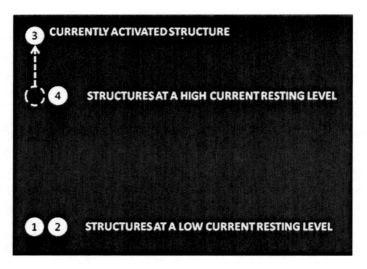

Figure 2.1 Activation with a memory store.

The more newly acquired items are activated, although they may not always compete successfully, the more their resting level rises and the better chance they will have in future when participating in the online assembly of a given chain (or network) of representations. One might conclude from this observation that enhancing some input might help the learner not only (a) to begin to acquire some linguistic feature but also, (b) once it has been (minimally) 'acquired', to raise its resting level. This will then give it better chance of beating any competition and playing a role in the comprehension and production of utterances. For an item in memory to be subject to growth, it has to be activated. What has been termed an 'item' here may be some structural feature which is available in the store anyway (i.e. it is an integral property of the system), or it may be a complex item, that is, a novel combination of structures required to handle the representation of the current input. The activation is triggered by input, but note this is not input from outside (the environment) but immediate input from some adjacent system: this virtually always means an *internal* system. In the following sections, an attempt will be able to recast linguistic IE in MOGUL terms assuming that most inputs to are internal ones. Only the impact on the immediate sensory systems triggered by environmental, that is, *external* input can be reasonably said to controllable by the input enhancer. The intended target lies within so that, actually, IE should, if possible, facilitate access to the relevant system within the learner and make such input robustly present at the right internal location. It is, as it were, not enough to knock loudly and frequently at the front gate. Something has to happen in the rooms *inside* the house. The essential point is that the important input, in discussions of IE, is one or other of the internal inputs, that is, within the learner's mind and not outside, in the environment.

Linguistic processing

Among the various subsystems involved in a language processing in general, there are two *specifically* dedicated to language and therefore two corresponding memory stores (see Fig 2.2):

a. phonological memory
b. syntactic memory.

As elsewhere, items in these two memories are processed according to unique rules and principles, and the contents of a memory are specific to that store. They can only combine in a way dictated by the system in which they reside. For example, phonological structures reside in the phonological memory and are different from syntactic structures. Each memory store has its own dedicated processor such that phonological items are processed by the phonological processor according to phonological principles and so on. Special interfaces match activated items in each memory with items in the adjacent store (the larger two-way arrows in Fig 2.2).

The resting levels and the arrangement of items in memory reflect the language experience of the individual language user. On encountering what

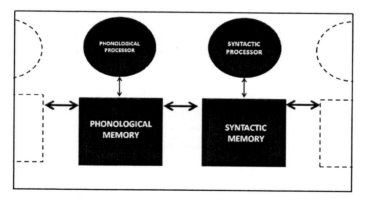

Figure 2.2 The two dedicated linguistic systems.

happens to be Polish auditory input, a Polish native speaker will activate different phonologically lawful combinations of items within the self-same phonological system than, say, a speaker of Spanish, English, Chinese or Japanese. The items are the same. The interrelationships and resting levels are different.

In L2 acquisition, strongly established L1 representations typically pose a big threat. Take an English-speaking learner of French. Due to the dominant L1 'rule',[1] an adjective will be expected to come before a noun even when the L2 rules require it to appear after the noun. English L1 requires 'red mill' (Adj + N), whereas its French equivalent requires 'moulin rouge' (N + Adj). The L2 order may already have been established in syntactic memory with a low resting level but initially the stronger L1 Adj + Noun order will still have much easier access into working memory and will tend to predominate in the learner's performance. Prior to the new, native-like order activated in the syntactic system, phonological strings like /mulẽ ruʒ/ will be matched up with Adj + N in the syntactic store, thus initially assigning adjective status to 'moulin' and noun status to 'rouge'. Thereafter, even when the native French order has been activated, it will face strong competition, as just mentioned, from the L1 English order until repeated processing has raised the relevant resting levels to a point where the L2 order can face off L1 competition. Note that in each system involved, competition is constrained by the processing principles of each processor involved.

IE recast in MOGUL terms

It is now appropriate to return to the three teacher-based types of IE mentioned earlier: perceptual, conceptual and affective IE. Recall that these categories were in terms of the teacher's intentions, not the actual psycholinguistic effects. It show now be clear that the most likely and in many case possible the only effect of IE of any kind is on the highly sensitive perceptual system. Provided the patterns of sound waves and light waves in which the enhancement material is delivered are registered (transduced), it is likely that the auditory and visual systems will make some sense of them and the corresponding items will be activated in one or other of these two systems. In the following discussion, not much will be said about affective enhancement although this topic is dealt with more extensively elsewhere.

Perceptual IE revisited

What does perceptual IE do? It seeks to optimize pre-linguistic input. The perceptual system being vital for survival is relatively easy to manipulate. The advertising world exploits this sensitivity. By increasing the auditory and visual aspects of selected linguistic features, teachers can perceptually enhance selected words or parts of words with a certain level of guaranteed success. Perceptual enhancement makes input as it were 'louder' or 'brighter'. Making any perceptual structure more salient by enhancing it will increase the chances of it being accepted for linguistic processing. As we already know, making some feature bright does not guarantee earlier processing. Some structures remain unacquired despite robust input. There are a number of reasons for this, an obvious one being that it is treated by the phonological system as auditory 'noise' and no matching phonological structures are searched for. The morphology marking object status in Spanish which figures in VanPatten's research in sentences like *A Maria la llama Juan* (literally: Maria$_{object}$ calls her$_{object}$ Juan$_{subect}$) is regularly ignored by English-speaking learners of Spanish (VanPatten and Cadierno 1993). Learners seem to be processing only some of the input linguistically and attributing to, respectively, 'Maria', 'llama' and 'Juan' properties that English word order would prompt so that the incorrect interpretation is reached (Maria$_{subject}$ calls Juan$_{object}$). The other possibility is that the object marker 'a' and the object pronoun 'la' are not treated as noise and are indeed processed linguistically but that they are given the wrong grammatical status. To recapitulate, making the visual and auditory input salient as possible so that good visual auditory representations are strongly activated has the effect of optimizing the chances of linguistic processing and no more than that. It is, as it were, up to the interfaces with the linguistic systems to take the processing to the next (linguistic) stage.

Conceptual IE revisited

The story for conceptual enhancement is similar. The first, simpler version simply means helping the learner to make all the appropriate associations online. Recall that, to process an utterance in this framework (following Jackendoff), a set of representations must be matched together, in parallel, and the resulting chain will produce an interpretation. If perceptual representations have been matched to phonological and syntactic representations, what we have so far is a chain of representations that still has no meaning. Completing that chain means adding a conceptual representation. This may not yield a successful outcome. In the Spanish example referred to above, English learners do complete the chain but come up with wrong analysis. Maria is not calling John: it is the other way round. By creating contexts that prejudice the learner against the wrong interpretation and bias them towards the correct one is a form of conceptual enhancement. VanPatten's processing instruction techniques provide examples of this. Whereas perceptual enhancement optimizes the *pre*-linguistic stage, this conceptual enhancement optimizes that *post*-linguistic stage. It is 'post-linguistic' in the narrow sense: the conceptual system where meaning is stored and processed is not part of the core linguistic system (phonology and syntax). And once again, it is still up to the linguistic processing stages (phonology and syntax) to respond and adjust to this optimized information outside. Both perceptual and conceptual enhancement clean up and optimize the periphery of the linguistic system, increasing the chances of comprehensive overall processing of an utterance but not guaranteeing it.

Metalinguistic conceptual enhancement

This means including in L2 input utterances conveying explicit information about language form, for example, telling learners that, say, 'adjectives *follow* nouns' in the L2. This kind of statement is intended to increase the understanding of the L2 works. Put another way, whatever the teacher's ultimate goal is, it actually targets the *conceptual* system and not the syntactic system. The MOGUL framework provides a way of making this observation more precise. The sentence 'adjectives follow nouns' is processed syntactically as, in simple terms: $Noun_{subject/plural} + Verb_{transive} + Noun_{object/plural}$. The syntactic system simply does not have the wherewithal to make any sense of this. 'Making sense' is literally the job of the conceptual processor. Metalinguistic knowledge about the way nouns and adjectives behave is encoded in conceptual structure. Conceptual structure is not in a code that the syntactic system can handle. The syntactic system cannot read and therefore benefit from what is coded in alien 'language'. It can only create a syntactic representation for what is presented to it. This means that the appropriate syntactic knowledge concerning the order with the noun phrase must develop separately in response to the syntactic processing of utterances.

Whereas information residing in the conceptual system can be projected into awareness, the items in syntactic memory and the way they are arranged and processed will remain forever inaccessible to conscious reflection. This means that if metalinguistic (explicit) information can help at all in the building of phonological and syntactic knowledge, it must be in the form of additional contextual assistance in making the post-linguistic stage of processing optimally meaningful.

Apart from its potential to enhance the meaning of utterances, the knowledge about language that is encoded in conceptual structure provides an extra resource for the older learner in producing more native-like performance. Here, MOGUL diverges to some extent from Krashen's classic views on the matter in that metalinguistic ability can to some extent become very fluent. This means that tests requiring spontaneous responses from learners will not necessarily exclude the possibility of them deploying knowledge that is metalinguistic in nature. It is, as Krashen suggested, limited in that conscious applications of online additions and self-corrections will impose an extra load on working memory. The point here is that it can still, to some extent, be automatized in rather the same way that experienced teachers can indulge in conscious reflection and adjustment to what they are saying in the middle of a class without breaking the flow of speech. Metalinguistic ability is deployed in L1 as well as in L2. For the experimenter, this means that separating out the particular contribution of metalinguistic knowledge in spontaneous speech will have to be done using more sophisticated techniques.

Affective IE revisited

Affective enhancement of linguistic input is a complex area that has been relatively unresearched in the way suggested by the present framework, but it may well prove to give important scientific backing to various teaching techniques whereby the learner is encouraged to assign positive and not negative value to aspects of the learning experience. Much more research is needed into the way affect can improve the activation of various relevant parts of system, raising resting levels and making features of the input more salient and 'brighter' in the way described with regard to perceptual enhancement (see Sharwood Smith forthcoming). This includes an interpretation, in MOGUL terms, of a growing body of work on affect and language (see, e.g. Dewaele 2005, 2010; Dörnyei 2001; Pavlenko 2008).

Final conclusions

The jury is still out on how far basic syntax and phonology can be influenced by teacher interventions of various kinds. A fair amount of empirical research has been carried out using various working hypotheses about what input is and how such external influence might operate. However, up until recently, there have only been only briefest and sketchiest accounts of the kind of processing involved that might move learners on from one developmental stage to the next. Recent attempts to fill this gap and provide a better, more fully fledged and cross-disciplinary account of developmental processing mechanisms should allow us to investigate more scientifically, with more precision, how and why and where: IE might work or fail to work. Applying the MOGUL framework to such questions suggests that various types of intervention can certainly optimize, in specific ways, various preconditions for the required grammatical growth to take place although the option of direct manipulation of syntactic and phonological growth mechanisms will always remain beyond the grasp of both teacher and learner.

Note

1   'Rule' is convenient shorthand for describing relationships among representations and does not imply that processors literally have a set of rules as such as part of their repertoire.

References

Alanen, R. (1995), 'Input enhancement and rule presentation in second language acquisition', in R. Schmidt (ed.), *Attention and Awareness in Second Language Acquisition*. Honolulu: University of Hawai'i Press, pp. 259–99.

Berent, G. P., Kelly, R. R., Schmitz, K. L. and Kenney, P. (2009), 'Visual input enhancement via essay coding results in deaf learners' long-term retention of improved English grammatical knowledge'. *Journal of Deaf Studies and Deaf Education*, 14, 190–204.

Carroll, S. (2001), *Input and Evidence: The Raw Material of Second Language Acquisition*. Amsterdam: John Benjamins.

Corder, P. (1967), 'The significance of learner's errors'. *International Review of Applied Linguistics*, 5, 161–70.

Cowan, N. (2005), *Working Memory Capacity*. New York: Psychology Press.

Dewaele, J.-M. (2005), 'Investigating the psychological and emotional dimensions in instructed language learning: obstacles and possibilities'. *Modern Language Journal*, 89, 367–80.

— (2010), *Emotions in Multiple Languages*. Basingstoke: Palgrave Macmillan.

Dijkstra, A. F. J. and van Heuven, W. J. B. (2002), 'The architecture of the bilingual word recognition system: from identification to decision'. *Bilingualism: Language and Cognition*, 5, 175–97.

Dörnyei, Z. (2001), *Teaching and Researching Motivation*. Harlow: Longman.

Doughty, C. (2005), 'Instructed SLA: constraints, compensation, and enhancement', in C. Doughty and M. Long (eds), *The Handbook of Second Language Acquisition*. Malden, MA: Blackwell, pp. 202–40.

Gascoigne, C. (2006), 'Explicit input enhancement: effects on target and non-target aspects of second language acquisition'. *Foreign Language Annals*, 39, 551–64.

Gass, S. (1997), *Input, Interaction, and the Second Language Learner*. Mahwah, NJ: Lawrence Erlbaum.

Grosjean, F. (1998), 'Transfer and language model'. *Bilingualism: Language and Cognition*, 13, 175–6.

— (2001), 'The bilingual's language modes', in J. Nicol (ed.), *One Mind, Two Languages: Bilingual Language Processing*. Oxford: Blackwell, pp. 1–22.

Han, Z. H., Park, E. S., and Combs, C. (2008), 'Textual enhancement of input: issues and possibilities'. *Applied Linguistics*, 29, 597–618.

Han, Z. H. and Peverly, S. T. (2007), 'Input processing: a study of *ab initio* learners with multilingual backgrounds'. *The International Journal of Multilingualism* 4, 17–37.

Izumi, S. (2002), 'Output, input enhancement, and the noticing hypothesis: an experimental study on ESL relativization'. *Studies in Second Language Acquisition* 24, 541–77.

Jackendoff, R. (1987), *Consciousness and the Computational Mind*. Cambridge, MA: MIT Press.

— (1997), *The Architecture of the Language faculty*. Cambridge, MA: MIT Press.

Krashen, S. (1982), *Principles and Practice in Second Language Acquisition*. Oxford: Pergamon.

Lee, S.-K. and Huang, H.-T. (2008), 'Visual input enhancement and grammar learning: A meta-analytic review'. *Studies in Second Language Acquisition*, 30, 307–31.

Leow, R. P., Egi, T., Nuevo, A. M., and Tsai, Y.-C. (2003), 'The roles of textual enhancement and type of linguistic item in adult L2 learners' comprehension and intake'. *Applied Language Learning*, 13(2), 1–16.

O'Grady, W. (2005), *Syntactic Carpentry: An Emergentist Approach to Syntax*. Mahwah, NJ: Erlbaum.

Overstreet, M. H. (1998), 'Text enhancement and content familiarity: the focus of learner attention'. *Spanish Applied Linguistics*, 2, 229–58.

Park, E. S. and Han, Z. H. (2008), 'Learner spontaneous attention in L2 input processing: an exploratory study', in Z. H. Han (ed.), *Understanding Second Language Process.* Clevedon: Multilingual Matters, pp. 106–32.

Pavlenko, A. (2008), 'Emotion and emotion-laden words in the bilingual lexicon'. *Bilingualism: Language and Cognition,* 11, 147–64.

Pienemann, M. (1998), *Language Processing and Second Language Development: Processability Theory.* Amsterdam: John Benjamins.

Schmidt, R. (2001), 'Attention', in P. Robinson (ed.), *Cognition and Second Language Instruction.* Cambridge: Cambridge University Press, pp. 3–32.

Schmidt, R. and Frota, S. N. (1986), 'Developing basic conversational ability in a second language: a case study of an adult learner of Portuguese', in R. R. Day (ed.), *Talking to Learn: Conversation in Second Language Acquisition.* Rowley, MA: Newbury, pp. 237–326.

Schumann, J. H. (1978), 'The acculturation model for second-language acquisition', in R. C. Gingras (ed.), *Second-Language Acquisition and Foreign Language Teaching.* Arlington, VA: Center for Applied Linguistics, pp. 27–50.

— (1997), *The Neurobiology of Affect in Language.* Malden, MA: Blackwell.

Schwartz, B. D. (1993), On explicit and negative data effecting and affecting competence and linguistic behavior. *Studies in Second Language Acquisition,* 15, 147–63.

Seliger, H. (1979), 'On the nature and function of rules in language teaching'. *TESOL Quarterly,* 1, 359–69.

Sharwood Smith, M. (1981), 'Consciousness-raising and the second language learner'. *Applied Linguistics,* 2, 159–68.

— (1985), 'Comprehension versus acquisition: two ways of processing linguistic input'. *Applied Linguistics,* 7, 239–56.

— (1991), 'Speaking to many minds: on the relevance of different types of language information for the L2 learner'. *Second Language Research,* 7, 118–32.

— (1993), 'Input enhancement in instructed SLA: theoretical bases'. *Studies in Second Language Acquisition,* 15, 165–79.

— (1996), 'The garden of Eden and beyond: on second language processing'. *CLCS Occasional Paper* no. 44, Trinity College, Dublin.

— (2014), 'Can you learn to love grammar and so make it grow? On the role of affect in L2 development', in L. Aronin, and M. Pawlak (eds) *Essential Topics in Applied Linguistics and Multilingualism. Studies in Honor of David Singleton.* Berlin: Springer Verlag.

Sharwood Smith, M. and Truscott, J. (2014), 'Explaining input enhancement'. *International Review of Applied Linguistics,* 52(3).

Sharwood Smith, M., Truscott, J. and Hawkins, R. (2013), 'Explaining change in transition grammars', in J. Herschensohn and Y.-S. Martha (eds), *A Handbook of Second Language Acquisition.* Cambridge: Cambridge University Press, pp. 560–80.

Simard, D. (2009), 'Differential effects of textual enhancement formats on intake'. *System,* 37, 124–35.

Terrell, T. D. (1991), 'The role of grammar instruction in a communicative approach'. *Modern Language Journal*, 75, 52–63.

Terrell, T. D., Baycroft, B., and Perrone, C. (1987), 'The subjunctive in Spanish interlanguage: accuracy and comprehensibility', in B. VanPatten, T. R. Dvorak, and J. F. Lee (eds), *Foreign Language Learning: A Research Perspective*. Rowley, MA: Newbury, pp. 119–32.

Trahey, M. and White, L. (1993), 'Positive evidence and preemption in the second language classroom'. *Studies in Second Language Acquisition*, 15, 181–204.

Trenkic, D. and Sharwood Smith, M. (2001), 'Reevaluating theoretical and methodological aspects of Focus on Form research'. Available at http://ltsc. ph-karlsruhe.de/Sharwood.pps.

Truscott, J. and Sharwood Smith, M. (2004), 'Acquisition by processing: a modular approach to language development'. *Bilingualism: Language and Cognition*, 7, 1–20.

— (2011), 'Input, intake, and consciousness: the quest for a theoretical foundation'. *Studies in Second Language Acquisition*, 33, 497–528.

VanPatten, B. (1996), *Input Processing and Grammar Instruction in Second Language Acquisition*. Norwood, NJ: Ablex.

— (2002), 'Processing instruction: an update'. *Language Learning*, 52, 755–803.

— (2004), 'Input Processing in SLA', in B. VanPatten (ed.), *Processing Instruction: Theory, Research, and Commentary*. Mahwah, NJ: Erlbaum, pp. 1–31.

VanPatten, B. and Cadierno, T. (1993), 'Explicit instruction and input processing'. *Studies in Second Language Acquisition*, 15, 225–43.

White, J. (1998), 'Getting the learners' attention', in C. Doughty and J. Williams (eds), *Focus on Form in Classroom Second Language Acquisition*. Cambridge: Cambridge University Press, pp. 85–113.

White, L., Spada, N., Lightbown, P. M., and Ranta, L. (1991), 'Input enhancement and L2 question formation'. *Applied Linguistics*, 12, 416–32.

Whong, M. (2011), *Language Teaching: Linguistic Theory in Practice*. Edinburgh: Edinburgh University Press.

3

Processing Instruction:
Where Research Meets Practice

James F. Lee
University of New South Wales, Australia

Processing Instruction (PI) is a type of focus-on-form, that is, grammar instruction, that addresses a processing problem associated with a particular linguistic structure. The function of PI is to alter a particular processing behaviour (problem) in order to increase the intake for possible acquisition. PI pushes learners to rely on forms in the input in order to derive meaning from an utterance. In essence, then, the learners are linking form with meaning and/or form with function. PI manipulates the input into what we refer to as structured input (VanPatten 1991). Importantly, by creating structured input and structured input activities, Processing Instruction promotes learners' connecting a linguistic structure with its meaning.

Before there was Processing Instruction, there was research on input processing. Input processing research shows us what learners do to make sense of the input. VanPatten (1996) contains the most elaborated presentation of the theoretical underpinnings for Processing Instruction. Lee and Benati (Chapter 1, 2009) provide an account of the evolution of the VanPatten's model of adult L2 input processing, particularly in his 2004 and 2007 works. PI has always been informed by input processing research. As VanPatten developed PI (VanPatten 1991, 1993), he also tested the effects of Processing Instruction empirically to demonstrate that it was an effective type of instruction, which indeed it is. (e.g. VanPatten and Cadierno 1993).

The purpose of this chapter is to explain and exemplify certain instructional aspects of PI; that is, I examine the I of PI. They are explicit information, structured input activities and corrective feedback. I then provide several suggestions for adapting Processing Instruction from its research instantiation to classroom practice.

Explicit information

As part of processing instruction, learners are provided a grammatical explanation of the target linguistic structure. They are given explicit information about the form and its function in order for them to develop metalinguistic knowledge of the structure. The distinguishing and innovative aspect of the explicit information in PI is that learners are provided information about input processing strategies, both the default, incorrect and target-language-inappropriate ones that learners rely on and the more effective, target-language-appropriate ones that they will be practising. Appendix A contains the English translation of the explicit information used in an investigation of the Spanish passive, titled 'Who does the action? Who receives the action?'. Learners accessed the explanation individually in a computer laboratory. The explanation was a self-guided, 16-slide PowerPoint presentation.

Beginning with the title, learners are focused on the processing problem, that is, correctly assigning the roles of agent and patient. The structure of the Spanish passive is nearly identical to that of its English counterpart in that the patient moves to sentence initial position and the agent moves to sentence final position and is marked with a preposition. A passive form of the verb is used based on a form of the verb 'to be'/*ser* plus the past participle as in (1) and (2).

1. John was criticized by Mary.
2. John fue criticado por Mary.

The processing problem that passive sentences present learners is the word order. VanPatten (2004) captured the problem in his First Noun Principle, which states that learners tend to interpret the first noun or pronoun they encounter in an utterance as the agent. That is, learners tend to interpret passive sentences as if they were active; they misassign the roles of agent and patient, which is quite detrimental to comprehension.

The explicit information on the Spanish passive voice begins with a review of word order in active sentences (slides 1–4). The passive voice is then introduced and exemplified (slides 5–7). The next part of the presentation involves forming the passive (slides 8–11). Slide 12 informs the learners about an inappropriate word-order-based processing strategy. Slide 13 informs them of a target-language-appropriate processing strategy, which, in this pedagogical context, we called a listening strategy.

Appendix B contains a second example of explicit information in a Processing Instruction context that was used in Benati et al. (2008). The target linguistic structure was the English simple past tense marker *–ed*. The processing problem that temporal morphology presents second-language learners is captured in VanPatten's (2004) Lexical Preference Principle, which states that learners tend to rely on lexical items rather than on grammatical form when both encode the same semantic information.

In contrast to the first example in which the explanation was delivered online to individuals, this example was delivered by the instructor to the whole class as if it were a typical lesson. The explicit information was presented in three parts. In the first part, the instructor introduced the form *–ed* and its function as a temporal marker and provided an example on the board. In the second part, the instructor related the form to different lexical temporal adverbials via a brainstorming activity recorded on the board. The instructor had a list of adverbial expressions as a guide to organize and stimulate the brainstorming activity. The instructor then supplied information about processing strategies. First, the instructor explained the inappropriate strategy of relying on lexical temporal adverbs and then presented the appropriate strategy of paying attention to the morphological marker *–ed*. To emphasize the verb form, she circled and underlined it in the example sentences on the board.

Because the information about processing strategies is the least familiar aspect of the explicit information in Processing Instruction, I am including three examples of that type of information. Figure 3.1 contains the information about processing strategies from three other investigations of Processing Instruction. The first of these is the Japanese passive (Benati et al. 2010). Active sentences in Japanese are typically SOV or Agent-Patient-Verb. The word order in passive sentences is Patient-Agent-Verb, in which the patient is morphologically marked as the grammatical subject and the agent is morphologically marked as the agent. The processing problem is captured in VanPatten's (2004) First Noun Principle, that is, the first noun is interpreted as the agent. The second linguistic structure is the French causative with *faire* (VanPatten and Wong 2004). The underlying structure of these causative sentences has two agents, one makes the other do something. The processing problem for learners is captured in VanPatten's (2004) First Noun Principle in that learners interpret the first noun as the only agent. The third example is the Italian future tense (Lee and Benati 2007b). The processing problem is captured in VanPatten's (2004) Lexical Preference Principle, that is, learners rely on lexical temporal adverbs rather than on verb morphology to assign tense. Typically, the information about processing strategies concludes the grammatical explanation and is the transition to the structured input activities.

1. Japanese passive. Benati, Lee and Hikima (2010, p. 155)

👁Keep in mind that the first noun is not an agent (the doer) in the following passive sentence.
Chris は Tomに たたかれました。Chris was hit by Tom.
Tom is an agent (the person who does the action.)
Chris is a patient (the person who is affected.)

Particle に is a little word but に has important role in the passive sentence. にshows
who does the action in the passive sentence.
Please listen or read carefully until the end of sentence.

The end of the verb form is a key to determine whether the sentence is a passive or an active form.

Please pay attention Who did what to whom!

2. French causative. VanPatten and Wong (2004, p. 115)

One of the problems the *faire causatif* presents is in listening comprehension. Second language
learners of French often misinterpret what they hear because the word order is different from
English. For example, it is not uncommon for learners of French to make the following mistake:

> They hear: "Jean fait faire la vaisselle à Paul."
> They incorrectly think: John is doing the dishes for Paul.

or

> They hear: "Marc fait couper les cheveux."
> They incorrectly think: Marc cuts hair.

In the activities that follow, we will practice hearing and interpreting the faire causatif.

3. Italian future tense. Lee and Benati (2007b, p. 43)

The future is used to talk about an action that has not yet taken place or making plans. . . . There
are two clues that will help you to recognize future tense forms:

**1. the future tense (first and third person) of regular verbs is formed by adding the ending ò or
à to the infinitive minus the final e.**

**2. the spoken stress on the first-and the third-person singular is on the final accented vowel of
the ending.**

> The second clue will be very useful in order to distinguish future forms from those forms of the
> present tense. An important difference is in the spoken stress of the final vowel of the future tense.

Future forms are usually accompanied by temporal adverbs that indicate that the action of the
verb occurred in the future. Here are some of these future temporal adverbs:

-domani –la semana prossima -el mese prossimo

However, although these adverbials are a good clue to know that an action has occurred in the
future they are not always present in the sentences you encounter. This is the reason why it will be
important for you to recognize future tense forms.

Figure 3.1 Three examples of explicit information about processing strategies.

Structured input activities

Structured input activities are the heart of Processing Instruction because we manipulate the input in these activities in order to make the target form more salient and essential to task completion. Salience is achieved by drawing and aligning the learners' attention. Essentialness is achieved because learners cannot complete the item if they do not process the form. The task-essential nature of structured input activities is the key to why they are successful in altering learners' processing behaviours. The most extreme demand a task can place on a linguistic structure or form is that 'the task cannot be successfully performed unless the structure is used' (Loschky and Bley-Vroman 1993, p. 132). In this context, we would substitute 'processed' or 'connected with its meaning' for 'used'.

It is important to note that structured input activities give learners practice processing the target form not producing it. Processing the target form allows for form-meaning connections to be made. Producing a form entails accessing it. Lack of production practice does not mean that the learners cannot produce the form after receiving processing instruction. In fact, they can as all investigations of the effects of PI have shown positive results on production measures (Lee and Benati 2009).

There are six guidelines for creating structured input activities which have been presented and discussed in previous works (Farley 2005; Lee and VanPatten 1995, 2003; VanPatten 1996; Wong 2004a, 2005). I will use the six guidelines to analyse structured input activities developed for the Spanish passive and the English simple past tense. The guidelines are as follows:

1. Present one thing at a time.
2. Keep meaning in focus.
3. Move from sentences to connected discourse.
4. Use both oral and written input.
5. Have the learners do something with the input.
6. Keep the learners' processing strategies in mind.

There are two types of structured input activities, referential and affective. Referential activities have a right and a wrong answer. Affective activities, in contrast, do not, but flood the input with positive evidence for the target structure and require the learner to respond with an opinion or other such evaluation. I will treat referential activities first.

Referential structured input activities

Figure 3.2 contains three sample items from a referential structured input activity for the Spanish passive. Note that in my research, presented in Chapter X, I had 58 items distributed into four referential activities. The left column contains the original Spanish version, whereas the right column is the English translation, provided for the benefit of the reader. How have the guidelines been accounted for in these items?

Original Spanish version	English translation
Escucha las oraciones. Escoge la respuesta correcta.	Listen to the sentences. Choose the correct answer.
1. ¿Quién recibe la acción?	1. Who receives the action?
Escucha: *Es admirada por todos.*	Hear: Is admired by everyone.
Escoge: a. Violeta b. Víctor c. Todos d. No estoy seguro/a.	Choose: a. Violeta b. Víctor c. Everyone d. I'm not sure.
2. ¿Quién hace la acción?	2. Who does the action?
Escucha: *Mirta y Liliana fueron elegidas por los otros alumnos para el premio.*	Hear: Mirta and Liliana were elected by the other students for the prize.
Escoge: a. Mirta y Liliana b. el profesor c. los otros alumnos. d. No sé la respuesta.	Choose: a. Mirta and Liliana b. the profesor c. the other students d. I don't know the answer.
3. ¿Quién hace la acción?	3. Who does the action?
Escucha: *María recuerda a Juan con cariño.*	Hear: María remembers Juan affectionately.
Escoge: a. María b. Juan c. los dos d. No estoy seguro/a.	Choose: a. María b. Juan c. both of them d. I'm not sure

Figure 3.2 Sample items from a referential structured input activity for the Spanish passive.

Present one thing at a time. This guideline points material developers to not approach grammar instruction from a paradigm perspective. That is, many textbooks present a grammatical form with all person-number combinations at one time. Processing Instruction seeks to focus instruction. The presentation and practice of the Spanish passive are limited to third-person forms in which the agent and patient are of different genders. First and second persons are not included. Limiting the forms eases the processing burden for the learners who are characterized as limited capacity processors. The learners to whom these materials were directed were enrolled in intermediate-level Spanish language classes and so I included both singular (item 1) and plural (item 2) items.

Keep meaning in focus. VanPatten developed his ideas about Processing Instruction within a communicative framework for language teaching (VanPatten 1991, 1993). His work moved away from the mechanical practices associated with what he referred to as traditional instruction in his research on Processing Instruction (e.g. VanPatten and Cadierno 1993). Because Processing Instruction is designed to promote learners connecting form and meaning, it is essential to keep meaning in focus. Meaning is kept in focus in these structured input activities because learners must identify either who performed the action or who received it. Correctly interpreting agent and patient roles is critical to successful communication.

Move from sentences to connected discourse. The learners' exposure to the target form or structure should, when possible, include both sentences and discourse as natural language samples would contain both. The sample items from the referential activities present the target form in sentences. When I present the affective structured input activities in Figure 3.3, the reader will find that they embed the target structure in discourse. I took the decision to associate referential items with sentences and affective items with discourse for the convenience of presenting them in our e-learning management system. There is no other rationale for doing so. The important point is that the target structure appears in both levels of language.

Use both oral and written input. VanPatten did not value oral input over written input but advocated the use of both. Learners both hear and see the target form. The three sample items in Figure 3.2 require the learners to hear the target structure. I took the decision to associate referential items with oral input and affective items with written input for the convenience of presenting them in our e-learning management system. There is no other rationale for doing so. The important point is that the target structure appears in both modes.

Have the learners do something with the input. The idea that learners should do something with the input is to require them to verify that they have correctly interpreted the target structure. The items in Figure 3.2 are multiple-choice items requiring the learners to physically identify the agent or patient.

Keep the learner's processing strategies in mind. This final guideline is arguably the most important. All the passive sentences used in the materials are reversible, that is, either entity is capable of performing the action. In this way, learners cannot rely on lexical semantics (one entity cannot perform the action) or event probabilities (one entity is more likely to perform the action) to process the meaning of the sentences. Each of the three sample items addresses a different aspect of the processing strategies we hope to instil in the learners. The explicit information provided to the learners advised them to pay attention to the verb form including the gender/number markings on the past participle. The Spanish sentence in (1) is a null-subject sentence in which the cue to the patient is found in the feminine gender marker –*a* at the end of the past participle; it does not translate well to English. The only possible answer is 'Violeta'. Item 2 asks learners to identify the agent. The input item is a full passive sentence with the patient fully expressed as the grammatical subject in a passive sentence. The explicit information provided to learners advised them not to rely on word order to determine agent/patient relations. If they process the verb form as a passive rather than active, they will arrive at the correct answer. The third item is an active sentence in which the word order aligns with agent and patient roles. The presence of actives in the input is part of the processing strategy training; the agent might appear in sentence initial position. Also, alternating active and passive sentences in the input helps prevent the learners from relying on a test-taking strategy of associating the patient with initial position and the agent with final position. VanPatten and Wong (2004) document that some of their learners adopted a second-noun strategy as a test-taking strategy, that is, they over-applied the instruction on word order and did not discriminately use their new processing strategy in accordance with the input sentences.

Figure 3.3 contains sample items from two investigations of Processing Instruction on the English simple past tense marker –*ed*. In both investigations, the learners practised with a total of six referential structured input activities with each containing ten items. How have the guidelines been accounted for in these activities?

Present one thing at a time. Because Processing Instruction does not take a paradigm approach, the past tense items in both investigations are limited to forms that are regular in the past tense such as 'talked' but not 'spoke'.

---

1. Benati, Lee and Houghton (2008, p. 101)

Your teacher's life!

Step 1

Read the following statements about things your teacher does and decide whether he/she does them now or did them last weekend:

He/She	Now	Last weekend
1. ... played tennis.	☐	☐
2. ... talks to the class.	☐	☐
3. ... talked to his mother.	☐	☐
4. ... argued with a friend.	☐	☐

[followed by 6 more items of identical structure]

Step 2

Now decide in pairs whether your teacher's weekend was an interesting or a boring weekend.

2. Benati (2005, p. 88)

Activity A

You will hear 10 sentences and you need to determine whether the action is taking place now (present) or has already taken place (past).

	Present	Past
1.	☐	☐
2.	☐	☐

Instructor's script
1. I listen to music.
2. I walked to the park.

(8 more activity items of identical structure)

Figure 3.3 Sample items from referential activities for English simple past tense.

Moreover, the items in the first activity are third-person only, whereas the items in the second are first-person only. *Keep meaning in focus.* The meaning that learners are to determine is when the action took place, in the past or present. *Use both oral and written input.* The first activity presents the input in written form, whereas the second presents it in oral form. *Have the learners do something with the input.* The learners record their decisions about temporal reference in these two activities by ticking a box. *Keep the learner's processing strategies in mind.* As indicated in the information the learners received about processing strategies, temporal verbal morphology is often accompanied by lexical temporal adverbials. As captured in the Lexical Preference Principle (VanPatten 2004), these temporal adverbials draw the learners' attention more than the morphology does. Therefore, we strip the input of lexical temporal markers, thereby structuring the input so that learners are forced to attend to the morphology. The learners are forced to read/listen for the *–ed* for past, the *–s* for third-person present or ø (silence) for first-person present.

Affective structured input activities

The purpose of affective structured input activities is to provide learners with positive evidence, that is, examples of how the target structure is used in the second language. There is no right or wrong answer to an affective activity, rather, the learners respond to the content of the items such as agreeing/disagreeing, providing an opinion or other such evaluation. Figure 3.4 contains two sample items from the affective activities for the Spanish passive. Note

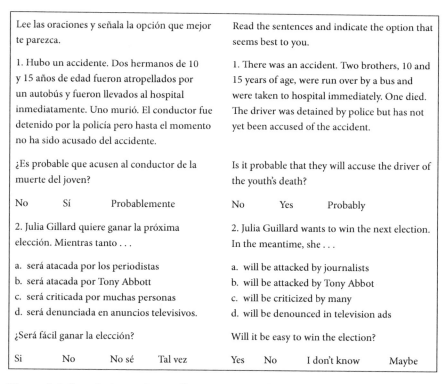

Lee las oraciones y señala la opción que mejor te parezca.	Read the sentences and indicate the option that seems best to you.
1. Hubo un accidente. Dos hermanos de 10 y 15 años de edad fueron atropellados por un autobús y fueron llevados al hospital inmediatamente. Uno murió. El conductor fue detenido por la policía pero hasta el momento no ha sido acusado del accidente.	1. There was an accident. Two brothers, 10 and 15 years of age, were run over by a bus and were taken to hospital immediately. One died. The driver was detained by police but has not yet been accused of the accident.
¿Es probable que acusen al conductor de la muerte del joven?	Is it probable that they will accuse the driver of the youth's death?
No Sí Probablemente	No Yes Probably
2. Julia Gillard quiere ganar la próxima elección. Mientras tanto . . .	2. Julia Guillard wants to win the next election. In the meantime, she . . .
a. será atacada por los periodistas b. será atacada por Tony Abbott c. será criticada por muchas personas d. será denunciada en anuncios televisivos.	a. will be attacked by journalists b. will be attacked by Tony Abbot c. will be criticized by many d. will be denounced in television ads
¿Será fácil ganar la elección?	Will it be easy to win the election?
Si No No sé Tal vez	Yes No I don't know Maybe

Figure 3.4 Sample items from affective structured input activities for the Spanish passive.

that in my research I had 58 items distributed into four affective activities. The learners performed one referential activity followed by an affective activity. The left column contains the original Spanish version, whereas the right column is the English translation, provided for the benefit of the reader. How have the guidelines been accounted for in these items?

Present one thing at a time. Like the referential activities, the affective activities contain only third-person forms. The first sample item contains both singular and plural items, whereas the second contains only singular ones. *Keep meaning in focus.* The affective activities are true-to-life scenarios. The first one about an accident was based on a Spanish news story that had been uploaded to YouTube. The second reflects the political culture of elections in Australia as two opposing party leaders seek to get their parties elected. *Move from sentences to connected discourse.* I chose to use discourse-level input for all the affective activities because the scenarios naturally led to the use of discourse. *Use both oral and written input.* The referential activities were constructed as oral input, whereas the affective activities were constructed as written input. *Have the learners do something with the input.* After reading each scenario, the learners are asked to respond to a question that elicits their opinion. The question requires them to assess the overall content of the scenario and chose an outcome. *Keep learner's processing strategies in mind.* Many feel that affective activities are adjuncts to referential activities (e.g. Farley 2005) or that the primary learning comes as a result of referential activities (e.g. McNulty 2011). An important characteristic of affective activities is that the target form and its meaning are brought together for the learner. The learner knows that the input is correct, that is, the input provides positive evidence.

Figure 3.5 contains two more examples of affective structured input activities. The first activity is from Benati (2005) that examined the English simple past tense and the second from Lee and Benati (2007b) that examined Italian future tense morphology. How do these activities incorporate the six guidelines for creating structured input activities?

Present one thing at a time. The linguistic items in both activities utilize only first person, regular forms. *Keep meaning in focus.* The learners' task in both activities is to indicate if the meaning of the sentence applies to them or not by saying if they did a particular activity over the weekend or if they will make the same resolutions as someone else. *Move from sentences to connected discourse.* These two activities present the input in sentences. A sample affective structured input activity that presents the English simple past tense in discourse form can be found in Benati et al. (2008, p. 102), in which the learners listened to a story

---

1. English simple past tense (Benati, 2005, p. 88)

Activity B
Listen to the instructor making a series of statements and indicate whether you did the same thing at the weekend.

 Me, too. I did not.
1. ☐ ☐
2. ☐ ☐

Instructor's script
1. I played sport.
2. I visited my friend.

(8 more activity items of identical structure)

2. Italian future tense (Benati and Lee, 2007, p, 44)

Activity A
Paolo is making New Year's resolutions. Look at the sentences and indicate whether or not each statement applies to you. Compare your response with someone else.
<u>Notice the spoken stress of the third person singular of the future tense.</u>

L'anno prossimo	Vale per me	Non vale per me
1. studierà tutti i giorni	☐	☐
2. arriverà all'Università in orario	☐	☐
3. metterà in ordine la mia camera	☐	☐

(7 more activity items of identical structure)

Figure 3.5 Sample items of affective structured input activities for English simple past tense and Italian future tense.

about someone's first day in London. A sample affective structured input activity that presents the Italian future tense in discourse can be found in Benati (2001, p. 124) in which two characters in a four-frame cartoon talk about what they will do next year. *Use both oral and written input.* The activity for the English simple past tense presents the input in oral form, whereas the activity for the Italian future tense presents it in written form. *Have learners do something with the input.* We keep meaning in focus by having learners selfevaluate. We verify that they are doing that by having them tick the appropriate box, thereby doing something with the input. *Keep learners' processing strategies in mind.* Both linguistic targets are affected by the processing problem captured in VanPatten's (2004) Lexical Preference Principle, which states that learners tend to rely on lexical items as opposed to grammatical forms when both encode the same semantic meaning. The input items are, therefore, stripped of any lexical temporal indicators. The only marker of time in the input sentences is the grammatical from ($-ed$ or $-\grave{a}$).

As can be seen in the two sample affective structured input activities, individual answers will vary. My weekend activities may or may not coincide with someone else's just as my New Year's resolutions may or may not. Houston (2010) examined learners' responses to affective structured input activities to determine if they were authentically paying attention to meaning. He defined 'authentic' as a combination of plausibility and consistency across learners' responses. He found that learners responded differently to individual items. They did not simply answer all the items the same way as evidenced by significantly different response frequencies between items. In other words, their answers were plausible. Second, he analysed responses across two-part activities. The learners provided answers to items in Part 1 and then performed an evaluation of their answers in Part 2. For example, the learners first indicated which items in a list of exotic foods they had eaten. They then rated their adventurousness according to their responses as falling into one of three categories. Houston found a significant correlation between Part 1 responses and Part 2 evaluations. In other words, the learners' answers were consistent. Because the learners' answers were authentic (consistent + plausible), Houston concluded that learners attended to meaning when they performed affective structured input activities.

Corrective feedback and explicit information + corrective feedback

The third instructional aspect of Processing Instruction that I will treat is that of corrective feedback, of which there are two types. Corrective feedback may be implicit, that is, an indication to the learners that their response or answer is incorrect but no indication as to the source of the error. Corrective feedback may be explicit, that is, an overt indication that a response or answer is incorrect and an indication as to the source of the error. The first mention of corrective feedback in the Processing Instruction literature is in VanPatten and Oikkenon (1996). They state the following:

> They [participants] were given feedback as to whether or not their interpretations were correct but were not given additional information; that is, they were not reminded of any rules or processing strategies. (VanPatten and Oikkenon 1996, p. 501).

VanPatten and Oikkenon provided the participants with implicit feedback. They go one to provide an example of their corrective feedback.

> For example, as the instructor asked subjects to match a picture to an utterance with OVS word order, if subjects responded incorrectly (by choosing the picture that showed they had interpreted the object as the subject) she simply responded *No. La respuesta es B* ("NO. The answer is B") (i.e., not A – referring to the letters under each picture). In this way, subjects were told when their interpretations were correct or not but did not receive information as to why. (VanPatten and Oikkenon 1996, p. 502)

Why did these researchers choose to provide very limited implicit corrective feedback? VanPatten and Oikkenon were carrying out an experimental study in which there were three groups of participants. One group received full PI, which consists of explicit information plus structured input activities. Another group received only the explicit information. The third group received only structured input activities. The researchers wanted to exert as much control over the experimental setting as possible so that feedback was provided consistently across groups. Moreover, the feedback needed to be minimal so that feedback itself did not become an extraneous variable.

Whereas VanPatten and Oikkenon controlled corrective feedback, Sanz (2004) isolated and manipulated it. She compared the performance of two groups of learners who received Processing Instruction on third-person direct object pronouns in Spanish, delivered online to individuals. One group received explicit corrective feedback that identified the incorrect use of a word-order-based processing strategy as the source of the error. The other group did not receive explicit corrective feedback but rather very limited, implicit corrective feedback ('Sorry, try again'). The explicit corrective feedback occurred immediately after a learner submitted an answer. A pop-up window appeared indicating the error and the source of the error. Neither group received explicit information. They only received structured input activities, thereby isolating the effects of explicit corrective feedback. Sanz found that both groups benefited significantly and equally from PI. In other words, the group that received explicit corrective feedback did not outperform the group that had not on any of the post-tests (interpretation task, sentence completion task, video retelling). The feedback did not make a difference, rather '. . . it is practice in decoding structured input that leads to a change in processing strategies with positive consequences for acquisition'. (Sanz 2004, p. 252).

Now, the topic of corrective feedback intersects with the first topic I treated, explicit information. Sanz and Morgan-Short (2004) carried out a more elaborate investigation on the effects of explicit corrective feedback ($+/-$ EF) and explicit information ($+/-$EI) on the Processing Instruction of direct object pronouns in Spanish. They compared the performance of four groups: [$+$EI $+$EF], [$+$EI $-$EF], [$-$EI $+$EF], [$-$EI $-$EF]. They provided explicit corrective feedback and implicit feedback in the same ways as Sanz (2004). Sanz and Morgan-Short found that all four groups benefited significantly and equally from PI. That is, the groups that received explicit corrective feedback did not outperform the groups that had not on any of the post-tests (interpretation task, sentence completion task, video retelling). Moreover, the groups that received explicit information did not outperform the groups that had not on any of the post-tests. They state, '. . . based on our findings, it appears that when learners are asked to complete a task in which they are presented with structured input and task-essential practice items, supplementary information about the language form provided a priori does not enhance their ability to use the form in subsequent interpretation or production measures'. (Sanz and Morgan-Short 2004, p. 69).

These findings lead to the question, Which is more important, the explanation or the practice? The research results point strongly to the practice when performance is measured as a product, that is, by tests of interpretation and production (e.g. Benati 2004a, 2004b; VanPatten and Oikkenon 1996; Wong 2004b). However, research has emerged that looks at a different aspect of learners' performance, a more process-oriented measure. Fernández (2008) introduced a measure she called trails-to-criterion, defined as the number of practice items a learner did before answering correctly four consecutive items, that is, three target items and one distractor item. I have referred to trails-to-criterion as learning rate (Lee 2013). Providing learners with explicit information in addition to structured input activities has been shown to significantly increase their learning rate with the Spanish subjunctive (Fernández 2008), German accusative case articles (Culman et al. 2009; Henry et al. 2009; VanPatten and Borst 2012a), but not with direct object pronouns in Spanish (Fernández 2008; VanPatten and Borst 2012b). VanPatten and colleagues point to the nature of the explicit information as an explanatory factor.

> The reason for the difference in findings, then, might be related to the nature of the EI and whether it was portable (i.e., whether the information can be kept in working memory while the learner is simultaneously processing novel incoming data) enough to use during processing. (Henry et al. 2009, p. 572)

Given the many different linguistic targets that have been investigated in Processing Instruction, future research can go back to the previous work and test for how portable the explicit information is.

Processing instruction and classroom practice

Research on Processing Instruction seeks to document why PI is effective, for whom and under what circumstances. To that end, learners in the PI groups only practise processing the linguistic structure; they never produce it during the treatment period. Do we recommend that classroom learners never practise producing a form, only processing it? We create groupings of participants such as the [−EI, −EF] group, who received neither explicit information about the target structure nor explicit corrective feedback about their incorrect answers (Sanz and Morgan-Short 2004). This grouping is tantamount to giving classroom learners a worksheet and telling them to simply fill it in as best they can or to try to figure it out as they go along. Do we recommend that teachers not give grammar explanations or withhold corrective feedback? In the following paragraphs, I will make several suggestions for classroom practice.

This chapter discusses various instructional aspects associated with Processing Instruction. It does not, however, review the findings of research that demonstrates how effective Processing Instruction is. Lee and Benati (2009) review the research in which Processing Instruction is compared to traditional instruction, meaning-based output instruction and other types of instruction or tasks. These findings underscore that as a result of processing instruction learners alter their processing strategies and, as a result, work with input differently creating more intake from the linguistic data. Importantly, the type of knowledge they develop of the target form also allows them to access the form for use in language production tasks, from fill-in-the-blank form production to video retellings. The first suggestion for classroom practice, is, therefore, that instructors incorporate Processing Instruction into their course materials. We have substantial evidence that Processing Instruction can be delivered equally effectively in classrooms to a group of learners as well as in computer laboratories to individuals. That is, one need not dedicate class time to Processing Instruction but develop it to support classroom practice.

One of the instructional aspects of Processing Instruction that I have discussed in this chapter is the role of explicit information in the results of PI research. Regarding explicit information, the research points to it not having an effect on the end result of learning. Given enough structured input practice, all learners seem to get to the same result. Newer research is, however, providing a more nuanced insight into the effects of explicit information, which is that learners who receive explicit information appear to benefit more quickly from structured input activities. The second suggestion for classroom practice is, therefore, that instructors don't not give students a grammatical explanation but know that input practices are the most important element in the instructional equation.

Another of the instructional aspects of Processing Instruction I have discussed in this chapter is the role of corrective feedback. It is somewhat surprising that so few studies of Processing Instruction have manipulated feedback as a variable given the importance placed on feedback in classrooms and in certain approaches to SLA (e.g. Gass and Mackey 2007; Lantolf and Thorne 2007). Sanz (2004) and Sanz and Morgan-Short (2004) varied whether learners received explicit feedback while providing all learners with implicit feedback. Explicit feedback does not appear to make a difference. But in the absence of a body of work that compares explicit corrective feedback to implicit corrective feedback to no corrective feedback whatsoever, the third suggestion for classroom practice is, therefore, that instructors don't not give the students corrective feedback. Learners tend to expect and accept corrective feedback. Many instructors conceive of their role as including the provision of corrective feedback.

The groups who receive Processing Instruction in our controlled experimental settings never produce the target form as part of the treatment. This research-driven decision leads to a confusion that we advocate a comprehension-based approach to teaching. VanPatten made the following point in the epilogue of his 1996 book. 'The reader should not conclude from this focus [on one particular input-based type of grammar instruction] that we are advocating an abandonment of the communicative classroom. We are not advocating that processing instruction occupy all of instructors' and learners' time to the exclusion of interaction, reading, and other components of a communicative classroom' (VanPatten 1996, p. 158). Our position has always been that input is essential but ultimately insufficient. 'While input is *necessary* for creating a [linguistic] system, input is not *sufficient* for developing the ability to use language in a communicative context' (Lee and VanPatten 1995, p. 117, emphasis original). The fourth suggestion for classroom practice is, therefore, that instructors sequence language practices moving from structured input to structured output to task-based interaction (Lee 2000; Lee and VanPatten 1995, 2003).

Acknowledgement

The materials on the Spanish passive presented in this chapter were developed as part of a Faculty Research Grant from the Faculty of Arts and Social Sciences, University of New South Wales.

References

Benati, A. (2001), 'A comparative study of the effects of processing instruction and output-based instruction on the acquisition of the Italian future tense'. *Language Teaching Research,* 5, 95–127.

— (2004a), 'The effects of structured input and explicit information on the acquisition of Italian future tense', in B. VanPatten (ed.), *Processing Instruction: Theory, Research, and Commentary.* Mahwah, NJ: Erlbaum, pp. 207–55.

— (2004b), 'The effects of processing instruction and its components on the acquisition of gender agreement in Italian'. *Language Awareness,* 13, 67–80.

— (2005), 'The effects of PI, TI and MOI in the acquisition of English simple past tense'. *Language Teaching Research,* 9, 67–113.

Benati, A. G., Lee, J. F., and Hikima, N. (2010), 'Chapter 5: Exploring the effects of processing instruction on discourse-level interpretation tasks with the Japanese passive construction', in A. Benati and J. F. Lee (eds), *Processing Instruction and Discourse.* London: Continuum, pp. 148–77.

Benati, A. G., Lee, J. F., and Houghton, S. D. (2008), 'Chapter 4: From processing instruction on the acquisition of English past tense to secondary transfer-of-training effects on English third person singular present tense', in A. Benati and J. F. Lee (eds), *Grammar Acquisition and Processing Instruction: Secondary and Cumulative Effects.* Bristol: Multilingual Matters, pp. 88–120.

Culman, H., Henry, N., and VanPatten, B. (2009), 'The role of explicit information in instructed SLA: an on-line study with processing instruction and German accusative case inflections'. *Die Unterrichtspraxis,* 42, 19–31.

Farley, A. P. (2005), *Structured Input: Grammar Instruction for the Acquisition-Rich Classroom.* New York: McGraw-Hill.

Fernández, C. (2008), 'Reexamining the role of explicit information in processing instruction'. *Studies in Second Language Acquisition,* 30, 277–305.

Gass, S. M. and Mackey, A. (2007), 'Input, interaction, and output in second language acquisition', in B. VanPatten and J. Williams (eds), *Theories in Second Language Acquisition: An Introduction.* Mahwah, NJ: Erlbaum, pp. 175–99.

Henry, N., Culman, H., and VanPatten, B. (2009), 'More on the effects of explicit information in instructed SLA: a partial replication and a response to Fernández (2008)'. *Studies in Second Language Acquisition,* 31, 559–75.

Houston, A. (2010), 'Affective structured input online: how authentic are learner responses?' *Hispania*, 93, 218–34.

Lantolf, J. and Thorne, S. (2007), 'Sociocultural theory and second language learning', in B. VanPatten and J. Williams (eds), *Theories in Second Language Acquisition: An Introduction*. Mahwah, NJ: Erlbaum, pp. 201–24.

Lee, J. F. (2000), *Tasks and Communicating in Language Classrooms*. New York: McGraw-Hill.

— (2013), 'Foci and general findings of research on processing instruction: moving beyond limitations', in J. F. Lee and A. G. Benati (eds), *Individual Differences and Processing Instruction*. London: Equinox, pp. 19–46.

Lee, J. F. and Benati, A. (2007a), *Delivering Processing Instruction in Classrooms and Virtual Contexts: Research and Practice*. London: Equinox.

— (2007b), *Second Language Processing: An Analysis of Theory, Problems and Possible Solutions*. Continuum: London.

— (2009), *Research and Perspectives on Processing Instruction*. Berlin: Mouton de Gruyter.

Lee, J. F. and VanPatten, B. (1995), *Making Communicative Language Teaching Happen*. New York: McGraw-Hill.

— (2003), *Making Communicative Language Teaching Happen* (2nd ed). New York: McGraw-Hill.

Loschky, L. and Bely-Vroman, R. (1993), 'Grammar and task-based learning', in G. Crookes and S. Gass (eds), *Tasks and Language Learning: Integrating Theory and Practice*. Clevedon, UK: Multilingual Matters, pp. 123–67.

McNulty, E. M. (2011), *On Activity Type and Activity Order in the Processing Instruction of Spanish Cuando Plus Subjunctive/Indicative*. Unpublished PhD dissertation. Indiana University, Bloomington, IN.

Sanz, C. (2004), 'Computer delivered implicit versus explicit feedback in processing instruction', in B. VanPatten (ed.), *Processing Instruction: Theory, Research, and Commentary*. Mahwah, NJ: Erlbaum, pp. 241–55.

Sanz, C. and Morgan-Short, K. (2004), 'Positive evidence versus explicit rule presentation and explicit negative feedback: a computer-assisted study'. *Language Learning*, 54, 35–78.

VanPatten, B. (1991), 'The foreign language classroom as a place to communicate', in B. Freed (ed.), *Foreign Language Acquisition Research and The Classroom*. Lexington, MA: D. C. Heath, pp. 54–73.

— (1993), 'Grammar instruction for the acquisition rich classroom'. *Foreign Language Annals*, 26, 433–50.

— (1996), *Input Processing and Grammar Instruction: Theory and Research*. Norwood, NJ: Ablex.

— (2004), 'Input processing in second language acquisition', in B. VanPatten (ed.), *Processing Instruction: Theory, Research, and Commentary*. Mahwah, NJ: Erlbaum, pp. 5–31.

— (2007), 'Input processing in adult second language acquisition', in B. VanPatten and J. Williams (eds), *Theories in Second Language Acquisition: An Introduction*. Mahwah, NJ: Erlbaum, pp. 115–35.

VanPatten, B. and Borst, S. (2012a), 'The roles of explicit information and grammatical sensitivity in Processing Instruction: nominative-accusative case marking and word order in German L2'. *Foreign Language Annals*, 45, 92–109.

— (2012b), 'The roles of explicit information and grammatical sensitivity in the processing of clitic object pronouns and word order in L2 Spanish'. *Hispania*, 95, 270–84.

VanPatten, B. and Cadierno, T. (1993), 'Explicit instruction and input processing'. *Studies in Second Language Acquisition*, 15, 225–43.

VanPatten, B. and Oikkenon, S. (1996), 'Explanation vs. structured input in processing instruction'. *Studies in Second Language Acquisition*, 18, 495–510.

VanPatten, B. and Wong, W. (2004), 'Processing instruction and the French causative: another replication', in B. VanPatten (ed.), *Processing Instruction: Theory, Research, And Commentary*. Mahwah, NJ: Erlbaum, pp. 97–118.

Wong, W. (2004a), 'The nature of processing instruction', in B. VanPatten (ed.), *Processing Instruction: Theory, Research, And Commentary*. Mahwah, NJ: Erlbaum, pp. 33–63.

— (2004b), 'Processing instruction in French: the roles of explicit information and structured input', in B. VanPatten (ed.), *Processing Instruction: Theory, Research, And Commentary*. Mahwah, NJ: Erlbaum, pp. 187–205.

— (2005), *Input Enhancement: From Theory and Research to the Classroom*. New York: McGraw-Hill.

Appendix A. Explicit information for the Spanish passive voice (translated from the original Spanish)

Note: The symbol $\otimes$ indicates that the sentence could also be heard.

Who does the action?

Who receives the action?

A presentation of the passive voice in Spanish

1. Review

The active voice

Typical word order

    S(ubject) + V(erb) + O(bject)

Who does the action? Subject = agent

Who receives the action? Object = patient

2. Example 1

Juan criticó a María. ⊗
John criticized Mary.

Who made the criticism?
Juan = the agent and the subject
Who received the criticism?
María = the patient and the object

3. Example 2

Carlos visitará a los abuelos. ⊗
Carlos will visit his grandparents.

Who will make the visit?
Carlos = the agent and the subject
Who will receive the visit?
The grandparents = the patient and the object

4. This is called the active voice because the verb form is active.

5. New Grammar Point

The passive voice
S(ubject) + V(erb) + O(bject of the preposition por)

Who does the action? The object of the preposition por
Who receives the action? The grammatical subject

6. Example 1

María fue criticada por Juan. ⊗
María was criticized by Juan.

Who made the criticism?
Juan = the agent and the object of the preposition por
Who received the criticism?
María = the patient and the grammatical subject

7. Example 2

Los abuelos serán visitados por Carlos. ⊗
The grandparents will be visited by Carlos.

Who will make the visit?

Carlos = the agent and the subject

Who will receive the visit?

The grandparents = the patient and the grammatical subject of the verb (third-person plural)

8. This is called the passive voice because the form of the verb is passive.

9. Formation of the passive (1)

The verb

María *fue criticada* por Juan.

The verb 'ser' (*fue*) and the past participle (*criticada*) are combined.

10. Formation of the passive (2)

The verb

Los abuelos *serán visitados* por Carlos.

The verb 'ser' (*serán*) and the past participle (*visitados*) are combined.

11. Formation of the passive (3)

The form of the past participle
It functions like an adjective.
What is the appropriate form of an adjective?

María -> criticad*a* (feminine, singular)
Grandparents -> visitad*os* (masculine, plural)

12. **NOTE!**

Many students hear 'María fue criticada por Juan' and they say that María made the criticism. They say that Juan received the criticism. This is not true. These students are relying on the order of the words.

Many students hear 'Los abuelos serán visitados por Carlos' and they say that the grandparents will make the visit. They say that Carlos will receive the visit. This is not true. These students are relying on the order of the words.

13. Listening Strategies

We will practise listening to and reading active and passive sentences.

NOTE! Listen for the form of the verb and do not rely only on the order of the words.

María . . . criticad*a*
Los abuelos . . . visitad*os*

14. Let's practise

Now, open the exercises in Blackboard.

You can refer to this explanation while you do the exercises.

Good luck!

Appendix B. Explicit information for the English simple past tense from Benati et al. (2008, p. 99)

Note: This instruction was carried out by the students' regular classroom teacher, who presented the lesson as if it were a typical lesson.

Teacher's instructions

The past simple tense is one of the tenses used to talk about events in the past. It refers to finished actions and events. Very often the English past simple tense ends in –*ed*. This is the regular past tense.

For example [*write on board*]:

> I played tennis with Paula.

When you talk about a finished time in the past, the English past simple tense is often accompanied by a temporal adverb or time expression.

For example [*write on board*]:

> *Yesterday*, I smoked 20 cigarettes.

Can anybody tell me some other adverbs?
[*brainstorm temporal adverbs and write them on board*]

last>	night		morning		afternoon
	week	yesterday>	afternoon	this>	morning
	month		evening		evening
	year				
	Saturday				

VERY IMPORTANT!

Do not rely on the temporal adverb to understand when the actions take place as sometimes you can hear a sentence without the temporal adverb.

You must pay attention to the tense ending to understand when the action takes place.

In the case of describing past events, pay attention to the ending of the verb: −ed. [*teacher circle and underline –ed in the examples*]

4

Collaborative Tasks and their Potential for Grammar Instruction in Second/Foreign Language Contexts

María del Pilar García Mayo

Universidad del País Vasco UPV/EHU, Spain

Recent research on SLA points to the need for a comeback to attention to formal aspects of language within a communicative context (Nassaji and Fotos 2011). One of the ways in which teachers can foster learners' attention to form in the classroom is by means of communicative tasks carried out in collaboration. This chapter will illustrate how several collaborative tasks such as dictogloss, text-reconstruction or jigsaw foster dialogue among the members of dyads carrying out communicative tasks and offer opportunities to improve the knowledge of the target language. It is precisely when performing these collaborative tasks that learners pay attention to formal aspects of language.

Grammar instruction in perspective

Still to this date, for many second/foreign language learners, learning another language means having to 'fight' with its grammar. As rightly pointed out by Larsen-Freeman, 'Perhaps no term in the language teaching field is as ambiguous as grammar' (Larsen-Freeman 2009, p. 518). Larsen-Freeman (2009) points out that the term grammar has been used to refer to seven different concepts: (i) mental grammar (an internal mental system that generates and interprets utterances), (ii) prescriptive grammar, (iii) descriptive grammar, (iv) linguistic grammar (the focus of a given linguistic theory), (v) reference grammar, (vi) pedagogical grammar and (vi) teacher's grammar. All of these terms, according to the author, are ambiguous and each of the definitions provided to clarify them is multidimensional.

For second/foreign language teachers, these definitional issues are beyond the scope of their daily classroom activity. What they are looking for is some way that might be helpful to convey the rules of the language they are teaching. Throughout time, different methods have dealt with the issue of how grammar should be taught (Howatt 1984; Larsen-Freeman 2003, 2009; Nassaji and Fotos 2011; Richards and Rodgers 2001) and teachers have gone from the use of the Grammar-translation method, introduced at the end of the eighteenth century and with a focus on learning grammar rules and no emphasis on communication skills, to the implementation of communicative-based approaches, with a total focus on meaning and language use within a communicative setting (Savignon 2001). In fact, the advent of the CLT approaches led to the oblivion of formal grammar teaching (Mitchell 2000).

Although CLT was successful in the sense of providing learners with tasks that were close to real-life experience and, therefore, increased their motivation (Grim 2009; Nunan 1989), some researchers raised their voices against the lack of attention to formal grammar aspects in the language classroom. Thus, Genesee (1994) warned that second language (L2) teaching must include *systematic attention* to the development of the learners' linguistic system. In a study published in 2002, Pica asked herself whether it would be possible to acquire L2 grammatical competence through communication and content study alone. In that study, Pica mentioned that meaning-centred instruction led to low levels of linguistic accuracy (i.e. non-target morphology and syntax) and to the overlooking of formal aspects in general.

Over the last three decades, the role of grammar teaching in the second/foreign language classroom has been reconsidered on the basis of findings in SLA research. Numerous studies, nicely summarized in Spada (2011), point to the fact that a mere exposure to meaningful L2 input is not enough for learners to reach proficiency in a second/foreign language and to foster their productive skills. All this research has led to a reconsideration of grammar teaching on the basis of at least four arguments (García Mayo 2011; Nassaji and Fotos 2011). The first comes from the empirical evidence collected in Canadian immersion programmes (Allen et al. 1990; Lyster 2007; Swain 1985). Different studies have shown that even though learners were exposed to large amounts of meaningful input, skills such as speaking and writing remained far from native-like and in stark contrast to listening and reading skills. Besides, it was observed that formal aspects of grammar were never acquired, which led researchers to suggest that a comeback to attention to language form was needed.

The second argument was provided by pioneering research by VanPatten (1990 *et passim*) in which he claimed that, because of processing limitations – especially at beginner levels –, learners will tend to rely on lexical items as opposed to grammatical form to obtain meaning. Therefore, there would be a need to identify effective strategies that would lead learners to draw attention to formal aspects of language. Work by Schmidt (1990, 2001) had already claimed that some type of attention to form was necessary for language learning to take place, attention that he operationalized as *noticing*. Last, but not least, a large amount of empirical studies had pointed to the idea that explicit attention to form was beneficial for language learning. The meta-analysis carried out by Norris and Ortega (2000) was groundbreaking in that sense and showed that explicit instruction resulted in significant gains that were maintained over time. This general finding has been reported more recently in the meta-analysis carried out by Spada and Tomita (2010).

Within this backdrop, it seems clear that formal aspects of language need to be considered seriously, and language teachers should be aware of ways in which they can draw learners' attention to those aspects always within a communicative setting. Ellis (2005) identified four ways in which we can manipulate tasks used in the classroom in order to draw learners' attention to issues that otherwise might go unnoticed: manipulating task components (Pica et al. 1993), manipulating task planning (Ellis 2005), providing corrective feedback (Nassaji and Simard 2010) and interacting in collaborative tasks. It is precisely this last option that this contribution will deal with. The rest of the chapter is structured as follows: the next section reviews the importance of interaction in SLA and argues for the relevance of collaborative dialogue as a tool to increase learners' attention to form. The chapter will then summarize several research studies that have used collaborative grammar tasks with specific grammatical targets in second and foreign language settings to illustrate how those tasks draw learners' attention to form. The final section will provide some ideas for future research within the realm of collaborative grammar tasks.

Interaction and collaborative dialogue

A large body of research in the field of SLA from the cognitive-interactionist perspective has provided support for the facilitative role of interaction in the process of L2 learning (García Mayo and Alcón Soler 2013; Gass and Mackey 2007; Keck et al. 2006; Long 1996; Mackey and Goo 2007; Pica 1994, among others). Interaction between learners and/or between learners and native speakers has been claimed to facilitate L2 learning because it seems to trigger opportunities where positive and negative input (feedback) as well as output opportunities are provided. It is this last construct in the interactional approach, output, that has been of utmost importance since the seminal work by Swain (1985 *et passim*). For Swain, output is not just the product of L2 acquisition but it also plays a crucial and unique role in L2 development. In fact, it is only when L2 learners are *pushed* to produce that they are aware of their lack of linguistic resources (they notice a hole in their interlanguage – Swain 1995) or of the mismatch between what they have said and the target form (they notice a gap – Schmidt and Frota 1986).

Swain (1985 *et passim*) proposed the Output Hypothesis, which claims that output cannot be seen merely as an end product of learning but, rather, as an important factor to promote the L2 learning process. She identified three by now well-known functions of output, which will be illustrated below with several examples.

    i. *The noticing function*: when learners produce output they are aware of the mismatch (the gap) between what they want to say and what they can produce in the target language. Consider the following examples:

1. Learner 1:   Instead of 'easier' it should be 'easily' . . . It's an adverb . . . Isn't it?

   Learner 2:   But this is the . . . easier stowage. . . . It's the comparative but not the superlative.

                 (Alegría de la Colina and García Mayo 2007, p. 99)

2. María: Yes. Eh . . . there are cookies in your picture?

   Iria: Eh . . . is . . . eh

   María: Are there no?

   Iria: What?

   María: Or there are or are there?

   Iria: Are there

   María: Are there cookies?

                    (Azkarai Garai 2013, p. 88)

In (1), two low-proficiency Spanish EFL learners are completing a text reconstruction task and they focus on whether they should be using the comparative or the superlative form of the adjective *easy*. In (2), the learners, now two low-intermediate Spanish-Basque EFL learners, have doubts about how to use the English existential construction *there are* when asking a question. In both examples, the learners focus their attention on formal aspects of the language they are learning.

ii. *Hypothesis formation and testing*: learners use their output as a way of trying out new language forms and structures. They may produce just to see what works and what does not (Swain 1997)

3. Learner 1: John arrive, arrove, arrove or arrive?
   Learner 2: arrove, in the past
   Learner 1: I mean, arrove or arrived?
   Learner 2: arrove the airplane
   Learner 1: arrived or arrove?
   Learner 2: arrove
   Learner 1: arrove the airport at 8:30.

(Adams 2007, pp. 48–9)

Example (3) features two Spanish ESL learners trying to complete a communicative task. Learner 1 has doubts about the past tense of the verb *arrive*, and learner 2 seems very sure that the answer is the wrong form *arrove*, which is the one finally adopted by his partner. Learner 1 was trying out the right and the wrong form while performing the task as if saying them aloud would lead him to choose the correct answer.

iii. *Metatalk*: this function refers to the language used by the learners to reflect consciously on their language use. They use language to indicate an awareness of something about their own or their interlocutor's use of language (Swain 1998, p. 68).

4. Learner 1: And the verb here?
   Learner 2: Check . . . well, actually, it is 'are not checked', passive, and 'remain', the other one . . .
   Learner 1: And if it is '-ed', isn't it 'has'? or is it 'are'?
   Learner 2: Let's see, the verb 'to be' in the same form as it is and then the participle . . .
   Learner 1: Ok, ok . . . are not checking, checked.

(Alegría de la Colina and García Mayo 2007, p. 105)

In example (4), two low-proficiency EFL learners, make use of terms such as 'passive' and 'participle' when deciding which form of the verb they should provide to complete a text-reconstruction task. Swain and colleagues (Swain 1995, 2005; Swain and Lapkin 1995, 2002) broadened the scope of work on learners' output by introducing the concept of *collaborative dialogue* and consider it from a sociocultural perspective (Vygotsky 1978). In the sociocultural tradition, human cognitive development is a socially situated activity mediated by language, that is, knowledge is socially constructed by interaction and is then internalized (see Gánem-Gutierrez 2013). Collaborative dialogue is thus seen as a form of output which allows learners to notice a gap between their interlanguage and the target language forms and to test their hypotheses about the target language and its use. In Swain's words, 'Collaborative dialogue is dialogue in which speakers are engaged in problem-solving and knowledge-building- in this case solving *linguistic* problems and building knowledge about *language*' (Swain 2005, invited talk, The University of Iowa). In recent work, Swain (2006, 2010) refers to the learners' engagement in trying to solve language-related problems while completing collaborative tasks such as *languaging*.

During collaborative tasks, learners may consciously reflect on their own language use and produce what has been referred to as *language-related episodes (LREs)*, which were originally defined by Swain as '. . . any part of the dialogue in which students talk about the language they are producing, question their language use, or other- or self-correct'. (Swain 1998, p. 70). LREs, which have been claimed to represent L2 learning in progress (Gass and Mackey 2007), have been categorized in different ways (Adams and Ross-Feldman 2008; Fortune 2005), but a generally accepted division is the one used by Williams (2001) where she classified LREs on the basis of their nature (grammatical or lexical) and their outcome (resolved – whether target-like or non-target-like – and unresolved). *Grammatical LREs* are interactions where the learners deal with aspects of morphology or syntax, whereas *lexical LREs* deal with word meanings, word choices, use of prepositions and spelling. In example (5), the learners talk about whether they should use the definite article:

5. Learner 1:   We will talk about the main advantages of containerization
   Learner 2:   aha
   Learner 1:   in general terms, containerization . . . I think we should omit 'the'
   Learner 2:   yes, I was going so say that too.

                (Alegría de la Colina and García Mayo 2007, p. 99)

Some collaborative tasks have been shown to elicit output from second/foreign language learners and have proved to be successful in drawing their attention to formal aspects of the language system they try to internalize. Among those, *dictogloss* (Wajnryb 1990) is probably one of the most researched (Alegría de la Colina and García Mayo 2007, 2009; García Mayo 2002a, 2002b; Kim 2008; Kowal and Swain 1997; Kuiken and Vedder 2002; Leeser 2004). In a dictogloss task, the teacher reads a pre-selected text (appropriate for the learner's proficiency level) once at normal pace and the learners just listen. In the second phase, the teacher reads the text again and the learners jot down notes individually about what they consider to be key words. At the third phase, the learners work in pairs or small groups and try to reconstruct the original text as genuinely as possible in terms of accuracy and cohesion. During the third phase, the learners have to pool their linguistic resources together to come up with a final product that would resemble the original text. The task pushes them to collaborate in the search for the appropriate word or expression or the appropriate grammatical form.

Other collaborative output tasks that have been used in several research studies are *text reconstruction* and *jigsaw*. In text-reconstructions, the learners are provided with a written text which has been deprived of function words that they have to insert in order to come up with an accurate product. This task has also been claimed to be effective to draw learners' attention to formal aspects of the language (García Mayo 2002a, 2002b; Kowal and Swain 1997; Storch 1998). The jigsaw is a two-way information task in which each participant has part of the necessary information to complete the task and must necessarily exchange it. It is a task intended to promote negotiation of meaning (Pica et al. 1993).

Over the last decade, by means of a careful description of learners' output while engaged in collaborative tasks, SLA researchers have demonstrated that collaborative dialogue facilitates language learning, and collaborative tasks are a good example of how attention to form can be drawn in the language learning classroom. For example, pioneering work by Storch (1999) considered the effect of collaborative work on the quality of learner's writing. Eleven intermediate-advanced ESL learners from different first language (L1) backgrounds took part in a study that showed that pair work had a positive effect on overall grammatical accuracy when the learners completed several form-focused tasks. The researcher found that a greater proportion of problematic items were not only detected but also correctly amended by the learners when working in pairs than when working individually. Swain and Lapkin (2002) studied the collaborative writing of a pair of adolescent French immersion students. The researchers analysed the transcripts of the learners while they were completing the writing task in collaboration and were comparing their text to a reformulated version. Couched within a sociocultural perspective, the paper documents how these two learners confront and resolve language-related problems. Swain and Lapkin (2002) claim that collaborative writing tasks offer multiple opportunities to discuss language which leads to learning.

In more recent work, Storch and Wigglesworth (2007) compared the writing performance of adult ESL learners on two tasks, a report task and an argumentative essay. The tasks were completed individually (n = 24) and in collaboration (n = 24 pairs). Their findings, similar to the ones obtained in a later study (Wigglesworth and Storch 2009) showed that the texts written in collaboration were more accurate than those written individually, although the differences in terms of fluency and accuracy were non-significant. More recent work by Fernández Dobao (2012) in Spanish as a foreign language setting compared the performance in the same writing task by groups of four learners, pairs and individual learners. She analysed the LREs in the learners' oral output while collaborating in the writing process and reported that '. . . groups produced more LREs and a higher percentage of correctly resolved LREs than pairs. As a result, the texts written by the groups were more accurate not only than those written individually, but also than those written in pairs' (Fernández Dobao 2012, p. 40).

Also in a foreign language setting, Alegría de la Colina and García Mayo (2007) analysed the oral interaction of 12 pairs of elementary EFL adult learners enrolled in Maritime Studies, who mastered a wide range of content-specific vocabulary but had discoursal and morphosyntactic deficiencies. Three tasks were used, all with content related to the participants' specialization – an aspect that had not been controlled for in García Mayo (2002a, 2002b): jigsaw (visual stimulus), text reconstruction (written stimulus) and dictogloss (oral stimulus). The authors concluded that all three tasks were effective in drawing learners' attention to formal aspects of language and engage them in metatalk. Collaboration seemed to be highly productive for these elementary learners because it allowed them to solve a high percentage of grammatical problems. More recently, McDonough and Sunithan (2009) analysed the LREs generated by 48 L1 Thai EFL learners when they completed a series of computer-based activities in a less-structured context: a self-access learning environment where '. . . review activities, teacher feedback, and modeling are unlikely to occur' (McDonough and Sunithan 2009, pp. 233–4). The findings showed that most LREs were successfully solved in collaboration.

All the studies briefly summarized above have reported numerous instances of both lexical and grammatical LREs but not many have used collaborative tasks with specific grammatical targets. In the following section, we will review a selection of those studies and comment on whether and how they actually drew learners' attention to formal aspects of language.

Collaborative grammar tasks: Some empirical studies in second/foreign language settings

This section summarizes research where collaborative tasks targeted specific grammar features and discusses the extent to which they helped learners in the language learning process.

Swain and Lapkin (2001) reported on a study in which two communicative tasks, dictogloss and jigsaw, with the same content, were used in two classes with 65 English adolescent learners of French at various proficiency levels. The grammatical form in focus was *French pronominal verbs*. The researchers hypothesized that there would be less attention to form when the students performed the jigsaw task because this is a typical meaning-focus task. Contrary to expectations, the learners focused on formal aspects equally in both tasks, although the researchers speculated that one of the reasons could have been that both had a written component, and it was the act of writing collaboratively that led students to discuss problems as they arose. Swain and Lapkin's (2001) study used a pre- and a tailor-made post-test developed on the content of the learners' dialogue but found no statistically significant differences in the learners' performance. The learners did focus on the target form but, sometimes, as in example (6), they overgeneralize the use of the pronominal form of the verb (probably influenced by a video-recorded mini-lesson they had watched before the task, as Swain and Lapkin mentioned:

6. Learner 1:   Yvonne va à l'école
    (Yvone goes to school)
   Learner 2:   Se parte à l'école
    (Yvone leaves [uses non-existent pronominal form] for school)
   Learner 1:   Oui. Elle . . . se marche
    (She walks [uses non-existent pronominal form]
   Learner 2:   Se part, parce que . . .
    (Leaves [uses non-existent pronominal form] because)

Learner 1:   Est-ce que c'est part ou se part?

             (Is it leaves or leaves [in the non-existent pronominal form])

Learner 2:   Part

             (Leaves)

Learner 1:   Part? Just part?

             (Leaves? Just leaves?)

Learner 2:   Ya

Learner 1:   Ok. Yvonne part à l'école, um . . .

             (Yvonne leaves for school)

García Mayo (2002a, 2002b) analysed the oral interaction of 14 high-intermediate/advanced adult EFL learners as they worked on several form-focused tasks (dictogloss, text reconstruction and editing passage – where learners had to actually correct grammatical problems so that the message could be conveyed more clearly) and other tasks such as cloze and multiple choice – which, although structured activities, were designed in such a way that the members of the pairs had to interact. After a quantitative and qualitative analysis of the data, she concluded that, except for the dictogloss (probably because of the learners' lack of familiarity with the task), all the other activities generated a high amount of LREs and led learners to reflect on their language choices by means of hypothesis testing strategies, one of the functions of output as claimed by Swain (1985). Consider the following example where the learners are completing a text-reconstruction task and are trying to decide whether the adjective *inclined* should be followed by the preposition *to* or by *–ing*:

7. Learner 1	Learner 2
	. . . *men are less incline* . . . it has to be an adjective . . . inclined to confess, you are inclined to do something . . .
to confession	to confess . . .
but after a proposition . . .	to confess . . . what?
to is a preposition . . .	yeah . . .
so it should be followed . . .	included to confessing . . .
by *ing* . . .	no, because *to* is part of the second verb . . . inclined to confess. . . yeah
ok, I trust you	

                                    (García Mayo 2002b, p. 329)

Each of the form-focused tasks had one or several grammatical target features[1] but, as the author reports, not all talk focused on the linguistic items targeted by the tasks. In Swain's words: 'Learners talk about what they *need* to talk about; that is, those aspects of language about which they are not sure. And that, in turn, will depend on their current internalized state of knowledge about language and its use.' (Swain 1998, p. 73). However, no pre-post-test design was used, so no impact on learning could be measured.

Kuiken and Vedder (2002) focused on the *English passive* and analysed the interaction of an experimental group of 20 EFL Dutch high-school students while they completed two dictogloss tasks. There was also a control group ($n = 12$) who completed the same tasks individually. Both groups took a pre-test to assess the knowledge of the target feature and both a post- and a delayed post-test. The quantitative analysis carried out led the researchers to conclude that the learners' collaboration '. . . did not result in a better recognition of passives and a higher score in the detection test, nor in a more frequent use of these structures in the text reconstruction task' (Kuiken and Vedder 2002, p. 350). However, as in Swain and Lapkin (2001), the qualitative analysis of the data shows numerous examples of learners' noticing the passive construction and being aware of their usage problems. Consider the following example, where the learners substitute an active structure by a passive:

8. Denise: 'Until now . . .'yes, 'it's still unclear . . . *who created them* and why.'
   Maarten: Yes
   Denise: 'Until now . . . who designed and *created them* and why.'
   Maarten: yes, 'who . . ., who built . . .'
   Tin Choi: . . . who copied . . .
   Denise: yes, that's possible, I think. Yes, sounds good.
   Maarten: 'Created', yes, 'created'.
   Maarteen: '*Pictures were created*', or . . . ehm . . . yes, '*were created*'
   Tin Choi: That's still better probably

                                          (Kuiken and Vedder 2002, p. 352)

Also in an EFL setting, Baleghizadeh (2009) analysed the performance of 42 Iranian intermediate learners while they completed a conversational cloze task under two conditions: collaboratively and individually. The cloze task had three types of grammatical targets: *articles, prepositions and coordinating conjunctions.* His findings showed that learners working in pairs outperformed those working individually on article and preposition use but there were no significant differences in coordinating conjunctions. The author speculates that '. . . more complex grammatical items (e.g. articles and prepositions) are better candidates to benefit from pair work than those which do not encompass a wide range of complicated rules'.

Adams (2007) studied the oral interaction of 25 adult ESL participants (13 of whom had Spanish as their L1) while they performed three interactive tasks (dinner seating, picture story and spot-the-difference). The target grammatical points the researcher was interested in were *question words, past tense and locative prepositions*. Based on the results of a tailor-made post-test, generated on the basis of the LRE discussions that the learners had engaged in, Adams argued for the effectiveness of learner collaboration in promoting L2 learning. The following example comes from her study:

9. Learner 1:   the man opened the suitcase and he find the suitcase
   Learner 2:   find got a mistake
   Learner 1:   got a mistake
   Learner 2:   yes, yes, yes, yes, man, the man opened, opened the suitcase, period. Suitcase.
   Learner 1:   and
   Learner 2:   and he found, F-O-U-N-D

(Adams 2007, p. 45)

While trying to complete the collaborative task, learner 2 realizes that his partner's utterances has a problem with the past tense of the verb *find*. He repeats the first part of his partner's utterance (The man opened the suitcase) and then he spells the correct form of the past tense of the verb.

The study by Nassaji and Tian (2010) uses *phrasal verbs* as the target grammatical feature. The authors used two types of output tasks, a reconstruction cloze task and a reconstruction editing task, to compare their effectiveness in helping the learning of the target feature. The participants of the study, which was carried out in two intact classes in an intensive ESL programme in Canada, were 26 low-intermediate adults from different first language backgrounds. The participants carried out each of the two tasks both collaboratively and individually and to eliminate task effects, the order of the tasks was counterbalanced. Once more, the findings point to the more successful completion of the tasks when learners worked collaboratively than individually but, as in the study by Kuiken and Vedder (2002), no significant differences were found regarding the impact of collaboration on the participant's knowledge of phrasal verbs between the pre-test and the post-test scores. Nassaji and Tian provide several possible reasons to explain this lack of significant differences such as the brief and limited interaction that took place among learners, the nature of the target form chosen, difficult for non-native speakers of English and, therefore, leaving little chance for learners to provide feedback to their peers and, finally, a lack of a training session so that learners might get acquainted with the procedure. What the researchers did find was an effect of task type: the editing tasks were more effective than the cloze tasks in promoting interaction and learning. Consider example (10), where learner 2 suggests the use of *pay off*, which is finally accepted by his partner.

10. Editing task: 'Wow. So it paid for to study French at school. I had not
                      trouble getting a job'
    Learner 1:   Ok. So it paid for to study French at school.
    Learner 2:   Pay off?
    Learner 1:   yeah, maybe this don't need 'to'. Paid off study.
    Learner 2:   Paid . . .
    Learner 1:   I think this don't need . . .
    Learner 2:   Um . . .
    Learner 1:   Maybe, maybe. I had no trouble getting job.
                                    (Nassaji and Tian 2010, p. 411).

A recent study by Basterrechea and García Mayo (2013) investigates the effect of collaborative work on production of the present *tense marker –s* by 81 English-as-a-foreign-language (EFL) and Content and Language Integrated Learning (CLIL) adolescent learners (age range, 15–16 years) while completing a dictogloss task. Learners in CLIL classrooms are exposed to more hours of target language input per week, and the interactive teaching approach followed in the classrooms is believed to enhance learning opportunities (Dalton-Puffer 2011). The target item was chosen because both anecdotal and empirical evidence has shown that L1 Spanish learners of English (Dulay and Burt 1973) and Basque-Spanish bilinguals (García Mayo et al. 2005; García Mayo and Villarreal Olaizola 2011) have difficulty producing it accurately in written and spoken discourse. Besides, some researchers have claimed that forms that are not crucial for successful communication, such as the marker –s, are appropriate candidates for form-focused tasks (Williams and Evans 1998). Following the regular dictogloss procedure, the learners listened to a text about a familiar topic (a social network) without writing anything down. They then listened to the passage again and were instructed to take notes in English. Finally, using their notes, the learners reconstructed the passage either collaboratively or individually. The findings show that both CLIL and EFL learners do indeed focus on formal aspects on language and, most importantly, they focus on the feature they have more problems with: the *–s* marker. Consider example (11):

11. Learner 1: and interesting people, who meet in parties *por ejemplo* (for example)

     Learner 2: who (*uttered while writing*)

     Learner 1: meet in parties

     Learner 2: she meets in parties

     Learner 1: no who meet in parties

     Learner 2: meets *no tiene que ser* (no it has to be) meets *porque es tercera persona* (because it is third person)

                                        (Basterrechea and García Mayo 2013, p. 35)

As seen in (11), learner 2 referred to the target form explicitly and resolved the LRE correctly. Learner 1 believed that *meet* should agree with *people* (from the main clause) instead of with the subject of the relative clause (*she*).

Results also showed that CLIL learners produced more LREs than EFL learners and, most importantly, that there was a positive correlation between the LREs focused on the target feature during collaboration with accurate use of that target feature in the text reconstruction. A statistically significant correlation was found between LREs (both all LREs involving third-person singular and those correctly solved) and accurate use of the target feature in the reconstructed texts for both CLIL and EFL learners. As for the impact of collaboration, pairs that completed the dictogloss tasks collaboratively outperformed learners who worked individually, and collaborative text reconstruction was more beneficial in the CLIL context than in the EFL context. However, although a correlation was found between LREs focused on the target feature, their resolution and the use of that feature in the reconstructed text, we should not infer that there is a direct causation, as see in Basterrechea (2012). She administered a grammaticality judgement task as a pre- and a post-test to the same group of learners who completed the dictogloss task and found that there was no significant impact on the learning of the target feature.

As we have seen, several studies in both ESL and EFL contexts have used collaborative tasks targeting specific grammatical issues. They have all showed that these tasks draw learners' attention to form, engage them in form-focused talk and seem to be beneficial for the language learning process.

Conclusion

This chapter has presented arguments in favour of the use of collaborative tasks in both second and foreign language learning settings. The studies reviewed have shown that when learners complete communicative tasks in collaboration, they identify gaps in their knowledge, they pool their linguistic resources together and solve most of the problems they are faced with. Collaborative work seems to activate mechanisms that have been claimed to facilitate the language learning process as learners voice their opinions about particular aspects of the task they are completing, thus focusing their attention on formal aspects of the language within a communicative context.

Among the research carried out on collaborative tasks, there is relatively little work that has considered specific grammatical features. Some of that work has already been summarized here, and the general findings also point to the positive impact of collaboration on drawing learners' attention to those specific aspects of languages the researchers were interested in. However, as rightly observed by Nassaji and Tian, 'Collaborative work facilitates learners' interaction and attention to target forms, *although it may not necessarily lead to superior learning in comparison to individual work*' (Nassaji and Tian 2010, p. 400).

As pointed out by Kim and McDonough (2011), some studies have suggested that LREs may be used by just a few learners and that their overall frequency in the discourse might be low (Carless 2003; Foster 1998; Philp et al. 2010). Considering the apparent benefits of the interaction that takes place in LREs, it would be necessary to identify ways by which we can make teachers aware of the benefits of collaborative tasks. In line with studies such as Swain and Lapkin (2001), learners could be provided with *explicit information about the target grammatical form(s)* before they carry out the tasks, as is done in Processing Instruction (Lee and Benati 2009; Lee and VanPatten 2003). Recently, Kim and McDonough (2011) suggested the use of *pre-task modelling* and examined whether this technique was pedagogically effective to '. . . encourage learners to adopt collaborative pair dynamics and generate LREs'. (Kim and McDonough 2011, p. 184). The participants in their study (44 Korean EFL learners) completed three tasks (dictogloss, text-reconstruction and information gap) and those who received pre-task modelling, operationalized as videotaped models of collaborative interaction, produced more LREs and correctly solved a greater proportion of those than learners who did not receive any models.

Another important aspect that needs to be taken into account when dealing with collaborative work is that we should be able to measure the impact of collaboration on learning by means of pre- and post-tests (and even delayed post-tests) to gauge whether that impact is lasting and has the potential to trigger restructuring of the learners' interlanguage system. We are all well aware of how difficult it is to carry out longitudinal studies in classroom settings but these are surely in dire need.

Of course, we cannot forget about individual and social factors when talking about learners' interaction. As pointed out by Philp et al. (2010), learners' willingness to attend to difficulties with language form during peer task-based interaction is affected by both task characteristics, individual and social factors. Among individual factors, personality, aptitude and motivation as well as learners' internal capacities should be studied in detail. Recent work by Mackey and Sachs (2012) has found that higher working memory capacity is likely to trigger more instances of modified output on the part of the learner. Among the social factors, in their three-week peer task-based oral interaction study, the learners felt more relaxed while doing group work than when there was whole-class interaction. More research is necessary on different educational settings, too. For example, the impact of collaborative grammar tasks might not be the same in traditional foreign-language classes and CLIL scenarios (Basterrechea and García Mayo 2013), and there is a clear need to carry out more research, as Dalton-Puffer (2011) observes.

All the research possibilities that lie ahead on the issue of collaborative grammar tasks should also lead to more knowledge transfer efforts on the part of researchers. In fact, the link between research findings and second language pedagogy needs to be strengthened in such a way that professional development is 'research-based and practitioner-informed', if we borrow part of the title of the book by Fortune and Menke (2010).

*Acknowledgements

This research was supported by the following research grants: FFI2012-32212 (Spanish Government), IT311-10 (Basque Government) and UFI11/06 (University of the Basque Country).

Note

1   Those were: articles and prepositions in the *multiple choice task*; articles, prepositions and connectors in the *cloze task*; verbal features, prepositions and connectors in the *text reconstruction task*; verbal features, prepositions and connectors in the *text-editing task* and articles, connectors and adverbs in the *dictogloss task*.

References

Adams, R. (2007), 'Do second language learners benefit from interacting with each other?', in A. Mackey (ed.), *Conversational Interaction in Second Language Acquisition*. Amsterdam: John Benjamins, pp. 29–52.

Adams, R. and Ross-Feldman, L. (2008), 'Does writing influence learner attention to form?', in D. Belcher and A. Hirvela (eds), *The Oral-Literate Connection*. Michigan: The University of Michigan, pp. 243–66.

Alegría de la Colina, A. and García Mayo, M. P. (2007), 'Attention to form across collaborative tasks by low proficiency learners in an EFL setting', in M. P. García Mayo (ed.), *Investigating Tasks in Formal Language Learning*. Clevedon: Multilingual Matters, pp. 91–116.

— (2009), 'Oral interaction in task-based EFL learning: The use of the L1 as a cognitive tool', *International Review of Applied Linguistics*, 47, 325–46.

Allen, P., Swain, M. Harley, B., and Cummins, J. (1990), 'Aspects of classroom treatment: toward a more comprehensive view of second language education', in B. Harley, P. Allen, J. Cummins, and M. Swain (eds), *The Development of Second Language Proficiency*. Cambridge: Cambridge University Press, pp. 57–81.

Azkarai Garai, A. (2013), *Gender and Task Modality in EFL Task-based Interaction*. Ph.D. dissertation. The University of the Basque Country (UPV/EHU).

Baleghizadeh, S. (2009), 'Investigating the effectiveness of pair work on a conversational cloze task in EFL classes'. *TESL Reporter*, 42, 1–12.

Basterrechea, M. (2012), *Interaction and Focus on Form in a Dictogloss Tasks in Secondary Education: A Comparative Study of CLIL and Mainstream Learner Production*. Ph.D. dissertation. The University of the Basque Country (UPV/EHU).

Basterrechea, M. and García Mayo, M. P. (2013), 'Language-related episodes during collaborative tasks: a comparison of CLIL and EFL learners', in K. McDonough and A. Mackey (eds), *Interaction in Diverse Educational Settings*. Amsterdam: John Benjamins, pp. 25–44.

Carless, D. (2003), 'Factors in the implementation of task-based teaching in primary school'. *System*, 31, 485–500.

Dalton-Puffer, C. (2011), 'Content-and-language integrated learning: from practice to principles?' *Annual Review of Applied Linguistics*, 31, 182–204.

Dulay, H. C. and Burt, M. K. (1973), 'Should we teach children syntax?' *Language Learning*, 23, 245–58.

Ellis, R. (2005), *Planning and Task Performance in a Second Language*. Amsterdam: John Benjamins.

Fernández Dobao, A. (2012), 'Collaborative writing tasks in the L2 classroom: comparing group, pair and individual work'. *Journal of Second Language Writing*, 21, 40–58.

Fortune, A. (2005), 'Learners' use of metalanguage in collaborative form-focused L2 output tasks'. *Language Awareness*, 14, 21–38.

Fortune, T. W. and Menke, M. (2010), *Struggling Learners and Language Immersion Education: Research-Based, Practitioner-Informed Responses to Educators' Top Questions*. Minneapolis, MN: University of Minnesota.

Foster, P. (1998), 'A classroom perspective on the negotiation of meaning'. *Applied Linguistics*, 19, 1–23.

Gánem-Gutierrez, G. A. (2013), 'Sociocultural theory and second language development: theoretical foundations and insights from research', in M. P. García Mayo, M. J. Gutiérrez Mangado and M. Martínez Adrián (eds), *Contemporary Perspectives on Second Language Acquisition*. Amsterdam: John Benjamins, pp. 129–52.

García Mayo, M. P. (2002a), 'The effectiveness of two form-focused tasks in advanced EFL pedagogy'. *International Journal of Applied Linguistics*, 12, 156–75.

— (2002b), 'Interaction in advanced EFL pedagogy: a comparison of form-focused activities'. *International Journal of Educational Research*, 37, 323–41.

— (2011), 'The relevance of attention to L2 form in communicative classroom settings'. *ELIA: Estudios de Lingüística Inglesa Aplicada*, 11, 11–45.

García Mayo, M. P. and Alcón Soler, E. (2013), 'Input, output. The interactionist framework', in J. Herschensohn and M. Young-Scholten (eds). *The Handbook of Second Language Acquisition*. Cambridge: Cambridge University Press, pp. 209–29.

García Mayo, M. P. Lázaro Ibarrola, A., and Liceras, J. M. (2005), 'Placeholders in the English interlanguage of bilingual (Basque/Spanish) children'. *Language Learning*, 55, 445–89.

García Mayo, M. P. and Villarreal Olaizola, I. (2011), 'The development of suppletive and affixal tense and agreement morphemes in the L3 English of Basque-Spanish bilinguals'. *Second Language Research*, 27, 129–49.

Gass, S. M. and Mackey, A. (2007), 'Input, interaction and output in second language acquisition', in B. VanPatten and J. Williams (eds), *Theories in Second Language Acquisition. An Introduction*. Mahwah, NJ: Lawrence Erlbaum, pp. 175–200.

Genesee, F. (1994), 'Integrating Language and content: lessons from immersion'. *The National Center for Research on Cultural Diversity and Second Language Learning, Educational Practice Report*, 11, 1–15.

Grim, F. (2009), 'Integrating focus on form in L2 content-enriched lessons'. *Foreign Language Annals*, 41, 321–46.

Howatt, A. (1984), *A History of English Language Teaching*. Oxford: Oxford University Press.

Keck, C. M., Iberri-Shea, G., Tracy-Ventura, N., and Wa-Mbaleka, S. (2006), 'Investigating the empirical link between task-based interaction and acquisition: a quantitative meta-analysis', in J. M. Norris and L. Ortega (eds), *Synthesizing Research on Language Learning and Teaching*. Amsterdam: John Benjamins, pp. 91–131.

Kim, Y. (2008). 'The contribution of collaborative and individual tasks to the acquisition of L2 vocabulary'. *The Modern Language Journal*, 92, 114–30.

Kim, Y. and McDonough, K. (2011), 'Using pretask modelling to encourage collaborative learning opportunities'. *Language Teaching Research*, 15, 183–99.

Kowal, M. and Swain, M. (1997), 'From semantic to syntactic processing. How can we promote it in the immersion classroom?', in R. K. Johnson and M. Swain (eds), *Immersion Education: International Perspectives*. Cambridge: Cambridge University Press, pp. 284–309.

Kuiken, F. and Vedder, I. (2002), 'The effect of interaction in acquiring the grammar of a second language'. *International Journal of Educational Research*, 37, 343–58.

Larsen-Freeman, D. (2003), *Teaching Language: From Grammar to Grammaring*. Boston: Thomson Heinle.

— (2009), 'Teaching and testing grammar', in M. H. Long and C. Doughty (eds), *The Handbook of Language Teaching*. Oxford: Blackwell, pp. 518–42.

Lee, J. F. and Benati, A. (2009), *Research and Perspectives on Processing Instruction*. Berlin: Mouton de Gruyter.

Lee, J. F. and VanPatten, B. (2003), *Making Communicative Language Teaching Happen* (2nd edn). New York: McGraw-Hill.

Leeser, M. J. (2004), 'Learner proficiency and focus on form during collaborative dialogue'. *Language Teaching Research,* 8, 55–81.

Long, M. H. (1996), 'The role of the linguistic environment in second language acquisition', in W. Ritchie and T. Bhatia (eds) *Handbook of Research on Second Language Acquisition*. New York: Academic Press, pp. 413–68.

Lyster, R. (2007), *Learning and Teaching Languages through Content: A Counterbalanced Approach*. Amsterdam/Philadelphia: John Benjamins.

Mackey, A. and Goo, J. (2007), 'Interaction research in SLA: a meta-analysis and research synthesis', in A. Mackey (ed.), *Conversational Interaction in Second Language Acquisition*. Amsterdam: John Benjamins, pp. 407–72.

Mackey, A. and Sachs, R. (2012), 'Older learners in SLA research: a first look at working memory, feedback, and L2 development'. *Language Learning*, 62, 704–40.

McDonough, K. and Sunithan, W. (2009), 'Collaborative dialogue between Thai EFL learners during self-access computer activities'. *TESOL Quarterly*, 43, 231–54.

Mitchell, R. (2000), 'Applied linguistics and evidence-based classroom practice. The case of foreign language grammar pedagogy'. *Applied Linguistics,* 21, 281–303.

Nassaji, H. and Fotos, S. (2011), *Teaching Grammar in Foreign Language Classrooms. Integrating Form-Focused Instruction in Communicative Contexts*. London: Routledge.

Nassaji, H. and Simard, D. (2010), 'Introduction: current developments in form-focused interaction and L2 acquisition'. *The Canadian Modern Language Review/La Revue Cannadienne des Langues Vivantes*, 66, 773–8.

Nassaji, H. and Tian, J. (2010), 'Collaborative and individual output tasks and their effect on learning English phrasal verbs'. *Language Teaching Research*, 14, 397–419.

Norris, J. and Ortega, L. (2000), 'Effectiveness of L2 instruction: a research synthesis and quantitative meta-analysis'. *Language Learning*, 50, 417–28.

Nunan, D. (1989), *Designing Tasks for the Communicative Classroom*. Cambridge: Cambridge University Press.

Philp, J., Walter, S., and Basturkmen, H. (2010), 'Peer interaction in the foreign language classroom: what factors foster a focus on form?' *Language Awareness*, 4, 261–79.

Pica, T. (1994), 'Review article: research on negotiation: what does it reveal about second-language learning conditions, processes and outcomes?', *Language Learning*, 44, 493–527.

— (2002), 'Subject matter content: how does it assist the interactional and linguistic needs of classroom language learners?' *Modern Language Journal*, 85, 1–19.

Pica, T., Kanady, R., and Falodun, J. (1993), 'Choosing and using communication tasks for second language instruction', in G. Crookes and S. M. Gass (eds), *Tasks and Language Learning. Integrating Theory and Practice*. Clevedon: Multilingual Matters, pp. 9–34.

Richards, J. C. and Rodgers, R. (2001), *Approaches and Methods in Language Teaching* (2nd edn). Cambridge: Cambridge University Press.

Savignon, S. (2001), 'Communicative language teaching for the twenty-first century', in M. Celce-Murcia (ed.), *Teaching English as a Second or Foreign Language* (3rd edn). Boston, MA: Heinle & Heinle, pp. 13–28.

Schmidt, R. (1990), 'The role of consciousness in second language learning'. *Applied Linguistics*, 11, 129–58.

— (2001), 'Attention', in P. Robinson (ed.), *Cognition and Second Language Instruction*. Cambridge: Cambridge University Press, pp. 3–32.

Schmidt, R. and Frota, S. (1986), 'Developing basic conversational ability in a second language. A case study of an adult learner of Portuguese', in R. Day (ed.), *Talking to Learn: Conversation in Second Language Acquisition*. Rowley, MA: Newbury House, pp. 237–326.

Spada, N. (2011), 'Beyond form-focused instructions: reflections on the past, present and future research'. *Language Teaching Research*, 44, 225–36.

Spada, N. and Tomita, Y. (2010), 'Interactions between type of instruction and type of language feature: A meta-analysis'. *Language Learning*, 60, 1–46.

Storch, N. (1998), 'A classroom-based study: insights from a collaborative text reconstruction task'. *ELT Journal*, 52, 291–300.

— (1999), 'Are two heads better than one? Pair work and grammatical accuracy'. *System*, 27, 363–74.

Storch, N. and Wigglesworth, G. (2007), 'Writing tasks: comparing individual and collaborative writing', in M. P. García Mayo (ed.), *Investigating Tasks in Formal Language Learning*. Clevedon: Multilingual Matters, pp. 157–77.

Swain, M. (1985). 'Communicative competence: some rules of comprehensible input and comprehensible output in its development', in S. Gass and C. Madden (eds), *Input in Second Language Acquisition*. Rowley, MA: Newbury House, pp. 235–53.

— (1995), 'Three functions of output in second language learning', in G. Gook and B. Seidlhofer (eds), *Principle and Practice in Applied Linguistics*. Oxford: Oxford University Press, pp. 125–44.

— (1997), 'Collaborative dialogue: its contributions to second language learning'. *Revista Canaria de Estudios Ingleses*, 34, 115–32.

— (1998), 'Focus on form through conscious reflection', in C. Doughty and J. Williams (eds), *Focus on Form in Classroom Second Language Acquisition*. Cambridge: Cambridge University Press, pp. 64–82.

— (2006), 'Languaging agency and collaboration in advanced second language Learning', in H. Byrnes (ed.), *Advanced Language Learning: The Contributions of Halliday and Vygotsky*. London: Continuum, pp. 95–108.

— (2010), 'Talking-it-through: languaging as a source of learning', in R. Baststone (ed.), *Sociocognitive Perspectives on Language Use and Language Learning*. Oxford: Oxford University Press, pp. 112–30.

Swain, M. and Lapkin, S. (1995), 'Problems in output and the cognitive processes they generate: a step towards second language learning'. *Applied Linguistics,* 16, 371–91.

— (2001), 'Focus on form through collaborative dialogue: exploring task effects', in M. Bygate, P. Skehan and M. Swain (eds), *Researching Pedagogic Tasks: Second Language Learning, Teaching, and Testing*. New York: Longman, pp. 99–118.

— (2002), 'Talking it through: two French immersion learners' response to reformulation', *International Journal of Educational Research*, 37, 285–304.

Swain, M. (2005), 'The output hypothesis: Theory and research', in E. Hinkel (ed.), *Handbook of Research in Second Language Teaching and Learning*. Mahwah, NJ: Lawrence Erlbaum, pp. 471–83.

VanPatten, B. (1990), 'Attention to form and content in the input. An experiment in consciousness'. *Studies in Second Language Acquisition,* 12, 287–301.

Vygotsky, L. S. (1978). *Mind in Society: The Development of Higher Psychological Processes*. Cambridge: Cambridge University Press.

Wajnryb, R. (1990). *Grammar Dictation*. Oxford: Oxford University Press.

Wigglesworth, G. and Storch, N. (2009), 'Pair versus individual writing: effects on fluency, complexity and accuracy'. *Language Testing*, 26, 445–66.

Williams, J. (2001), 'The effectiveness of spontaneous attention to form'. *System*, 29, 325–40.

Williams, J., and Evans, J. (1998), 'What kind of focus and on which forms?', in C. Doughty and J. Williams (eds), *Focus on Form in Classroom Second Language Acquisition*. Cambridge: Cambridge University Press, pp. 139–55.

5

Interactional Feedback: Insights from Theory and Research

Hossein Nassaji
University of Victoria, Canada

Classroom research has indicated that instruction that integrates attention to form in the context of meaning-focused communication is more effective than instruction that deals with language forms in an isolated and decontextualized manner (e.g. Doughty and Williams 1998; Ellis 2001; Nassaji and Fotos 2010; Spada 1997). There are different ways of drawing learners' attention to form in the context of communication. This chapter discusses one of those ways, which is through interactional feedback. It defines interactional feedback and its different types and subtypes and then discusses how it assists SLA. It also examines factors that may influence its effectiveness. The chapter ends with suggestions for L2 instruction.

Introduction

The notion that second language (L2) learners need to attend to linguistic forms in order to acquire an L2 has become fundamental to current theories and research in the field of SLA. Although there has been a debate on the degree to which learners need to pay attention to form, SLA researchers seem to generally agree that some degree of noticing is required for effective language learning. Different approaches exist as to how to deal with language forms in L2 classrooms. Traditional approaches have prescribed proactive structured-based lessons in which language forms are taught explicitly and mainly in an isolated manner. The literature on form-focused instruction, however, has shown that such a manner of teaching grammatical forms is not necessarily very effective.

Therefore, researchers are now advocating a more communicative way of dealing with grammar, in which attention to form in integrated into a meaning-focused communicative context. This kind of instruction has been called *focus-on-form* (FonF) and has been distinguished from a traditional form-focused instruction, which has been called *focus on forms* (Long 1991; Long and Robinson 1998). There are different ways of drawing learners' attention to form in a meaning-focused context (Doughty and Williams 1998; Nassaji and Fotos 2010). In this chapter, I discuss one of those ways, which is through interactional feedback. I begin by defining interactional feedback and then presenting a taxonomy of its different types. Then, drawing on both theory and research in this area, I examine and discuss a number of key issues including whether and how interactional feedback assists SLA and also the factors that may mediate its effectiveness. I conclude with a discussion of the implications of this examination for classroom pedagogy.

What is interactional feedback?

Interactional feedback refers to feedback generated in response to linguistically erroneous or communicatively inappropriate utterances that learners produce during conversational interaction. This can take place through the use of various forms of negotiation and conversational modification strategies, such as recasts, clarification requests, confirmation checks and repetition, happening in the course of conversation. Interactional feedback is a kind of *reactive FonF* because it occurs in response to a problem or an error of some kind that the learner has already made. This is distinguished from *preemptive FonF* that occurs when learners' attention is drawn to form in the absence of any actual error (Ellis 2001). Interactional feedback draws learners' attention to form both implicitly, through strategies used to negotiate meaning (i.e. those used to deal with communication difficulty) and, more explicitly, through negotiation of form, in which the teacher attempts more deliberately to focus the learner's attention to a particular linguistic form irrespective of any communication breakdown. Interactional feedback can be in response to a wide range of linguistic forms including grammatical, lexical, phonological or even pragmatic forms. Since interactional feedback occurs during meaning-focused exchanges, attention to form occurs at the point where learners' attention is on communicating meaning. Therefore, this kind of FonF provides learners with opportunities to connect form and meaning required for L2 development (e.g. Doughty and Varela 1998; Long and Robinson 1998). The following example from Nassaji (2007a, p. 529) provides an example of an interactional feedback exchange.

Example 1

1	Student:	One of the ladies, a little girl, she wear a short … short … short skirt … a short skirt.	**Initiation**
2	Teacher:	She's wearing a short skirt?	**Feedback**
3	Student:	Yeah, she's wearing a short skirt.	**Uptake**

An interactional feedback exchange consists of three main moves: an initiation move that triggers the feedback, a feedback move in response to the trigger move and an optional uptake move, which is the student's response to the feedback move. In the above example, the erroneous utterance in turn 1 produced by the learner is the initiation move, which has triggered the feedback move in turn 2 by the teacher. The utterance in turn 3 is the uptake move, in which the student has responded to the feedback by repeating the feedback utterance. Uptake is an optional move in the sense that the student has a choice as to whether or not to respond to the feedback.

Types of interactional feedback

Research that has examined interactional feedback in classroom contexts has identified a number of feedback types used by the teacher in reaction to learner's errors in the course of interaction (e.g. Ellis et al. 2001; Lyster and Ranta 1997; Panova and Lyster 2002). These feedback types can be generally grouped into two main types: reformulation and elicitation (Nassaji 2009). Reformulation strategies are those that rephrase the learner's erroneous utterance and provide the learner with the correct form. These types of feedback have also been called *input-providing* because they provide the learner with target-like input (Ellis 2009). Elicitation strategies are those that do not provide the learner with the correct from but rather attempt to prompt the learner to correct his or her original erroneous output. Therefore, they are called *output-prompting* or prompts (Ellis 2009; Lyster 2004). Since elicitations do not supply the correct form, they allow the learner to discover the correct form of their initial erroneous utterance. In other words, they provide opportunities for self-repair (Ellis et al. 2001; Lyster and Ranta 1997). Examples of reformulation strategies are *recasts* and *direct corrections*. Examples of elicitation strategies that prompt self-repair are *clarification requests, repetition, metalinguistic feedback* and *direct elicitation*. In what follows, a brief description of these different feedback strategies along with examples is provided.

a. Reformulation strategies

Recasts

Recasts refer to utterances following the learner's erroneous utterance that reformulate the whole or part of that utterance into a correct form without changing the overall meaning. This kind of feedback is usually implicit in nature, as it does not provide a clear and explicit indication that the learner's utterance contains an error. Therefore, they are considered to provide feedback in an unobtrusive way and without interrupting the flow of communication. The following example from Mackey and Philp (1998, p. 342) provides a recast.

Example 2

NNS	I think some this girl have birth-day and and its big celebrate
NS	big celebration
NNS	Oh

Direct correction

Direct correction refers to feedback that rephrases the learner's erroneous utterance into a correct form but also clearly indicates to the learner that his or her utterance is erroneous in some way (Example 3). Since explicit correction directly informs the learner about the error, it can be considered to be motivated by a deliberate intention to linguistic problems.

Example 3

| Student | He has catch a cold |
| Teacher | Not catch, caught. |

b. Elicitation strategies

Clarification requests

Clarification requests refer to the feedback that occurs when the teacher or an interlocutor does not fully understand a learner's utterance and asks for clarification. It usually occurs through phrases such as 'pardon me?' 'sorry?' and 'excuse me?'. An important characteristic of clarification requests as feedback is that they do not provide the correct form, and therefore, they provide the learner with opportunities to self-correct (Lyster 1998, 2004). Here is an example of clarification requests.

Example 4

Learner	What happen for the boat?
NS	What?
Learner	What's wrong with the boat? (McDonough 2005, p. 86)

Repetition

Repetition refers to feedback that repeats all or part of the learner's erroneous utterances with a rising intonation (Example 5). Similar to clarification requests, this kind of feedback does not provide the correct form. Therefore, it provides an opportunity for self-repair.

Example 5

Student	He play soccer everyday.
Teacher	He play?

Metalinguistic feedback

Metalinguistic feedback refers to feedback that provides the learner with metalinguistic information. This can include comments about language rules or structures and how it works or statements or question about grammaticality of the students' utterance. Metalinguistic feedback can be provided in the form of metalinguistic clues without providing the correct from, which can then promote self-repair (such as in Example 6). It can also be combined with correction, in which case it does not provide opportunities for self-repair (such as in Example 7).

Example 6

Learner	He has two child.
Teacher	Child is singular. You need the plural form.

Example 7

Student	I explained him my reasons.
Teacher	You need a preposition. Explained to him.

Direct elicitation

Direct elicitation is feedback that attempts to elicit the correct form more overtly. This can happen when the interlocutor repeats the learner's utterance up to the error and then waits for the learner to complete the utterance or when the interlocutor asks more directly for a reformulation of an ill-formed utterance (Example 8).

Example 8

Student	. . . on the street there was a policeman, and she was skippingrunning.
Teacher	I am sorry, she was . . .?
Student	Skipping running, the thief.

(Nassaji 2009, p. 429)

The role of interactional feedback

Theoretically, the argument for the role of interactional feedback relates closely to the notion of whether or not there is any need for corrective or negative feedback in language acquisition. In L1 acquisition, one theoretical position, the nativist approach, claims that there is limited explicit corrective feedback in the context of L1 learning, and therefore, L1 children rarely receive explicit corrective feedback on their ill-formed utterances (Brown and Hanlon 1970; Demetras et al. 1986). In this view, language learning becomes possible through an innate ability called UG. Some L2 researchers have argued that similar innate knowledge is also available to L2 learners and that L2 learners either do not need corrective feedback, or if they do, it is only in rare cases where the learners are not able to get the correct form from exposure to the target language evidence (e.g. Flynn 1988, 1996; Schwartz 1993; White 1991). However, despite such a perspective, many SLA researchers believe that L2 learning is different from L1 child acquisition and that in order to acquire an L2 successfully, L2 learners, particularly adults, need ample exposure not only to the correct form of the language but also to negative feedback (i.e. information about what is not correct in a given language) (DeKeyser 1998; Doughty 2001, 2003; Doughty and Varela 1998; Ellis 2002, 2008; Gass 1997, 2003; Long 1991, 1996, 2006; Long and Robinson 1998; Pica 1994, 1996, 2002; Swain 1998).

Negative feedback can be obtained in various ways (Long 2006). It can be obtained directly through explicit correction or explanation of language rules or indirectly through various forms of interactional feedback in the context of meaning-focused communication. It is suggested that when learners interact with a more competent interlocutor, they not only communicate meaning but can also receive negative feedback on their interlanguage production through various interactional modifications and adjustments in the course of interaction (e.g. Gass 2003; Long 1996; Pica 1996).

How does interactional feedback assist SLA?

Within SLA, a major argument for the role of interactional feedback comes from Long's interaction hypothesis and the importance attributed to the role of negotiation of meaning in communicative interaction (e.g. Gass 2003; Long 1996). Negotiation of meaning occurs as a result of the various conversational adjustments and modifications when learners perceive difficulties in understanding message during interaction. Negotiation of meaning is suggested to facilitate SLA by not only making input comprehensible but also by providing opportunities for negative feedback (e.g. Gass 2003; Long 1996; Pica 1994). It is suggested that feedback obtained through interaction is particularly beneficial for L2 development because 'such feedback connects input, internal learner capacities, particularly selective attention, and output in productive ways' (Long 1996, pp. 451–2). Negotiation also provides opportunities for output that has been considered to facilitate L2 development (e.g. Gass 2003; Long 1996; Mackey and Gass 2006; Pica 1994). Swain (1993, 2005) has emphasized the importance of output by numerating a number of functions for it, including noticing interlanguage problems, testing hypotheses, promoting conscious reflection and internalizing target language knowledge, all of which have been claimed to be beneficial for L2 acquisition.

Within the interaction perspective, an important process whose role has been emphasized and is suggested to be promoted through interaction is noticing. Noticing refers to the input that is detected and mentally registered (e.g. Schmidt 1990, 1993). Extensive discussions and debate exist in the literature about the role and degree of attention and how it mediates learning (e.g. Leow 1998; Tomlin and Villa 1994; Wong 2001). However, it is generally agreed that learning cannot take place without some degree of awareness. Two kinds of noticing have been distinguished, noticing the gap and noticing the hole. Noticing the hole occurs when learners are pushed to produce output and then realize that they are not able to say what they want to say in the target language (Swain 1993; Swain and Lapkin 1995). Noticing the gap occurs when the learner compares his or her original output with the teacher's output and then realizes that his or her interlanguage differs from the target language (Swain 1998; Williams 2005).

It is believed that when learners interact and negotiate meaning, it is highly possible that they notice the linguistic forms in the input. They may become aware of their non-target-like utterance as a result of the various conversational adjustments that take place during interaction. In particular, depending on the kind of feedback they receive, they may notice either a hole or a gap in their interlanguage. For example, when the teacher or an interlocutor reformulates a learner's erroneous utterance into a correct form, the learner may notice a gap in their interlanguage, because the learner may compare his or her original output with the teacher's output and then realize that his or her interlanguage differs from the target language (Doughty and Varela 1998; Williams 2005). This process is also called 'cognitive comparison' and has been suggested to be facilitative of language acquisition (Doughty 2001; Long and Robinson 1998). In this respect, the comparison can signal to the learner that his or her original utterance was erroneous, thus providing the learner with implicit negative evidence. It can also trigger cognitive processes that may lead to the restructuring of the learner's interlanguage (Doughty 2001).

Elicitation strategies, such as clarification requests or repetition of the learner's utterance with a rising intonation, assist acquisition by promoting noticing the hole. As noted earlier, these strategies do not provide the learner with the correct form. Rather they push learners to correct his or her original output. When learners are pushed to self-correct, they become aware of the potential difficulties they have in expressing their meaning. In other words, such feedback makes learners aware of their interlanguage hole. Interactional strategies such as direct correction and metalinguistic feedback help acquisition in various ways. First, when learners receive correction that directly indicates or explains what their errors are, learners are provided with explicit knowledge. Explicit knowledge, as defined by Ellis (e.g. Ellis 1997; Ellis et al. 2009), refers to conscious and declarative knowledge of linguistic rules; it is different from implicit knowledge that is intuitive and is not available for conscious analysis and verbalization. Although the nature of the connection between explicit knowledge and language acquisition has been a matter of debate, it has been argued that explicit knowledge contributes, if not leads, to acquisition by promoting awareness of linguistic forms, which is argued to be needed, even if to a small degree (Schmidt 1993, 1995).

Research examining the beneficial effect of interactional feedback

Given the theoretical importance attributed to interactional feedback and the role of negotiation in L2 learning, a considerable body of research has been conducted in recent years to empirically examine the role of such feedback in L2 acquisition (e.g. Braidi 2002; Doughty and Varela 1998; Ellis et al. 2001; Lyster 1998, 2001; Lyster and Izquierdo 2009; Lyster and Ranta 1997; Mackey 1999; Mackey et al. 2010; Mackey et al. 2003; Mackey and Philp 1998; McDonough and Mackey 2008; Nassaji 2007a, 2009; Oliver 2000; Oliver and Mackey 2003; Panova and Lyster 2002; Philp 2003; Saito and Lyster 2011; Sheen 2007). This research has been conducted in both classroom and laboratory settings and has examined a variety of issues not only those related to whether such feedback occurs during L2 interaction but also whether or not there is any effect of such feedback on L2 acquisition. The findings have been reported in numerous individual studies and also summarized in a number of recent reviews and meta-analyses (e.g. Li 2010; Lyster and Saito 2010; Mackey and Goo 2007; Russell and Spada 2006). A detailed discussion of the findings is beyond the scope of this chapter. However, in general, and as confirmed in the several meta-analyses mentioned, interactional feedback has been found to facilitate L2 acquisition. For example, in their meta-analysis of 15 feedback studies, Russell and Spada (2006) found a mean effect size of 1.16 for feedback effectiveness, suggesting that feedback has a substantial effect on language learning. Mackey and Goo (2007), in their meta-analysis of 28 interaction studies, found a large mean effect size for feedback effects on both immediate and delayed post-tests. Finally, Lyster and Saito (2010), in their meta-analysis of 15 classroom-based studies, reported significant and durable effect for interactional feedback in general. The effect varied depending on the outcome measures used in the studies, but it was particularly large when the measures involved free constructed response formats (i.e. measures the involved non-controlled meaning-focused communication).

What types of feedback is most effective?

In addition to the general role of feedback, researchers have also been interested in the relative efficacy of different feedback types and also the conditions under which they might be more effective. Although there is a strong argument and research evidence for the beneficial effects of interactional feedback in general, there has not been an agreement on the extent to which learners benefit from different feedback types. For example, some researchers have argued that recasts are potentially effective because they provide students with both positive evidence (correct models of the language) as well as negative evidence (e.g. Long 2006, Doughty 2001). Others have argued that recasts are potentially ambiguous and thus not very effective (e.g. Lyster 2004, Panova and Lyster 2002). It has been argued that when learners receive recasts in communicative contexts, it is quite possible they would interpret the recast as a reaction to content rather than to form. Therefore, learners may not notice recasts as a kind of corrective feedback (Lyster 1998). Others have contended that that although recasts can be ambiguous, learners are still able to perceive a good amount of recasts and are able to learn from them (e.g. Long 2006). Long (2006) has also argued that elicitations cannot assist acquisition of new knowledge and can only assist the deployment of old knowledge.

Such debates have led to a growing number of studies in recent years, examining the differential effectiveness of different feedback types. However, although this research has confirmed the facilitative effect of feedback in general, its results with respect to what type of feedback is more effective have been mixed. For example, a number of classroom-based observational studies have examined the occurrence and effectiveness recasts and its comparison with other types of feedback such as elicitations (e.g. Ellis et al. 2001; Loewen and Philp 2006; Lyster and Ranta 1997; Nassaji 2007a; Panova and Lyster 2002; Sheen 2004). These studies have shown different and at times conflicting results. For instance, Lyster and Ranta (1997) examined the role of six different feedback types (e.g. recasts, clarification requests, repetition, direct correction and metalinguistic feedback) in French immersion classrooms. They found that while recasts were the most frequently occurring type of feedback, they were one of the least effective ones in terms of learner repair (18%). Panova and Lyster (2002) also found a very low rate of repair following recasts (13%) compared to other types of feedback such as repetition (83%) and elicitation (73%) in an ESL classroom. However, Ellis et al. (2001), examining the role of feedback in ESL classrooms in New Zealand, found both a high rate of recasts and also a very high rate of successful uptake following recasts (the rate of uptake was about four times higher than that found in Lyster and Ranta's study). Sheen (2004) also found that recasts were both highly frequent (accounting for 83% of all instances of feedback) and also highly successful in terms of learner repair (71%) in the EFL classes that she examined.

Of course, these studies have used uptake as a measure of feedback effectiveness, which has been simply defined as the learner's spontaneous responses to feedback in the course of interaction. Many researchers have argued that the presence of uptake does not provide any evidence for learning even though it may indicate that the learner has noticed the feedback (Ellis and Sheen 2006). However, even experimental and quasi-experimental studies, which have used various pre-test–post-test measures, have not found conclusive results.

For example, Ammar and Spada's (2006) and Lyster's (2004) experimental classroom-based studies both reported that elicitation strategies that pushed the learner to produce the target form was more effective than recasts in terms of accuracy of post-tests. However, McDonough (2007), investigating the effects of recasts and clarification requests (prompts) on learning simple past test, found a significant effect for both recast and clarification requests and no superiority of clarification requests over recasts. Ellis et al.'s (2006) classroom-based study investigated the effects of recasts and metalinguistic feedback on learning English past tense. They did not find a significant effects of recasts, but they did find such effects of metalinguistic feedback (see also Carroll and Swain 1993). However, Loewen and Nabei's (2007) classroom-based study found no difference between recasts and metalinguistic feedback on the acquisition of English question formation. McDonough and Mackey (2006) found a significant effect of recasts in a treatment group who received recasts on their non-target-like English question forms as compared to a group who did not receive recasts.

Thus, although in general, feedback studies demonstrate that interactional feedback can have a beneficial effect on L2 acquisition, research has not been able to provide a straightforward answer as to what kind of feedback is most effective. Therefore, the issue of whether there is any particular type of feedback that is better than others has remained unresolved.

Of course, if feedback is generally effective, the question arises as to why there is such a discrepancy among research results when it comes to the effectiveness of different feedback types. There can be many reasons for this, some of which are methodological relating to how studies have been conceptualized and designed, and some others have to do with how feedback is provided. Interactional feedback is also a complex phenomenon, and there are a number of factors that may mediate its effectiveness. It is beyond the scope of this chapter to discuss all these issues and factors. However, I will briefly examine some of them below.

Factors affecting the effectiveness of feedback

Feedback strategies such as recasts have been usually considered to be fairly implicit in nature. Thus, one fundamental issue related to such feedback concerns the extent to which learners can notice the targeted form in the recast. As noted earlier, it has been argued that when learners receive recasts in communicative contexts, it is quite possible they would interpret the recast as a reaction to content rather than to form. Therefore, learners may not notice the recast as a kind of corrective feedback. However, not all recasts are the same, and in fact, they can greatly vary in terms of their degree of implicitness depending on how they are provided. Recasts, for example, can be provided in the form of unstressed confirmation checks, in which case, they can be fairly implicit such as in Example 9. They can also be used in conjunction with various interactional features such as added stress, rising intonation or other types of verbal prompts or signals (such as in Examples 10 and 11), in which case they can be considered to be more explicit. It is quite possible that when recasts are combined with such features, its explicitness may be enhanced and therefore the feedback can be more effectively noticed as corrective feedback.

Example 9

Student: Her hair is bind above her head.
Teacher: Oh her hair is tied back.
Student: Yeah.

Example 10

Student:	And she catched her.
Teacher:	She CAUGHT [stressed] her?
Student:	Yeah caught her.

Example 11

Student:	She wear glasses and uh
Teacher:	Do you mean she is wearing glasses?
Student:	Yeah, she's wearing glasses.

(from Nassaji 2007b)

Recasts can also rephrase part of the erroneous utterance or it may rephrase the whole utterance. It may single out and correct the error only or it may correct the error and also expand on the learner's utterance. Such differences in the way recasts are provided can also change its explicitness and, therefore, the degree to which they can be noticed as feedback. Philp (2003) found that shorter recasts (five or fewer morphemes) were more accurately noticed and recalled than longer recasts (more than five morphemes). Egi (2007) found that L2 learners interpreted recasts more accurately as corrective feedback when they involved fewer changes than when they involved multiple changes.

Another factor that can affect the explicitness of feedback, and thus, its effectiveness, is whether the feedback is targeting incidentally a wide range of forms or whether it targets intensively and repeatedly a predetermined linguistic form (Ellis 2001; Ellis and Sheen 2006). When feedback is provided on a single target form repeatedly, it can be assumed that the feedback becomes more explicit, and thus, learners may become more effectively aware of the corrective force of the feedback. On the other hand, when the feedback targets a variety of linguistic forms, it can become less focused and thus less likely to draw learners' attention to form. As noted earlier, Lyster (2004) investigated the differential effects of recasts versus prompts when learners received instruction in conjunction with feedback in the classrooms and found that elicitation strategies were more effective than recasts. However, conducting a similar study, Lyster and Izquierdo (2009) provided learners with instruction in the classroom but with feedback in dyadic interaction outside the classroom. Using pre-test–post-test measures, they found that both recasts and elicitations were equally effective. The effectiveness of both recasts and elicitations in dyadic interaction outside the classroom could be due the fact that, in dyadic interaction, learners may not only receive the feedback more intensively but they also receive them in individualized one-on-one fashion, which can then increase the likelihood of learners' attention to form.

There are a number of other factors that can influence the effectiveness of feedback such as the nature of the linguistic target, learners' orientation to form, as well other individual learner differences such as age, language proficiency, anxiety, motivation, personality and attitude. For example, recasts have been shown to be better perceived as feedback in response to lexical errors than morphosyntactic errors (Mackey et al. 2000) and also more beneficial to learners who are linguistically more advanced than less advanced (Mackey and Philp 1998). Context of instruction, such as EFL versus ESL, has also been found to influence the effectiveness of feedback. Sheen (2004), for example, found that recasts were more effective when provided in EFL contexts than in ESL context. In their meta-analysis, Mackey and Goo (2007) found a large mean effect size for feedback in research conducted in foreign language contexts than in research in second language contexts. One reason, for such findings could be that, in foreign language contexts, the pedagogy may be more form-oriented than in second language contexts. When students receive feedback in a context where the focus is on form, they are more likely to notice the corrective intention of feedback than when they receive the feedback in a context where the language is used as a means of communication (Ellis and Sheen 2006).

Conclusion and implications for classroom pedagogy

In this chapter, I have discussed the interactional feedback as a particular way of drawing learners' attention to grammatical forms. As briefly reviewed, there is an extensive body of research that has recently examined the role of interactional feedback in SLA. Findings suggest that, in general, interactional feedback can facilitate L2 acquisition. However, the effectiveness of such feedback varies depending on the number of learner- and context-related variables. Although there is still a need for far more research in this area to better understand how feedback works and under what conditions it affects acquisition, a number of guidelines can be drawn from such research that can be helpful for classroom instruction.

First, it is now well-established that noticing is an important requirement for language learning and that the degree of effectiveness of feedback depends largely on the extent to which students are able to notice the feedback as correction. This suggests that, when providing feedback, teachers should make sure that the feedback is salient or explicit enough so that students can realize its corrective intent. This is particularly true of recasts, which due to their implicit and ambiguous nature may go unnoticed.

The explicitness of recasts can be increased in a number of ways. It can be increased, for example, by adding extra stress to the feedback or using additional intonational or verbal prompts in conjunction with recasts. As discussed earlier, the length of recasts can also affect its explicitness. Shorter recasts that target fewer errors are more noticeable than longer recasts that target multiple errors. Partial recasts that reformulate the erroneous part only might be more effective than full recasts that reformulate the whole utterance. Thus, when recasting learner errors, teachers should consider these different kinds of recasts and provide them in such a way that students can recognize their corrective intent.

Second, research seems to indicate that feedback strategies that do not supply the correct form are more effective than those that provide the correction. This then suggests that teachers should use or at least begin with feedback strategies that encourage learners to self-correct themselves. This provides a discovery-based approach to error correction, which can be considered as not only motivating but also helping learners to make inferences, and test their hypothesis, about the target language forms (see Angelovska and Hahn, this volume). Of course, it should be noted that elicitations can promote immediate self-repair only if learners have already declarative knowledge of the target form. If the learner does not have the declarative knowledge, pushing the learner further may not lead to self-repair. In such cases, additional more explicit clues that can help learners to discover the form might be needed (Nassaji 2011). As Long (2006) pointed out, pushing learners too much to provide self-repair when learners are not able to do so may also be embarrassing to learners as they may make their lack of knowledge or understanding public. Furthermore, elicitation strategies such as clarification requests can be ambiguous, and similar to recasts, they may simply be interpreted as a communicative move or a request to repeat the original utterance. This suggests that when using elicitation strategies, the teacher should make sure that they are explicit enough. In particular, in cases where learners have no knowledge of the target structure, it may be helpful to combine the feedback with input that provides the learner with more clear information about the correct form.

Research suggests that instruction and feedback are effective if they target language forms for which learners are developmentally ready (e.g. Mackey and

Philp 1998; Pienemann 1984, 1998; Spada and Lightbown 1999). This suggests that teachers should take into account learners' developmental level and that they should provide feedback in such a way that it matches learners' developmental readiness. Of course, as Ellis (2005) pointed out, it is not always easy for teachers to determine developmental readiness of individual learners. Furthermore, even though there are theoretical accounts of how L2 learners acquire certain syntactic structures, empirical research on the details of learners' developmental paths is limited. It has also not yet provided evidence of developmental sequences for many linguistic forms. This then suggests that teachers may not be able to reliably determine what form to target with what kind of feedback and, hence, should consider other possibilities. One possibility here is to be flexible and make use of different types of feedback so that students can be exposed to a variety of feedback forms (Ellis 2009). Another possibility is providing feedback with scaffolding. For example, following Aljaafreh and Lantolf (1994), Nassaji and Swain (2000) took a sociocultural perspective (Vygotsky 1978) towards corrective feedback and found that effective feedback was feedback in which the learner received gradual and step-by-step help in a scaffolding manner. One characteristic of scaffolded feedback is that it involves multiple feedback moves rather than single feedback moves. It also begins with indirect feedback and then moves progressively towards more direct feedback moves as needed.

Finally, to choose the appropriate type of feedback, teachers should also take into account other factors such as the nature of the error targeted, the context in which the feedback is provided and also various individual differences that exist among learners such as age, language proficiency, personality, anxiety, attitude and motivation. These factors can all play a role in facilitating feedback effectiveness. Thus, when providing feedback, it is important that teachers consider the role of these variables.

References

Aljaafreh, A. and Lantolf, J. (1994), 'Negative feedback as regulation and second language learning in the zone of proximal development'. *Modern Language Journal*, 78, 465–83.

Ammar, A. and Spada, N. (2006), 'One size fits all?: Recasts, prompts, and L2 learning'. *Studies in Second Language Acquisition*, 28, 543–74.

Braidi, S. M. (2002), 'Reexamining the role of recasts in native-speaker/nonnative-speaker interactions'. *Language Learning*, 52, 1–42.

Brown, R. and Hanlon, C. (1970), 'Derivational complexity and order of acquisition in child speech', in J. Hayes (ed.), *Cognition and the Development of Language*. New York: Wiley, pp. 11–53.

Carroll, S. and Swain, M. (1993), 'Explicit and implicit negative feedback: An empirical study of the learning of linguistic generalizations'. *Studies in Second Language Acquisition*, 15, 357–86.

DeKeyser, R. (1998), 'Beyond focus on form', in C. Doughty and J. Williams (eds), *Focus on Form in Classroom Language Acquisition*. Cambridge: Cambridge University Press, pp. 42–63.

Demetras, M., Post, K., and Snow, C. (1986), 'Feedback to first language learners: The role of repetitions and clarification questions'. *Child Language*, 13, 275–92.

Doughty, C. (2001), 'Cognitive underpinning of focus on form', in P. Robinson (ed.), *Cognition and Second Language Instruction*. Cambridge: Cambridge University Press, pp. 206–57.

— (2003), 'Instructed SLA: Constraints, compensation, and enhancement', in C. J. Doughty and M. H. Long (eds), *The Handbook of Second Language Acquisition*. Oxford: Blackwell, pp. 256–310.

Doughty, C. and Varela, E. (1998), 'Communicative focus on form', in C. Doughty and J. Williams (eds), *Focus on Form in Classroom Second Language Acquisition*. Cambridge: Cambridge University Press, pp. 114–38.

Doughty, C. and Williams, J. (eds) (1998), *Focus on Form in Classroom Second Language Acquisition*. Cambridge: Cambridge University Press.

Egi, T. (2007), 'Interpreting recasts as linguistic evidence: The role of linguistic target, length, and degree of change'. *Studies in Second Language Acquisition*, 29, 511–37.

Ellis, R. (1997), *SLA Research and Language Teaching*. Oxford: Oxford University Press.

— (2001), 'Introduction: Investigating form-focused instruction'. *Language Learning*, 51, 1–46.

— (2002), 'Does form-focused instruction affect the acquisition of implicit knowledge?'. *Studies in Second Language Acquisition*, 24, 223–36.

— (2005), 'Principles of instructed language learning'. *System*, 33, 209–24.

— (2008), *The Study of Second Language Acquisition* (2nd edn). Oxford: Oxford University Press.

— (2009), 'Corrective feedback and teacher development'. *L2 Journal*, 1, 3–18.

Ellis, R., Basturkmen, H., and Loewen, S. (2001), 'Learner uptake in communicative esl lessons'. *Language Learning*, 51, 281–318.

Ellis, R., Loewen, S., Erlam, R., Philp, J., Elder, C., and Reinders, H. (eds). (2009). *Implicit and Explicit Knowledge in Second Language Learning and Teaching*. Clevedon, UK: Multilingual Matters.

Ellis, R. and Sheen, Y. (2006), 'Reexamining the role of recasts in second language acquisition'. *Studies in Second Language Acquisition*, 28, 575–600.

Flynn, S. (1988), 'Nature of development in L2 acquisition and implications for theories of language acquisition in general', in S. Flynn and W. O'Neill (eds), *Linguistic Theory in Second Language Acquisition*. Dordrecht: Kluwer, pp. 277–94.

— (1996), 'A parameter-setting approach to second language acquisition', in W. Ritchie and T. Bhatia (eds), *Handbook of Second Language Acquisition*. San Diego: Academic Press, pp. 121–58.

Gass, S. (1997), *Input, Interaction, and the Second Language Learner*. Mahwah, NJ: Erlbaum.

— (2003), 'Input and interaction', in C. Doughty and M. Long (eds), *The Handbook of Second Language Acquisition*. Oxford: Blackwell, pp. 224–55.

Leow, R. (1998), 'Toward operationalizing the process of attention in SLA: Evidence for tomlin and villa's (1994) fine-grained analysis of attention'. *Applied Psycholinguistics*, 19, 133–59.

Li, S. (2010), 'The effectiveness of corrective feedback in SLA: A meta-analysis'. *Language Learning*, 60, 309–65.

Loewen, S. and Nabei, T. (2007), 'Measuring the effects of oral corrective feedback on L2 knowledge', in A. Mackey (ed.), *Conversational Interaction in Second Language Acquisition: A Series of Empirical Studies*. Oxford: Oxford University Press, pp. 361–78.

Loewen, S. and Philp, J. (2006), 'Recasts in adults English L2 classrooms: Characteristics, explicitness, and effectiveness'. *Modern Language Journal*, 90, 536–56.

Long, M. (1991), 'Focus on form: A design feature in language teaching methodology', in K. DeBot, R. Ginsberge and C. Kramsch (eds), *Foreign Language Research in Cross-Cultural Perspective*. Amsterdam: John Benjamins, pp. 39–52.

— (1996), 'The role of the linguistic environment in second language acquisition', in W. Ritchie and T. Bhatia (eds), *Handbook of Second Language Acquisition*. San Diego: Academic Press, pp. 413–68.

— (ed.). (2006), *Problems in SLA*. Mahwah, NJ: Lawrence Erlbaum.

Long, M. and Robinson, P. (1998), 'Focus on form: Theory, research and practice', in C. Doughty and J. Williams (eds), *Focus on Form in Classroom Language Acquisition*. Cambridge: Cambridge University Press, pp. 15–41.

Lyster, R. (1998), 'Recasts, repetition, and ambiguity in L2 classroom discourse'. *Studies in Second Language Acquisition*, 20, 51–81.

— (2001), 'Negotiation of form, recasts, and explicit correction in relation to error types and learner repair in immersion classrooms'. *Language Learning*, 51, 265–301.

— (2004), 'Differential effects of prompts and recasts in form-focused instruction'. *Studies in Second Language Acquisition*, 26, 399–432.

Lyster, R. and Izquierdo, J. (2009), 'Prompts versus recasts in dyadic interaction'. *Language Learning*, 59, 453–98.

Lyster, R. and Ranta, L. (1997), 'Corrective feedback and learner uptake: Negotiation of form in communicative classrooms'. *Studies in Second Language Acquisition*, 19, 37–66.

Lyster, R. and Saito, K. (2010), 'Oral feedback in classroom SLA'. *Studies in Second Language Acquisition*, 32, 265–302.

Mackey, A. (1999), 'Input, interaction and second language development: An empirical study of question formation in ESL'. *Studies in Second Language Acquisition*, 21, 557–87.

Mackey, A. and Gass, S. (eds) (2006). 'Pushing the methodological boundaries in interaction research (special issue)'. *Studies in Second Language Acquisition*, 28(2), 169–78.

Mackey, A. and Goo, J. (2007), 'Interaction research in SLA: A meta-analysis and research synthesis', in A. Mackey (ed.), *Conversational Interaction in Second Language Acquisition: A Collection of Empirical Studies*. Oxford: Oxford University Press, pp. 407–52.

Mackey, A. and Philp, J. (1998), 'Conversational interaction and second language development: Recasts, responses, and red herrings?' *Modern Language Journal*, 82, 338–56.

Mackey, A., Gass, S., and McDonough, K. (2000), 'How do learners perceive interactional feedback?' *Studies in Second Language Acquisition*, 22, 471–97.

Mackey, A., Oliver, R., and Leeman, J. (2003), 'Interactional input and the incorporation of feedback: an exploration of NS-NNS and NNS-NNS adult and child dyads'. *Language Learning*, 53, 35–66.

Mackey, A., Adams, R., Stafford, C., and Winke, P. (2010), 'Exploring the relationship between modified output and working memory capacity'. *Language Learning*, 60, 501–33.

McDonough, K. (2005), 'Identifying the impact of negative feedback and learners' responses on esl question development'. *Studies in Second Language Acquisition*, 27, 79–103.

— (2006), 'Interaction and syntactic priming: EnglishL2 speakers' production of dative constructions'. *Studies in Second Language Acquisition*, 28, 179–207.

— (2007), 'Interactional feedback and the emergence of simple past activity verbs in L2 English', in A. Mackey (ed.), *Conversational Interaction in Second Language Acquisition*. Oxford: Oxford University Press, pp. 323–38.

McDonough, K. and Mackey, A. (2008), 'Syntactic priming and ESL question development'. *Studies in Second Language Acquisition*, 30, 31–47.

Nassaji, H. (2007a), 'Elicitation and reformulation and their relationship with learner repair in dyadic interaction'. *Language Learning*, 57, 511–48.

— (2007b), 'Focus on form through recasts in dyadic student-teacher intercton: A case for recast enhancement', in C. Gascoigne (ed.), *Assessing the Impact of Input Enhancement in Second Language Education*. Stillwater, OK: New Forums Press, pp. 53–69.

— (2009), 'Effects of recasts and elicitations in dyadic interaction and the role of feedback explicitness'. *Language Learning*, 59, 411–52.

— (2011), 'Correcting students' written grammatical errors: The effects of negotiated versus nonnegotiated feedback'. *Studies in Second Language*, 1, 315–34.

Nassaji, H. and Fotos, S. (2010), *Teaching Grammar in Second Language Classrooms: Integrating Form-Focused Instruction in Communicative Context*. London: Routledge.

Nassaji, H. and Swain, M. (2000), 'Vygotskian perspective on corrective feedback in L2: The effect of random versus negotiated help on the learning of English articles'. *Language Awareness*, 9, 34–51.

Oliver, R. (2000), 'Age differences in negotiation and feedback in classroom and pairwork'. *Language Learning*, 50, 119–51.

Oliver, R. and Mackey, A. (2003), 'Interactional context and feedback in child ESL classrooms'. *Modern Language Journal*, 87, 519–33.

Panova, I. and Lyster, R. (2002), 'Patterns of corrective feedback and uptake in an adult ESL classroom'. *TESOL Quarterly*, 36, 573–95.

Philp, J. (2003), 'Constraints on "noticing the gap": Nonnative speakers' noticing of recasts in NS-NNS interaction'. *Studies in Second Language Acquisition*, 25, 99–126.

Pica, T. (1994), 'Research on negotiation: What does it reveal about second-language learning conditions, processes, and outcomes?' *Language Learning*, 44, 493–527.

— (1996), 'Do second language learners need negotiation?'. *International Review of Applied Linguistics in Language Teaching*, 34, 1–21.

— (2002), 'Subject-matter content: How does it assist the interactional and linguistic needs of classroom language learners?' *Modern Language Journal*, 86, 1–19.

Pienemann, M. (1984), 'Psychological constraints on the teachability of languages'. *Studies in Second Language Acquisition*, 6, 186–214.

— (1998), *Language Processing and Second Language Development: Processability Theory*. Amsterdam: John Benjamins Publishing Company.

Russell, J. and Spada, N. (2006), 'The effectiveness of corrective feedback for second language acquisition: A meta-analysis of the research', in J. Norris and L. Ortega (eds), *Synthesizing Research on Language Learning and Teaching*. Amsterdam: Benjamins, pp. 131–64.

Saito, K. and Lyster, R. (2011), 'Effects of form focused instruction and corrective feedback on L2 pronunciation development of /r/ by Japanese learners of English'. *Language Learning*, 62, 1–39.

Schmidt, R. (1990), 'The role of consciousness in second language learning'. *Applied Linguistics*, 11, 129–58.

— (1993), 'Awareness and second language acquisition'. *Annual Review of Applied Linguistics*, 13, 206–26.

Schwartz, B. (1993), 'On explicit and negative data effecting and affecting competence and linguistic behavior'. *Studies in Second Language Acquisition*, 15, 147–63.

Sheen, Y. (2004), 'Corrective feedback and learner uptake in communicative classrooms across instructional settings'. *Language Teaching Research*, 8, 263–300.

— (2007), 'The effects of corrective feedback, language aptitude, and learner attitude on the acquisition of English articles', in A. Mackey (ed.), *Conversational Interaction in Second Language Acquisition: A Collection of Empirical Studies*. Oxford: Oxford University Press, pp. 301–22.

Spada, N. (1997), 'Form-focused instruction and second language acquisition: A review of classroom and laboratory research'. *Language Teaching*, 29, 1–15.

Spada, N. and Lightbown, P. (1999), 'Instruction, first language influence, and developmental readiness in second language acquisition'. *Modern Language Journal*, 83, 1–22.

Swain, M. (1993), 'The output hypothesis: Just speaking and writing aren't enough'. *Canadian Modern Language Review*, 50, 158–64.

— (1998), 'Focus on form through conscious reflection', in C. Doughty and J. Williams (eds), *Focus on Form in Classroom Second Language Acquisition*. Cambridge: Cambridge University Press, pp. 64–81.

— (2005), 'The output hypothesis: Theory and research', in E. Hinkel (ed.), *Handbook on Research in Second Language Teaching and Learning*. Mahwah, NJ: Lawrence Erlbaum Associates, pp. 471–83.

Swain, M. and Lapkin, S. (1995), 'Problems in output and the cognitive-processes they generate: A step towards second language-learning'. *Applied Linguistics*, 16, 371–91.

Tomlin, R. and Villa, V. (1994), 'Attention in cognitive science and second language acquisition'. *Studies in Second Language Acquisition*, 16, 183–202.

Vygotsky, L. S. (1978), *Mind in Society: The Development of Higher Psychological Processes*. Cambridge, MA: Harvard University Press.

White, L. (1991), 'Adverb placement in second language acquistion: Some effects of positive and negative evidence in the classroom'. *Second Language Research*, 7, 133–61.

Williams, J. (2005), 'Form-focused instruction', in E. Hinkel (ed.), *Handbook on Research in Second Language Teaching and Learning*. Mahwah, NJ: Lawrence Erlbaum Associates, pp. 673–91.

Wong, W. (2001), 'Modality and attention to meaning and form in the input'. *Studies in Second Language Acquisition*, 23, 345–68.

Part Two

Empirical Research

6

Instructed SLA as Parameter Setting: Evidence from Earliest-stage Learners of Japanese as L2

Megan Smith and Bill VanPatten
Michigan State University, United States

As VanPatten and Rothman (this volume) argue, a good deal of instructed SLA is concerned with rule learning. In this chapter, we take a generative approach to the nature of instructed SLA and, in agreement with VanPatten and Rothman, take the position that acquisition of a mental representation for language does not involve rule learning in the classic sense. Instead, we argue that classroom learners, just like child L1 learners and L2 learners who acquire language without formal instruction, process exemplars in the input and that these exemplars are used to fix parametric variations of the language. The aspects of language that look like rules evolve from the interaction of external data (i.e. input) and learner-internal language-making mechanisms. We also argue that just like all other cases of language acquisition, those undergoing instructed SLA project beyond the data they are exposed to and create grammars that are underdetermined by the data available to them in the input.

Our chapter is organized as follows. We first briefly outline the nature of head directionality, contrasting Japanese and English. Second, we discuss the nature of poverty of the stimulus (POS) and what this means in terms of grammar creation in the minds of learners. Third, we describe a study in which we taught English L1 speakers Japanese as an L2 in a controlled laboratory setting, testing them after only 30 minutes of exposure. We conclude with a discussion of how instructed L2 learners are no different from other learners and do indeed make use of the language-making mechanism used by both L1 learners and non-classroom learners.

Head directionality in Japanese and English

Head directionality (e.g. Baker 2001; Dryer 1992) describes major cross-linguistic differences in the relative ordering of the subject, object and verb in different languages and within the basic organizational unit of the sentence, namely, the phrase. Words are not strung together like beads on a string to create sentences, but instead are organized into units with an internal structure. These units are called phrases, and phrases are arranged hierarchically into sentences. Consequently, phrase structure is a fundamental building block of language. Phrases are structured in a certain way: a grammatical category, such as a noun, a verb or a preposition, will 'choose' another grammatical category, and these two will combine to form a phrase. Certain grammatical categories can only select for other grammatical categories; prepositions, for example, select for nouns (in English, these nouns are usually selected with an article) and not verbs:

1. a. At the table, on the phone, in the pool . . .
   b. *At jump, *on talk, *in swim . . .[1]

Once a preposition has selected for a noun, these two categories combine to form prepositional phrases (PPs). Similarly, verbs combine with nouns to form VPs. Exactly what elements select for which other elements is beyond the scope of our discussion here; the important idea here is that any grammatical category can head a phrase, and depending on the properties of that particular category, may also select for another phrase. The category that does the selecting is called the head of the phrase. The phrase for which the head selects is called the complement. So, prepositions are the heads of PPs, and the noun phrases they select for are the complements of those PPs. All phrases have heads and complements, and all sentences are made up of phrases (Carnie 2002).

   Phrase structure is a universal of language, but the relative ordering of heads and complements varies. Consider the Japanese phrases in (2):

2. a. Teiburu-ni   (prepositional phrase
      table-on   [PP])
      'on the table'
   b. Ringo-o taberu   (verb phrase [VP])
      apple-acc[2] eat
      'eat the apple'

    c. Hanako-ga   ringo-o   taberu.   (sentence or

       Hanako-nom apple-acc eat   tense phrase

       'Hanako eats an apple.'   [TP])

    d. John-wa Hanako-ga   ringo-o   taberu toh   itta.   (embedded clause or

       John-top Hanako-nom apple-acc eat   that said   complementizer

       'John said that Hanako eats an apple.'   phrase [CP])

It should be obvious, particularly from the English glosses in the second line, that the way in which Japanese orders heads and complements is different from that of English. In (2a), for example, the particle *ni*, which is the Japanese equivalent of *at*, comes *after* the noun it selects for, and not before, as it would in English. VPs (2b) show the same pattern – the verb follows the object.[3] In addition, and particularly important for our purposes, the subject, object and verb are ordered differently (subject, object and then verb) than they would be in English (subject, verb, and then object). (2d) is the most complicated of these sentences because it involves embedding another sentence within the main sentence. In English, the heads of clauses precede the complement, while in Japanese the heads of clauses follow the complement (i.e. English = that/which + clause; Japanese = clause + that/which). In the present case, the important features of (2d) are the location of the matrix verb, *itta* 'said', the location of the complementizer, *toh*[4] 'that' and the position of the embedded sentence. First, the main clause verb *itta* comes at the end of the sentence, and the phrase for which it selects, CP, precedes it. This is evident from the position of the complementizer, *toh*, between the matrix verb and the embedded sentence. Second, the complementizer, *toh*, which selects for the embedded clause, comes *after* the clause for which it selects – just like the order of the particle *ni* and noun we noted in (2a). In sum, all of the phrases in (2) demonstrate complement-head word order, and Japanese syntax differs from English syntax in that in English, heads precede their complements, but in Japanese, heads follow their complements.

    Head directionality captures this difference: although the basic building blocks of sentences in all languages are phrases with heads and complements, the relative order of heads and complements varies from language to language. Head-initial languages are languages like English, in which heads precede their complements, and head-final languages are languages like Japanese, in which heads follow their complements (Baker 2001). The relative order of the verb and the object (VO or OV) is thought to determine the relative order of heads and complements throughout the grammar. In addition to being a useful way of describing some of the differences between Japanese and English, head directionality also makes one important prediction for language acquisition. This prediction is that the language learning mechanism that L1 and L2 learners bring to the table 'knows' that the language being learnt will have phrases, and that these phrases will either be head-initial or head-final. Then, once the language learning mechanism has fixed the relative order of the verb and the object in the VP, it will project this order to all phrases throughout the grammar – without necessarily having been exposed to exemplars of these phrases in the input (e.g. Boeckx 2011; Boeckx 2010; Chomsky 1981). Following VanPatten and Rothman (this volume), then, language learners don't learn a rule, such as 'place the verb before/after the object', for sentence structure; the language acquisition device processes the input for verbs and objects and then builds an implicit mental representation that reflects this structure (but see Newmeyer 2005, 2004, for an alternative view). If this is the case, learners do not have to re-learn a word order rule for each novel structure, such as embedded clauses and polar (i.e. *yes/no*) questions, but instead the internal mechanisms responsible for language extend the structure they already have.

Poverty of the stimulus in L2 situations

Poverty of the stimulus (POS) situations are situations in which people come to know more about something than they could have learnt based on the experiences or explanations available to them. With reference to language, a POS situation occurs when people have implicit knowledge about language that they can't possibly have gotten from the data around them (e.g. Boeckx 2010; White 2003). We offer two examples, one involving a universal principle and one involving a parametric setting.

Languages fall into two broad groups: null-subject and non-null-subject languages. Null-subject languages, such as Spanish, allow overt subjects or subject pronouns to be absent in simple declarative sentences (i.e. imperative sentences are excluded from this categorization) whereas non-null-subject languages, like English, do not (see Rizzi 1982; Roberts and Holmberg 2010 for a discussion of null subjects). This is exemplified in (3) and (4) below.

3. *Did call your Mom?
4. ¿Llamaste a tu mamá?
3. is infelicitous because English requires subject pronouns except in very
   reduced situations (e.g. after conjunctions). However, (4) is perfectly fine

in Spanish and is even preferred over a sentence with an overt subject pronoun, assuming that there is no topic change. Null-subject languages are governed by a universal constraint that says that overt subject pronouns cannot take a quantified noun (or NP) as an antecedent. In this case, a quantified antecedent includes such things as negated nouns (e.g. 'nobody', 'not a single person') and those with *wh*-words (e.g. 'which person', 'who'). In (5) below, the overt pronoun *él* 'he' is barred from taking the Q word *quién* 'who' as its antecedent. The overt pronoun has to refer to someone else. However, in (6), the null-subject *pro* is free to take any antecedent that agrees with the verb in person and number, including the noun that precedes it in the main clause, *mi amigo* 'my friend'.

5. ¿Quién$_i$ dice que él$_{*i/j}$ entiende la sintaxis más que yo?
   'Who says he understands syntax more than I do?'
6. Mi amigo$_i$ dice que *pro*$_{i/j}$ entiende la sintaxis más que yo.
   'My friend says that (he) understands syntax more than I do'

This constraint is referred to as the overt pronoun constraint (OPC) and is universal (Montalbetti 1984). No child learning null-subject languages like Spanish or Turkish is taught the OPC. Nor are second language learners of null-subject languages taught the OPC. What is more, the OPC does not appear in the input. That is, there is nothing in the data 'out there' to tell a child or a language learner that overt subject pronouns cannot take a quantified antecedent. This is a clear POS situation, then. People come to know more about languages like Spanish and Turkish than what they are exposed to. Because the OPC is a universal, it is simply there once the learner's grammar (L1 or L2) determines that the language being learnt is a null-subject language (Kanno 1997; Perez-Leroux and Glass 1999).

A second example comes from parametric variation. Once learners' grammars have determined that a language is null subject or non-null subject, certain other aspects of language fall out of one option or the other. For example, in languages like Spanish and Italian, null subjects are required in non-referential situations. In languages like English and French, dummy subjects (like 'it' or 'there') are required in non-referential situations. Non-referential situations are those in which the subject of the sentence does not refer to anything in the real word. Examples include time expressions, existential statements and weather.

7. Es la una/*Ello es la una.
   *Is one o'clock/It's one o'clock.

8. Hay café/*Allí hay café (if *allí* = subject).
   *Is coffee./There's coffee.
9. Está lloviendo/*Ello está lloviendo.
   *Is raining/It's raining.

So, the learner of Spanish gets the knowledge that Spanish requires null subjects in referential sentences 'for free' once the null-subject nature of a language is determined. It is a by-product of the null-subject parameter. As in the case of the OPC, this is a clear POS situation. The child or L2 learner does not get this knowledge from the input or from learning it explicitly.

POS situations clearly show that there are aspects of language that are not and cannot be due to rule learning. The OPC and the grammaticality of null subjects in non-referential sentences are due to and derived from a universal property of human language. Both of these aspects of the grammar of null-subject languages are subtle enough that speakers of these languages are unaware of them, and they are rarely, if ever, discussed in language courses. Yet, both L1 and L2 speakers acquire these features of the grammar. At this juncture, it's reasonable to ask how these features are acquired. We suggest that learners acquire these features of grammar – universals and parameters – through the interaction of input and the mind's language-making mechanisms. In other words, the mind does not learn or store the structural properties of language in terms of long lists of rules, but in terms of structural properties based on language universals. Learners figure out what the structural properties of the target language are through exposure to linguistic input and then project from the input to the structure. If this is the case, we would expect to see evidence – in the form of POS situations – of structure building in language learners who have received no overt instruction on linguistic rules.

While POS situations are often examined from the perspective of an endpoint (i.e. adult native speaker knowledge or very advanced/near-native speakers of an L2), POS situations can arise at any point in the learning process (e.g. Schwartz 1998). That is, L2 learners need not be at some endpoint in their acquisition to demonstrate a POS situation. In the present study, we will explore to what extent a POS situation arises very early in the L2 grammars of instructed English L1/Japanese L2 learners, after exposure to just 100 simple SOV input sentences in Japanese.[5] Our specific question is this:

> Do very early-stage learners of Japanese as an L2, with no knowledge of or experience with a head-final language, assume that novel structures display the same headedness as simple SOV sentences? That is, do learners show evidence of knowledge about those things that they have not yet been exposed to or taught?

The present study

Participants

Participants were 60 people affiliated in some way with Texas Tech University in the spring of 2012. Fifty-three of these participants were undergraduates, four were graduate students, and three were employed by the university. Participants were recruited through an announcement posted on TechAnnounce, the university's listserv. All participants were monolingually raised, native speakers of English who had had no exposure to Japanese and who, if they had had experience studying a foreign language, had only studied French or Spanish. Crucially, prior to the study, they had had no knowledge of or exposure to a head-final language.

Materials

Treatment

The researchers created all the materials used in this study. This study contained two parts: a treatment portion and a post-treatment assessment. Because these participants had had no knowledge of Japanese, the treatment portion was constructed to teach participants basic vocabulary and to expose them to basic word order. Participants heard a pre-recorded sentence while also looking at a picture that illustrated the sentence. To provide additional input, the written version of the sentence was included below the picture. All sentences were presented using the Hepburn Romanization system (see below). Sentences were presented in groups of five, followed by a set of three 'quiz' questions about the sentences participants had just heard. Five names were used in the materials and recycled throughout the sentences. Participants were exposed to 100 sentences in total.

The first ten sets of five sentences, as well as the quiz sentences that followed them, were all declarative sentences consisting of a proper name for the subject, an inanimate noun for an object and a non-finite verb. These sentences demonstrated basic SOV word order and served to introduce vocabulary to participants. Participants saw the instructions given in (10) and then the first set of five sentences, which are given in (11) (see Appendix for sample drawings used):

10. You will hear a series of sentences about Taro, accompanied by a picture. Listen to each sentence carefully. You will hear each sentence twice.

11. a. Taro-ga   banana-o   taberu.
       Taro-NOM   banana-ACC   eat[6]
       'Taro eats a banana.'
    b. Taro-ga   ringo-o   taberu.
       Taro-NOM   apple-ACC   eat
       'Taro eats an apple.'
    c. Taro-ga   orenji-o   taberu.
       Taro-NOM   orange-ACC   eat
       'Taro eats an orange.'
    d. Taro-ga   meron-o   taberu.
       Taro-NOM   melon-ACC   eat
       'Taro eats melon.'
    e. Taro-ga   keiki-o   taberu.
       Taro-NOM   cake-ACC   eat
       'Taro eats cake.'

After participants completed this set of five sentences, they saw the set of instructions given in (12) and completed a quiz in which they had to match the sentence they heard with the picture on the screen. Participants heard three sentences, and for each sentence they heard, they had to choose between two pictures. The quiz sentences that followed the sentences in (11) are given in (13):

12. Now listen to the sentence and select the picture that goes with that sentence.

13. a. Taro-ga banana-o taberu.
    b. Taro-ga ringo-o taberu.
    c. Taro-ga orenji-o taberu.

This procedure was repeated throughout the treatment portion, and participants were quizzed after each set of five sentences. The first 5 sets of sentences, or the first 25 sentences, used the same 5 names and the same verb, but varied the object. The next 5 sets of five sentences, or sentences 26–50, varied the verb and kept the object constant:

14. a. Mary-ga   shinbun-o   nageru.
       Mary-NOM   newspaper-ACC   throw.
       'Mary throws the newspaper.'
    b. Mary-ga   shinbun-o   miru.
       Mary-NOM   newspaper-ACC   see
       'Mary sees the newspaper.'

    c. Mary-ga   shinbun-o   sawaru.
       Mary-NOM   newspaper-ACC   touch
       'Mary touches the newspaper.'
    d. Mary-ga   shinbun-o   kaku.
       Mary-NOM   newspaper-ACC   write
       'Mary writes a newspaper.'
    e. Mary-ga   shinbun-o   yomu.
       Mary-NOM   newspaper-ACC   read
       'Mary reads the newspaper.'

The last 50 sentences added postpositional phrases to the basic sentence. For all of these sentences, the location varied, but the subject, verb and object were kept the same:

15. a. Taro-ga   toshokan-de   hon-o   sagasu.
      Taro-NOM   library-LOC   book-ACC   look for
      'Taro looks for books in the library.'
   b. Taro-ga   kyoushitsu-de   hon-o   sagasu.
      Taro-NOM   classroom-LOC   book-ACC   look for
      'Taro looks for books in the classroom.'
   c. Taro-ga   kichin-de   hon-o   sagasu
      Taro-NOM   kitchen-LOC   book-ACC   look for
      'Taro looks for books in the kitchen.'
   d. Taro-ga   heya-de   hon-o   sagasu.
      Taro-NOM   bedroom-LOC   book-ACC   look for
      'Taro looks for books in (his) bedroom.'
   e. Taro-ga   kouen-de   hon-o   sagasu.
      Taro-NOM   park-LOC   book-ACC   look for
      'Taro looks for (his) book in the park.'

Immediately after completing the treatment portion of this study, participants completed the assessment portion. At no time did participants receive instruction on word order in Japanese. Instead, as per the instructions in (12) above, they were told to listen carefully. The quiz questions asked about the content of the sentences and not word order as per (13) above.

Assessment

The materials used in the assessment portion contained three sentence types: declarative sentences to which the learners had been exposed, and two novel structures not contained in the treatment materials – embedded clauses and polar questions with *ka*. The purpose of adding these novel structures was to see if participants projected head-directionality beyond the input of the treatment. In polar questions, *ka* appears in head final position in the CP, and in embedded clauses the head, *toh*, appears in final position in the CP, as illustrated in (17) and (18) below. Participants were randomly split into two groups. All participants read simple SOV sentences of the same kind as they saw in the treatment portion. Half of the participants also read polar questions with *ka*, and the other half read embedded clauses headed by *toh*. There were 12 sentences of each type; six were grammatical and six were ungrammatical, either by moving the question particle to the front of the sentence (for sentences with *ka*) or by moving the complementizer *toh* to the front of the embedded clause (for sentences with *toh*). Both of these violate head-final nature of Japanese. Participants read each sentence and then answered a question, in English, about each sentence. The Japanese sentences were presented first and then participants moved to the next screen for the comprehension question. Examples (16)–(18) demonstrate items for SOV sentences, polar questions and embedded clauses, respectively.

16. a. Reiko-ga orenji-o miru.
    b. *Reiko ga miru orenji-o
      'Reiko sees an orange.'

    Q: This sentence is about Reiko
      A. Seeing an orange   B. Seeing the scissors

17. a. Taro-ga banana-o taberu ka?
    b. *Ka Taro-ga banana-o taberu?
      'Is Taro eating a banana?'

    Q: This question is about Taro
      A. Eating a banana   B. Eating an apple

18. a. John-wa Hanako-ga ringo-o taberu toh[7] itta.
    b. *John-wa toh Hanako-ga ringo-o taberu itta
      'John said that Hanako eats an apple.'

    Q: This sentence is about
      A. Hanako eating an apple   B. John eating an apple

In total, participants read 24 sentences, 12 simple SOV sentences and then 12 sentences that contained either polar questions or 12 sentences that contained embedded clauses. Sentences were blocked and counterbalanced so that participants did not read the ungrammatical versions of the grammatical sentences (e.g. one-half of participants read grammatical versions of sentences 1–3 and ungrammatical versions of 4–6 for SOV sentences, while the other half read ungrammatical versions of 1–3 and grammatical versions of 4–6). Because the 12 novel sentences did not form part of the treatment, they served as distractors for the SOV sentences and vice versa.

It is important to note that participants were given no information beyond what was presented in the treatment portion for the assessment portion of the study. Polar questions were marked with a question mark to serve as a clue that those sentences were questions. No other information was given about questions. For embedded clauses, prior to assessment, participants read on screen that they would encounter one new verb while reading: *itta*, 'said'. No information about the structure of embedded clauses was given.

Procedure

All instructions and materials were delivered via computer using SuperLab 4.0. All participants were tested individually in the Psycholinguistics Lab at Texas Tech University. After completing a consent form and background questionnaire, participants began the treatment, working at their own pace. Once they'd completed the treatment, they moved to the assessment task. Participants took on average 30 minutes to complete the treatment.

For the assessment task, participants pressed a button to read each test sentence and then pressed a button that caused the test sentence to disappear and the comprehension question to appear. After selecting either A or B to indicate comprehension (see the assessment section of Materials), participants were prompted to press a button to move to the next test sentence. Participants took on average 10 minutes to complete the assessment.

Scoring

Scoring consisted of reading times for the grammatical and ungrammatical sentences, a method of testing for sensitivity to grammatical violations used in other research (e.g. VanPatten et al. 2012). In this kind of assessment, ungrammaticality generally results in longer reading times compared to grammatical sentences while the participant's attention is focused on meaning (via expected content questions; see the section above on assessment). First, we needed to establish if learners had internalized something about basic word order; that is, if they had internalized the correct headedness for objects and verbs. To this end, we examined individual reading times on the grammatical and ungrammatical versions of SOV sentences. Participants who did not demonstrate sensitivity to these grammatical violations by showing longer reading times on ungrammatical sentences were deemed not to have captured basic word order and were then eliminated from the study. On this basis, five participants were eliminated from the *ka* group and 14 participants were eliminated from the *toh* group. Next, the comprehension questions from the assessment portion were scored. Participants had to demonstrate at least 65% accuracy (or at least 16 out of 24) on the comprehension questions in the assessment portion to be included in the final results. On this basis, two more participants were eliminated from the *toh* group. The final participant pool was the following: *ka* group, n = 20; *toh* group, n = 19.

For all remaining participants, mean reading times for the following structures were tabulated: grammatical SOV word order, ungrammatical SVO word order, grammatical sentence-*ka* word order, ungrammatical *ka*-sentence word order, grammatical embedded clause-*toh* word order and ungrammatical *toh*-embedded clause word order.

Results

Ka group

Mean reading times and standard deviations for the *ka* group are given in Table 6.1. This group read sentences containing grammatical SOV and ungrammatical SVO word orders as well as grammatical and ungrammatical polar questions containing the particle *ka*. For both structures, mean reading times on ungrammatical sentences are longer than those on grammatical sentences. To see whether these perceived differences were significant, paired samples *t*-tests were performed on the grammatical and ungrammatical structures. For the SOV sentences, the *t*-tests revealed a significant difference between grammatical and ungrammatical structures, $t(19) = -4.547, p < .001$. For the sentences containing *ka*, the *t*-test also revealed a significant difference in reading times between grammatical and ungrammatical sentences, $t(19) = -3.524, p = .002$. Just in case the means were not normally distributed, a non-parametric Wilcoxon test was also performed. The results are the same as for the *t*-tests, $Z = -3.771, p < .001$, for SOV sentences, and $Z = -3.621, p < .001$, for sentences containing *ka*. The participants in the *ka* group, then, demonstrated significantly longer reading times on both the ungrammatical SVO and *ka* sentence word orders.

Table 6.1 Means and standard deviations in milliseconds for reading times on SOV and *Ka* sentences

	Mean	SD
SOV grammatical	3048	990
SOV ungrammatical	3907	1412
Ka grammatical	3739	1394
Ka ungrammatical	5032	2023

Table 6.2 Means and standard deviations in milliseconds for reading times on SOV and *To* sentences

	Mean	SD
SOV grammatical	4719	1467
SOV ungrammatical	5723	2009
To grammatical	8697	2880
To ungrammatical	8601	2455

Toh group

Mean reading times and standard deviations for the *toh* group are given in Table 6.2. This group read the same SOV/SVO sentences as the other group, plus sentences containing embedded clauses, marked with the particle *toh*. For the SOV sentences, the *t*-tests revealed a significant difference between grammatical and ungrammatical sentences, $t(19) = -3.864, p = .001$. For the sentences containing embedded clauses, the *t*-tests failed to show a significant difference in reading times, $t(19) = .221, p = .827$. Again, in the event that the means were not normally distributed, a non-parametric Wilcoxon test was also performed. The results are the same as for the *t*-tests, $Z = -3.173, p = .002$, for SOV sentences, and $Z = -0.037, p = .970$, for sentences containing *toh*. The participants in this group as a whole did not demonstrate significantly longer results on ungrammatical embedded clauses than on grammatical embedded clauses.

Individual results

Because the previous results relate to group means, the data for individual patterns of behaviour were also examined. Table 6.3 presents individual reading times for all 59 participants for grammatical and ungrammatical sentence structures. As can be seen, 100% of the population demonstrated knowledge

Table 6.3 Individual reading times in milliseconds for all participants

Group 1: SOV and *Ka* Sentences

Participant #	SOV grammatical	SOV ungrammatical	*Ka* grammatical	*Ka* ungrammatical
1	1494.83	2700.83	1706.5	3013
2	3220.33	4552.33	4277	5016.83
3	4153.5	6096.5	5358.17	6590.33
4	2324.67	3084.17	2951	4593.83
5	3276.5	3906.33	4946	6394.5
6	2048.67	2383.33	2223.5	2610.67
7	1070.33	1362.67	1129.17	2521
8	3583.33	3409.3	4360	5296.5
9	3859.33	4988.17	3575.17	11131.33
10	4702	5063.33	5108.83	5580
11	2999.83	4477.5	3220.17	4324
12	3437	3195.83	3699.5	6308.83
13	4290.33	5883.67	5815.5	6828.67
14	3469.17	6920.17	5080.33	5744
15	2746	3215.83	3843.67	5353.33
16	1389	1864.67	1589	1862.83
17	2846.5	3384.5	3561	5116.17
18	2815.83	3877.83	2296.17	3323
19	3210.67	3531	5094	4645.33
20	4018.83	4236.83	4950.3	4404.5

Group 2: SOV and *To* Sentences

Participant #	SOV grammatical	SOV ungrammatical	*To* grammatical	*To* ungrammatical
1	3735.83	4521.83	6137.67	7152.33
2	2121.17	2262.17	4836.5	5588.67
3	6550.33	7603.67	9711	10018.17
4	5797.33	8992.83	11581.67	13769.17
5	4813.83	6634.5	8168.17	8675.83

(Continued)

Table 6.3 (*Continued*)

Participant #	SOV grammatical	SOV ungrammatical	*To* grammatical	*To* ungrammatical
6	3938.17	5489.67	8153.83	9161
7	2676	3406.83	3741	6567.67
8	3373.83	3930.83	9234.83	10167.67
9	6045	10046.5	10516.83	12879.17
10	5671.5	7724	12388	8954.33
11	4507	4708.83	8856.5	7999.33
12	4220.5	5422.5	7588	5762
13	8004.83	8651.67	16861.83	12463.83
14	6178.33	7065.33	10364.17	9036.5
15	5475.5	5928.83	9869.17	9795.67
16	3472.83	5080	9027	8073
17	5551.67	6748.33	10113.67	9255.83
18	4496.5	4728.67	8241	5250.33
19	3425.17	5034.5	9410.17	6409.5

of the head-directionality of SOV sentences with longer mean reading times on SVO sentences than on SOV sentences. In the *ka* group, two of the participants (numbers 19 and 20) did not demonstrate longer reading times on ungrammatical sentences. In the *toh* group, ten participants demonstrated longer reading times on ungrammatical sentences with *toh* compared with grammatical sentences. The others demonstrated the reverse (i.e. longer reading times on grammatical sentences). These data suggest that about 50% of the subjects may have sensitivity to grammatical violations of head-directionality with embedded clauses. For this 50% of the *toh* group, mean reading time for grammatical sentences was 8009 milliseconds (SD = 2628) while the mean reading time for ungrammatical sentences was 9331 (SD = 2745). We ran a paired samples t-test on just these subjects and the results yielded a significant difference: $t(8) = -0.4.414$, $p = .002$. A Wilcoxon test confirmed these results: $Z = -2.666$, $p = .008$. In short, a significant subgroup within the *toh* group appeared to have projected beyond the input data to head-directionality with clause structure.

Discussion and conclusion

We believe our results to be clear and uncontroversial. The learners in the present study received minimal exposure to Japanese as an L2 and yet, demonstrated awareness of the head-final nature of Japanese as measured by longer reading times on ungrammatical sentences to which they had not been exposed. Although the learners in the group who read embedded clauses were not as consistent in their sensitivity to violations of complement-head order as those who read polar questions were, given that learners were only exposed to 100 stimulus sentences, the fact that 50% of them demonstrated sensitivity to violations of headedness in embedded clauses is impressive. What do these results mean for instructed SLA and particularly for the 'grammar dimension', the focus of the present volume?

First, these results demonstrate that instructed learners are no different from other learners (including L1 learners) in that they build mental grammars as a result of processing exemplars in the input. These earliest-stage instructed learners are clearly establishing a head-final language from the get-go – and they did not need any explicit instruction or intervention to do. To be sure, our treatment involved carefully laid out sequences of input sentences. That was necessary for testing headedness. But what we have shown is that the mind's language-making mechanisms are powerful and effective, which is the topic of our next point.

Our results also demonstrate that the mechanism classroom learners use to create language is the same mechanism that other learners, both L1 and uninstructed L2, use – namely, the architecture of the human mind that allows for parameterization in languages. Access to this architecture resulted in a POS situation after only 30 minutes of instruction. Our L2 learners showed knowledge of the head final nature of polar questions and embedded clauses – without being exposed to the relevant input or explanations. This means that instruction need not always explicitly teach such things as 'remember that *toh* is placed after the clause' or, 'to form *yes-no* questions, Japanese uses the particle *ka* and places it at the end of the sentence'. Learners will automatically place complementizers at the end of embedded clauses and question markers at the ends of sentences in a language like Japanese. All these learners needed to know was what *toh* and *ka* are. In other words, they didn't need a grammar lesson as such; what they needed was to learn a vocabulary item.

By making these claims, we do not mean to project beyond our own data (no pun intended) by implying that learners don't need to be taught anything, or that they will automatically 'pick everything up'. This is a wrong interpretation of our claim, and, as VanPatten and Rothman (this volume) argue, language can be divided into three levels: those things that can't be taught (universals), those things that don't need to be taught (derived aspects of language due to parameterization) and things that need to be learnt from the input. What we have shown is that learners do not need to learn the syntax of *ka* and *toh*; this underlying knowledge comes for free after getting exposure to basic sentences in Japanese. But they do need to learn what *ka* and *toh* are. That is, they need to map the relevant functions and meanings onto these morpho-phonological units. This poses an interesting question for instructed SLA. Clearly, there is a relationship between lexicon and syntax, but how do we go about specifying which aspects of the lexicon need to be taught and which don't? In our study, we explicitly told subjects what *toh* was before they began reading the test sentences. We did not tell them anything about how it was used or how embedded clauses were formed. We did this because it was necessary for the testing instrument we used. But in acquisition, do learners even need to be told what something like *toh* is? We believe that it is highly likely they would pick it up anyway. Because they have headedness already projected for the entire grammar (the basic results in our study), once learners encounter embedded clauses and hear or see *toh* and where it is located, their internal processes are almost forced to conclude that it is something residing in CP and thus must be the head of the phrase. So, in the end, even something like *toh* doesn't have to be explicitly taught. The same argument holds for polar questions and *ka*.

Although we can argue that the aspects of the lexicon, such as *ka* and *toh*, that have a syntactic function do not need to be taught in a language like Japanese, we cannot claim that nothing needs to be taught in any language. What we see, then, as an appropriate research agenda for the 'grammar dimension' in instructed SLA is to determine what needs to be taught and what doesn't. What is more, what we mean by 'need' is just that; that is, what kinds of things in the input would never get processed by the internal learning mechanisms without the aid of instruction? There is a consensus in the literature that instruction *may* (and we stress *may*) speed up the acquisition of some surface aspects of language. However, the fact that instruction might speed up the acquisition of some things is, in our minds, trivial from a theoretical viewpoint, and not that earth-shattering from a pedagogical viewpoint. In our study, we have shown that word order in Japanese doesn't need to be taught and that the mind of the learner comes to the task of acquisition ready to deal with headedness – and therefore ready to construct the basic architecture of Japanese grammar.

We have also suggested that the lexical items that head CP, namely *ka* and *toh*, probably do not need to be taught. This is good news for teachers. Time can be better spent on developing curricula and materials that maximize the work of the internal language-making mechanisms rather than explicitly teaching things that don't need to be taught and aren't ultimately learnt explicitly anyway. Again, it is the job of research to determine what, if anything, in language actually *needs* to be taught.

Authors' note

We are grateful to the editors, Cécile Laval, María J. Arche and Alessandro Benati for their comments, as well as to the anonymous reviewers for their comments. The data for this chapter also inform another paper that we have in progress, and we thank the editors for allowing us to include this chapter here.

Notes

1   English does have some expressions, such as 'at work', 'at play', 'on call' and 'on display' that seem like they might be instances of prepositions selecting for verbs. In these cases, however, the second word is better analysed as a noun, not a verb, given that these words cannot inflect: *at works/*at working, *at played/*at playing, *on called and *on displayed.

2   Japanese nouns are marked with a particle that reflects their role (subjects are marked with 'ga' and objects are marked with 'o') in the sentence. The important thing, for our purposes, is not these particles, but the order of the noun and the verb.

3   For those readers wondering about the ordering of subject-verb, we point out that subjects are not heads of a phrase (in this case TP) but are Specifiers, which do not figure into directionality in any language.

4   Here, and throughout this chapter, we use the non-standard Romanization *toh* to represent the Japanese complementizer と. This would normally be rendered in the Latin alphabet as *to*, and pronounced like *toe*, but due to its orthographic similarity with the English preposition 'to', we have chosen to use *toh* to help the reader keep the Japanese complementizer separate from the English preposition. See, also, note 6.

5   A reviewer queried why we do not review the literature on early stage acquisition in this chapter given the scope of our inquiry. The answer is that such research is irrelevant to the present study in that it focuses on aspects of acquisition other than representation and the role of parameters. See, for example, the special issue of Language Learning edited by Gulberg and Indefrey (2010).

6 For all sentences, English glosses are provided for the convenience of the reader. In both the treatment and assessment portions of the study, participants saw only the Japanese sentences.

7 *Toh* is meant to represent the Japanese complementizer と, which would normally be Romanized as '*to*'. The non-standard Romanization *toh* was used to help learners keep this form separate from the English preposition 'to'. See, also, note 4.

References

Baker, M. (2001), *The Atoms of Language: The Mind's Hidden Rules of Grammar.* New York: Baker Books.

Boeckx, C. (2010), *Language in Cognition.* Oxford: Wiley-Blackwell.

— (2011), 'Approaching parameters from below', in A. Di Sciullo and C. Boeckx (eds), *The Biolinguistic Enterprise: New Perspectives on the Evolution and Nature of the Human Language Faculty.* Oxford: Oxford University Press, pp. 205–21.

Carnie, A. (2002), *Syntax: A Generative Introduction.* Maden, MA: Wiley-Blackwell.

Chomsky, N. (1981), *Lectures on Government and Binding.* Dordrecht: Foris.

Dryer, M. (1992), 'The Greenbergian word order correlations'. *Language,* 68, 81–138.

Gullberg, M. and Indefrey, P. (eds) (2010), 'The earliest stages of language learning [Issue supplement]'. *Language Learning,* 60(s2), 1–283.

Kanno, K. (1997), 'The acquisition of null and overt pronominals in Japanese by English speakers'. *Second Language Research,* 13, 265–87.

Montalbetti, M. (1984), *After Binding: On the Interpretation of Pronouns.* Unpublished PhD thesis, Massachusetts Institute of Technology.

Newmeyer, F. (2004), 'Against a parameter-setting approach to typological variation'. *Linguistic Variation Yearbook,* 4, 181–234.

— (2005), *Possible and Probable Languages.* Oxford: Oxford University Press.

Perez-Leroux, A. T., and Glass, W. (1999), 'Null anaphora in Spanish second language acquisition: probabilistic versus generativist approaches'. *Second Language Research,* 15, 220–49.

Roberts, I. and Holmberg, A. (2010), 'Introduction: parameters in minimalist theory', in T. Biberauer, A. Holmberg, I. Roberts, and M. Sheehan (eds), *Parametric Variation: Null Subjects in Minimalist Theory.* Cambridge: Cambridge University Press, pp. 1–57.

Rizzi, L. (1982), *Issues in Italian syntax.* Dordrecht: Foris.

Schwartz, B. (1998), 'The second language instinct'. *Lingua,* 106, 133–60.

VanPatten, B., Keating, G., and Leeser, M. (2012), 'Missing verbal inflections as a representational issue: evidence from on-line methodology'. *Linguistic Approaches to Bilingualism,* 2, 109–40.

White, L. (2003), *Second Language Acquisition and Universal Grammar.* Cambridge: Cambridge University Press.

Appendix

Sample drawings used during treatment

Taro-ga ringo-o taberu

Taro-ga orenji-o taberu

Mary-ga kichin-de hon-o miru

7

The Relationship between Learning Rate and Learning Outcome for Processing Instruction on the Spanish Passive Voice

James F. Lee
University of New South Wales, Australia

Second language learners have a tendency to use an inappropriate word-order-based processing strategy to (mis)interpret passive sentences. When asked to identify the agent in a passive sentence, they tend to select the first noun, which in passive sentences is not the agent but the patient. In relying on word order, they ignore formal features of the language that mark agent/patient relationships. The aims of the study are to determine if processing instruction will be effective for teaching Spanish passive constructions and to examine the relationship between learning rate and learning outcome. Learning rate is also referred to in the literature on processing instruction as trials to criterion (e.g. Fernández) which is the number of items processed before the learner correctly processes three target items in a row. Learning outcome is the number of items processed correctly on a post-test. The study uses a pre-test/post-test/delayed post-test design. The results indicate that processing instruction on the Spanish passive was successful in that learners improved significantly as a result of instruction. Also, learning rate was significantly correlated with learning outcome in that the learners who more quickly began to process correctly had higher learning outcomes. Learning rate accounted for quite a bit of the variance in learning outcome scores in the immediate post-test.

Introduction

VanPatten (1996, 2004, 2007) developed a set of principles that account for adult second language processing, some of which are framed by the construct of capacity. Comprehension for second language learners is quite effortful in terms of cognitive processing and available working memory. Effort imposes limits on processing and so has consequences for what learners can process (process being defined as the connection of a form to its function/meaning).

In addition to the processing of form, VanPatten has articulated a basic parsing routine for beginning L2 learners: the First Noun Principle (VanPatten 2004). It states that 'Learners tend to process the first noun or pronoun they encounter in a sentence as the subject [or agent]' (VanPatten 2007: 122). Second language learners' reliance on a word-order-based processing strategy to assign agent/patient roles has been documented in a variety of languages and for a variety of linguistic structures. Native speakers of English learning other languages tend to process sentences as if the word order was SVO or Agent-Action-Patient. That is, they impose canonical word order on sentences even if the sentence's word order is not canonical.

For example, canonical word order in Japanese is SOV with the verb always appearing in sentence final position (see Smith and VanPatten, this volume). Japanese uses NNV sequences in both active and passive sentences. In both sentence types, the grammatical role of subject is marked は and the subject occurs in sentence initial position. The patient in an active sentence is marked as such を and occurs in second position. The agent in a passive sentence is marked に as such and occurs as the second noun in the string. Benati et al. (2010) found that L2 learners of Japanese overwhelmingly misinterpreted passive sentences presented in isolation. L2 learners misinterpreted 89% of passive sentences as active sentences because they used a first noun strategy to assign the role of agent. When the sentences were presented in the contexts of a story and a dialogue, first noun strategy use decreased somewhat, but was still 79% and 80%, respectively.

French has a causative construction formed with the verb *faire* 'to make' yielding sentences with two agents. The agent of the verb *faire* is in sentence initial position, followed by *faire* + infinitive. The patient of the infinitive verb is next in the sequence followed then by the agent of the second verb which is marked with *à*. Wong (2010) found that learners misinterpreted causative sentences embedded in discourse from 95.5% to 100% of the time. Learners indicated, for example, that the first noun was the agent of the infinitive. They tended to identify the second agent as involved with the patient of the infinitive. Similar results for misinterpreting French causative sentences in isolation have been reported in Allen (2000) and VanPatten and Wong (2004).

Culman et al. (2009) examined word order in German with specific regard to accusative case marking on the masculine form of the definite article. Typical word order in German is SVO but due to case marking on the definite article, German allows OVS sentences. Culman et al. found that learners misinterpreted the OVS sentences from 85% to 92% of the time. Overwhelmingly they identified the first noun in the OVS sentences as the subject or agent. Similar results for misinterpreting German OVS sentences were found by LoCoco (1987), Henry et al. (2009) and VanPatten and Borst (2012a).

First noun strategy use among second language learners of Spanish is particularly well-documented with O$_{pro}$VS strings for which learners identify the first noun, an accusative case-marked pronoun, as the agent. Learners' rates of first noun strategy use in these types of stings has been documented as between 35% and 70% (VanPatten 1984), 27% and 73% (Lee 1987), 48% (Houston 1997), 84% (VanPatten and Houston 1998), 32% and 56% (Malovrh 2006), 42% and 50% but decreasing to 16% among advanced learners (Lee and Malovrh 2009), 35% and 50% but decreasing to 13% among advanced learners (Malovrh and Lee 2010) and 40% and 50% but decreasing to 14% among advanced learners (Malovrh and Lee 2013).

The linguistic target of the present study is the Spanish passive voice, which, like its English counterpart, does not reflect canonical word order. We could say it reverses it in that the agent appears in sentence final position and is marked with a preposition. The patient appears in sentence initial position and is the grammatical subject of the passivized VP. Learners use the first noun strategy to assign agent/patient roles in passive sentences in English (Qin 2008) and French (Ervin-Tripp 1974) as second languages. Will Processing Instruction alter L2 learners reliance on word order when processing Spanish passive sentences? Will how quickly they learn to process accurately be related to their ultimate learning success?

Background

Processing passive sentences is a challenge for children acquiring English as a first language (Bever 1970; Fraser et al. 1963; Slobin 1966). Baldie (1976) found that children's imitation, comprehension and production of passives improved with age. For example, accurate production of passive sentences was 0% at age 3 but had increased to 80% at age 7;6–7;11. In other words, passives are late-acquired in English as a first language.

The L2 acquisition of Spanish passives has been carried out in light of the acquisition of the Spanish copula system. The research all indicates that the passive with *ser*, or the true passive, is the last of the copular functions to be acquired by classroom learners (Briscoe 1995, cited in Geeslin 2005) and Peace Corps volunteers at the time they completed intensive in-country language training and 1 year later at the end of their in-country work experience (Guntermann 1992a, 1992b). The level of learner examined in the present study will not have acquired the Spanish passive with *ser*. In fact, the Spanish passive with *ser* is not even presented in the instructional materials used in the courses in which they were enrolled.

Processing Instruction has successfully altered learners' inaccurate use of a word–order-based processing strategy. The research has demonstrated that learners' interpretation and production improve significantly after receiving Processing Instruction on the Japanese passive (Benati et al. 2010), English passive (Qin 2008; Uludag and VanPatten 2012-see IRAL), French causative constructions with faire (VanPatten and Price 2012; VanPatten and Wong 2004; Wong 2010), German accusative case pronouns (e.g. Culman et al. 2009; and several others) and Spanish object pronouns in preverbal position (VanPatten and Cadierno 1993; and many others). I anticipate that Processing Instruction on the Spanish passive will yield similar results.

A recent innovation in measuring the effects of Processing Instruction has been to count trials-to-criterion, an indication of when learners begin and then maintain the correct processing strategy. This measure is a process-oriented one, whereas the vast majority of Processing Instruction research relies on product-oriented measures of interpretation and production post-tests. Fernández operationalized trials-to-criterion as '. . . the number of items that participants completed up to the point when they correctly answered three target items and one distracter item in a row' (2008, p. 289). The measure of trials-to-criterion has been related to the effects of explicit information (+ / −) in Processing Instruction research. Learners who received explicit information in addition to structured input activities have been shown to significantly decrease their trials-to-criterion, that is, process accurately more quickly, with the Spanish subjunctive (Fernández 2008) and German accusative case articles (Culman et al. 2009; Henry et al. 2009; VanPatten and Borst 2012a), but not with direct object pronouns in Spanish (Fernández 2008; VanPatten and Borst 2012b). Discussion of these divergent findings centres on the question of the portability of the explicit information, that is, if it is useable during practice, and the nature of the linguistic structure examined.

I refer to trials-to-criterion as learning rate, which is how quickly we see the effects of instruction during practice (Lee 2013). Trials-to-criterion has been treated as a dependent variable in all the investigations cited in the previous paragraph. The independent variable was the presence or absence of explicit information. In the present study, I refer to trials-to-criterion as an indication of learning rate and I do not treat it as a dependent variable. Rather, I treat it as an individual difference and correlate learning rate with learning outcomes.

Research questions

The previous research on the acquisition of the passive voice, word-order-based processing in L1 and L2 and the results of previous research on Processing Instruction contribute to the formulation of the research questions that guide the present study. They are as follows.

1. Are there significant learning outcomes associated with Processing Instruction on the Spanish passive voice as measured by an interpretation task?
2. Is there a relationship between learning outcomes and learning rate, that is, between scores on the interpretation task and how quickly learners begin to process sentences correctly?

Method

Participants

The participants in the present study were all enrolled in intermediate-level Spanish language classes at the University of New South Wales at the time of the investigation. Data collection took place in Semester 2 of 2010 (Intermediate B) and Semester 1 of 2011 (Intermediate A). The potential pool of participants was 175, but the pool on whom data were analysed numbers 56. All participants signed an informed consent form. They must have participated in the three administrations of the assessment task to be included in the Processing Instruction group, which reduced the participant numbers considerably. Additionally, they all scored less than 60% on the pre-test and they all accessed the explicit information provided on the target structure. Those who skipped the explanation of the target structure were not included in the present study.

Finally, only learners who completed all the items in the instructional materials were included in the final pool.

Thirty-seven of the fifty-six participants were assigned to the Processing Instruction group, whereas nineteen acted as a control group for the pre-test and immediate post-test (Times 1 and 2). The week after the administration of the immediate post-test, the control group then received the instructional materials on the Spanish passive (as per the agreement with the Human Ethics Review Committee not to withhold instruction from any one enrolled in the course). This means that there is no control group comparison for the delayed post-test.

Target form

The Spanish passive voice is structurally similar to its English counterpart. The function of the passive is to bring the patient into focal sentence-initial position. The agent becomes less important to the communicative event and in many passives, the agent need not be expressed in the surface structure. The sentence in (1) is in the active voice. It is passivized in (2).

1. Juan visitará a los abuelos.
   Juan – will visit – ACC marker – the grandparents
   Juan will visit his grandparents.
2. Los abuelos serán visitados por Juan.
   The grandparents – will be – visited – by – Juan
   The grandparents will be visited by Juan.

The patient in the active sentence moves to sentence initial position and becomes the grammatical subject of the passive sentence. The agent of the active sentence moves to a post-verbal position and is marked with a preposition. The passive form of the verb is a compound form with the verb *ser* 'to be' agreeing in number and person with the patient/grammatical subject. The -*n* on the verb is the marker for third-person plural. The other verbal element is the past participle form of the verb used in the active sentence. The past participle has an adjectival function in passive sentences which means that it agrees in number and gender with the patient/grammatical subject. The -*o* on the end of the participle reflects masculine gender and the -*s* is the plural marker. The sentence in (3) shows a singular form of *ser* and a feminine form of the participle,-*a*.

3. María es admirada por todos.
   María – is – admired-FEM – by – everyone.
   María is admired by everyone.

Materials

The materials developed for the present study include an interpretation task, a grammatical explanation and a set of referential and affective structured input activities. The interpretation task consisted of 80 items, 20 of which were passive sentences. The other 60 served as distracters and consisted of sentences with object pronouns, gender-cued cataphoric reference and null-subject sentences. The sentences were recorded into a PowerPoint presentation in which there were 10 sentences per slide. The participants heard a sentence in Spanish and then were asked a question in English. Their responses to these questions revealed how they assigned agency. For example, had sentences (2) and (3) above been used in the assessment, the corresponding questions would have been 'Who will do the visiting?' and 'Who does the admiring?', respectively. The presentation was timed such that learners had 5 seconds to respond before the next sentence started. The participants recorded their responses on a paper-and-pencil worksheet set.

After hearing 10 sentences, the PowerPoint advanced itself. In short, the participants did not control the delivery of the assessment items. I created 8 different versions of the assessment task by systematically re-ordering the slides so as to avoid a presentation bias. The testing took place in a language laboratory with individuals wearing headsets. The learners accessed the version of the assessment task indicated on the worksheet placed at the individual workstations. The worksheet consisted of 10 multiple-choice items per page. The multiple choices were such that the 'a' choice was the first person mentioned in the input sentence. The 'b' choice was the second person mentioned. The 'c' choice was 'both' for sentences with singular agents/patients or 'all 4' for those with plural agents/patients. Finally, participants had the 'd' choice of 'not sure'. One version of the assessment task was used as a pre-test in week 3 of the semester and different versions as the post-tests in weeks 5 and 7.

The instructional materials were presented, described and explained in detail in Chapter 3 of this volume. Both the explanation and the structured input practices were designed to be delivered to individuals working in a language laboratory. All participants were instructed to open a 16-slide, recorded PowerPoint presentation that provided the forms and functions of the Spanish passive voice. They had access to this explicit information all during the instructional treatment. After completing the presentation of the target linguistic structure, the participants were directed to open and carry out the structured input activities one at a time. There were 8 activities consisting of a total of 116 items equally divided between referential and affective items. All referential activities were presented in oral mode, whereas all affective activities were presented in written mode. The participants first performed a referential activity followed by an affective activity and so on. The participants had to submit one activity before moving to the next. Once submitted, the system displayed the activity with their answer marked as correct with a green tick or incorrect with a red x. The correct answer was indicated for each item that was incorrect. As there was no correct answer for affective activities, the system accepted any answer the participants provided.

Scoring

Performance on the assessment task, in all its administrations, was to tally the number of correct answers. The changes in the number of correct answers from pre-test to the two post-tests reflect a learning outcome. I then scored the learners' performance on the practice items in order to determine learning rate. The score for learning rate indicates the number of the practice item on which the learners began to answer three items in a row correctly. Only responses given to referential activity items were used to calculate learning rate. The affective response items were not included in this calculation as they have no correct answer.

Procedures

All procedures took place in a language laboratory during the learners' regularly scheduled class time. The learners took the pre-test in week 3 of the semester and I refer to this as Time 1. They then received Processing Instruction in week 5 in a 2-hour block of time. They took the immediate post-test after completing the instructional materials and I refer to this as Time 2. The Processing Instruction group took the delayed post-test in week 7. The control group took the pre-test in week 3 and the immediate post-test in week 5. During the class session in week 5, the instructor carried out activities in the language laboratory that did not involve the Spanish passive. The agreement with the Human Ethics Review Committee was that all the students enrolled in Intermediate Spanish would receive instruction on the Spanish passive, that is, no one would be left out. The control group needed to receive Processing Instruction on the Spanish passive, and our only access to the language laboratory was in week 7. There is, therefore, no control group comparison data for the delayed post-test.

Results

The comparison of the performance of the Processing Instruction group and the control group involves only Times 1 and 2. The means and standard deviations for these two groups' correct answers are presented in Table 7.1. The maximum score is 20. The means for Time 1 were submitted to a one-way Analysis of Variance (ANOVA) to determine that the two groups began the treatments with equivalent knowledge of the Spanish passive. The results of the ANOVA revealed that there were no significant differences between the two groups prior to treatment (F (1, 54) = 2.9733, p = .0904). Any differences that emerge after treatment will, therefore, be attributed to the treatment. The means for Times 1 and 2 were then submitted to a repeated measures ANOVA. The independent variable was Treatment, and the repeated measure was Time. The dependent variable was the number of passive sentences for which the learner had correctly identified the agent. The results of the ANOVA revealed a significant main effects for Treatment (F (1, 54) = 171.1121, p < .0001) and Time (F (1, 54) = 150.2590, p < .0001) as well as a significant interaction between the two (F (1, 54) = 177.3045, p < .0001). Two one-way ANOVAs were performed on the means contributing to the significant interaction. The results of the ANOVA on the control group's scores indicated that there was no significant difference between their Time 1 and Time 2 scores (F (1, 18) = 1.8303, p = .1928). The results of the ANOVA on the Processing Instruction group's scores showed that there was a significant difference between their Time 1 and Time 2 scores (F (1, 36) = 348.096, p < .0001). These results indicate that the effects for Treatment and Time are exclusively due to the performance of the Processing Instruction group who benefitted from instruction.

The next set of analyses explores the delayed effects associated with the processing instruction on the Spanish passive. The control group did not

Table 7.1 Means and standard deviations by Treatment and Time for the correct selection of the agent in passive sentences

Treatment	Time 1	Time 2
Processing Instruction	3.243	17.243
(n = 37)	(3.175)	(3.847)
Control	1.895	1.316
(n = 19)	(1.696)	(1.668)

Table 7.2 Means and standard deviations by Time for the correct selection of the agent in passive sentences by the Processing Instruction group

Time 1	Time 2	Time 3
3.243	17.243	14.568
(3.175)	(3.847)	(5.374)

participate in the Time 3 data collection. Therefore, the means and standard deviations for correct selection of the agent in passive sentences, presented in Table 7.2, are for the Processing Instruction group alone. A repeated measures ANOVA revealed a significant effect for Time ($F(1, 36) = 530.8258, p < .0001$). A series of one-way ANOVAs was performed to test for the differences between each pair of means. The results revealed that the scores for Time 2 were significantly higher than for Time 1 ($F(1, 36) = 606.903, p < .0001$) and significantly higher than for Time 3 ($F(1, 36) = 9.2799, p < .0043$). The latter result indicates that effects of instruction had begun to deteriorate in the 2-week gap between instruction and the delayed post-test. The results do, however, show that the scores at Time 3 are significantly higher than those at Time 1 ($F(1, 36) = 180.833, p < 0.0001$). This result indicates that the learners retained some of the benefits of instruction.

The final analyses relate to learning rate, that is, when learners began processing three items in a row correctly. The mean score for learning rate is 8.135 with a standard deviation of 9.256. The scores ranged from 1 to 53. I performed pairwise correlations between learning rate and the scores at Times 1, 2 and 3, the results of which are presented in Table 7.3. All three correlations presented in Table 7.3 are negative and demonstrate the desired effect. Specifically, a low score for learning rate indicates that the learner quickly began to process correctly. A high score for learning rate indicated that the learner took longer to process correctly. A high score for correct processing demonstrates that the learners did well on the assessment tasks; a low score demonstrates the learner did not do well. The results revealed two significant correlations between learning rate and the scores at Times 2 and 3. The correlation coefficient for Time 2 shows a significant and strong correlation between learning rate and learning outcome. The R^2 value indicates that learning rate is accounting for a very large 43% of the variance in Time 2 scores. The correlation coefficient for Time 3 shows a significant and moderate

Table 7.3 Pairwise correlations between learning rate and scores at Times 1, 2 and 3

Pair	Correlation	Significance probability	R^2
Learning rate × Time 1	−0.2224	.1859	0.04946
Learning rate × Time 2	−0.6562	.0001*	0.4308
Learning rate × Time 3	−0.3596	.0288*	0.1293

* indicates a significant correlation.

correlation between learning rate and learning outcome, accounting for only 13% of the variance. As expected, there is a non-significant correlation between Time 1 pre-test scores and learning rate.

Discussion and conclusion

The research presented in this chapter was guided by two research questions. They are:

1. Are there significant learning outcomes associated with Processing Instruction on the Spanish passive voice as measured by an interpretation task?
2. Is there a relationship between learning outcomes and learning rate, that is, between scores on the interpretation task and how quickly learners begin to process sentences correctly?

The results of the statistical analyses provided affirmative responses to both questions. Prior to receiving Processing Instruction, learners rarely assigned the agent correctly in passive sentences. The group's mean score of 3.243 indicates that learners assigned the agent correctly only 16% of the time. Learners used an incorrect word-order-based processing strategy to identify the agent in the vast majority of sentences. As a result of receiving Processing Instruction, learners became very successful in assigning the agent in passive sentences. The group's mean score of 17.243 on the immediate post-test and 14.568 on the delayed post-test indicate that learners assigned the agent correctly 86% and 73% of the time, respectively. The improvement from Time 1 was 70% but retreated to 57%. These figures represent an impressive learning outcome. The vast majority of

Processing Instruction research has found that the effects of instruction do not diminish in the short term of a 2-week period (Lee and Benati 2009). Why did the effects of instruction on the Spanish passive diminish so quickly? I believe the answer is not related to processing instruction or to the target linguistic structure. Rather, in between instruction in week 5 and the delayed post-test in week 7, the participants took the first major assessment in the course in which they were enrolled. It covered four chapters of material including four grammar points. Perhaps their intense focus on grammatical structures other than the Spanish passive immediately after instruction influenced how much information on the passive they could access during the assessment task.

Exciting research framed by the First Noun Principle has emerged since 2004, at which time, all but one work done in the area referred to Spanish object pronouns (e.g. Sanz 1997; VanPatten and Cadierno 1993; VanPatten and Fernández 2004). Allen (2000) attempted to expand the research on Processing Instruction to include the French causative construction with *faire*. Her study did not find a superior effect for Processing Instruction over traditional instruction. VanPatten and Wong (2004) replicated Allen (2000) but controlled for lexical semantics and event probabilities in the materials and assessment tasks. Furthermore, they added non-causative *faire* sentences to the materials so that learners had to distinguish when the first noun was and was not the agent. These changes to the materials resulted in a superior effect for Processing Instruction on the interpretation task. More research on the French causative construction has emerged (Benati et al. 2008, 2009; Laval 2013; VanPatten et al. 2013; Wong 2010). We now also have Processing Instruction research on English passives (Qin 2008; Uludag and VanPatten 2012), Japanese passives (Benati et al. 2010; Hikima 2011) and with the present study, Spanish passives. The research on Japanese passives had very few participants and so is in need of replication. Also, Japanese allows a direct as well as an indirect passive, the pragmatics of which indicate a certain irritation on the part of the speaker with the agent. Hikima (2011) included both types of passives in her materials but because of their pragmatic differences, these could be examined separately.

Another possible direction for future research involves gender-cued cataphoric reference as in (4) and (5). The subordinate clause is fronted and contains a null subject. The resolution of the subject is cued by the gender marker on the adjective (underlined in each sentence). My preliminary analysis of the L2 processing of these sentences is that learners overwhelmingly select the first noun as the subject of the subordinate clause, no matter the gender cue.

4. Mientras estaba enferm*a*, Luis hablaba con Silvia cada tarde.
5. Mientras estaba enferm*o*, Luis hablaba con Silvia cada tarde.

In the second part of this investigation, I found a relationship between learning outcome and learning rate. That is, the more quickly a learner consistently applied the target-language appropriate processing strategy they were taught, the higher their learning outcome, a finding that supports that of Culman et al. (2009) but not that of VanPatten et al. (2013) as the effect may depend on the intersection of target structure and processing problem. The effect of learning rate was still significant even after 2 weeks; likewise, the effect of instruction was still significant after 2 weeks (Time 1 vs. Time 3). The results do show a tapering off effect in that the amount of the variance learning rate accounts for at Time 3 is less than that at Time 1. Likewise, the Time 3 accuracy scores are significantly lower than those at Time 2. These results suggest that there may be a time beyond the 2 weeks examined in the present study at which the effect of learning rate may disappear. What we would then be left with would be the effect of instruction, which VanPatten and Fernández (2004) documented as being present 8 months after instruction. That is, the instruction itself may be more important in the long term than the initial rate of learning. This hypothesis could be easily researched. More research examining learning rate (or trials-to-criterion) independently of variables such +/− explicit information is certainly worth pursuing. Researchers can easily incorporate learning rate into their designs as long as they have access to the instructional materials learners carried out.

To conclude, there are significant learning outcomes associated with Processing Instruction on the Spanish passive voice as measured by an interpretation task immediately after instruction and after a 2-week delay, although the effect of instruction did diminish. There is a strong correlation between learning outcomes and learning rate such that higher scores on the interpretation task are associated with how quickly learners began to process sentences correctly, although the strength of the correlation diminished as did the effect of instruction.

Acknowledgement

The research reported in this chapter was supported by a Faculty Research Grant and a Research Promotion Grant from the Faculty of Arts and Social Sciences at the University of New South Wales, for which I am grateful. I also wish to acknowledge the contribution of two research assistants who worked with me on different aspects of this project, Henar Vicente and Henar Perales.

References

Allen, L. Q. (2000), 'Form-meaning connection and the French causative: an experiment in processing instruction'. *Studies in Second Language Acquisition*, 22, 69–84.

Baldie, B. J. (1976), 'The acquisition of the passive voice'. *Journal of Child Language*, 3, 331–48.

Bates, E. and MacWhinney, B. (1989), 'Functionalism and the competition model', in B. MacWhinney and E. Bates (eds), *The Crosslinguistic Study of Sentence Processing*. Cambridge: Cambridge University Press, pp. 3–73.

Benati, A., Lee, J. F., and Hikima, N. (2010), 'Exploring the effects of processing instruction on discourse-level interpretation tasks with the Japanese passive construction', in A. G. Benati and J. F. Lee (eds), *Processing Instruction and Discourse*. London: Continuum, pp. 148–77.

Benati, A., Lee, J. F., and Laval, C. (2008), 'Chapter 5: from processing instruction on the acquisition of French *imparfait* to secondary transfer-of-training effects on French subjunctive and to cumulative transfer-of-training effects with French causative constructions', in A. Benati and J. F. Lee (eds), *Grammar Acquisition and Processing Instruction: Secondary and Cumulative Effects*. Bristol: Multilingual Matters, pp. 121–57.

— (2009), 'Secondary and cumulative effects in attaining L2 proficiency in the classroom: the acquisition of French', in A. Benati (ed.), *Issues in Second Language Proficiency*. London: Continuum, pp. 189–201.

Bever, T. (1970), 'The cognitive basis for linguistic structures', in J. Hayes (ed.), *Cognition and The Development of Language*. New York: Wiley, pp. 279–362.

Briscoe, G. (1995), *The Acquisition of Ser and Estar by Non-Native Speakers of Spanish*, (unpublished PhD dissertation). University of Pennsylvania, Philadelphia, PA.

Culman, H., Henry, N., and VanPatten, B. (2009), 'The role of explicit information in instructed SLA: an on-line study with processing instruction and German accusative case inflections'. *Die Unterrichtspraxis/Teaching German*, 42, 19–31.

Ervin-Tripp, S. M. (1974), 'Is second language learning really like the first?'. *TESOL Quarterly*, 29, 11–28.

Fernández, C. (2008), 'Reexamining the role of explicit information in processing instruction'. *Studies in Second Language Acquisition*, 30, 277–305.

Fraser, C., Bellugi, U., and Brown, R. (1963), 'Control of grammar in imitation, comprehension and production'. *Journal of Verbal Learning and Verbal Behavior*, 2, 121–35.

Geeslin, K. (2005), *Crossing Disciplinary Boundaries to Improve the Analysis of Second Language Data: A Study of Copula Choice with Adjectives in Spanish*. Munich: Lincom GmbH.

Guntermann, G. (1992a), 'An analysis of interlanguage development over time: part I, *por* and *para*'. *Hispania*, 75, 177–87.

— (1992b), 'An analysis of interlanguage development over time: part II, *ser* and *estar*'. *Hispania*, 75, 1294–303.

Henry, N., Culman, H., and VanPatten, B. (2009), 'More on the effects of explicit information in instructed SLA: a partial replication and a response to Fernández (2008)'. *Studies in Second Language Acquisition*, 31, 559–75.

Hikima, N. (2011), *The Effects of Processing Instruction and Re-Exposure on Interpretation Discourse Level Tasks: The Case of Japanese Passive Forms*. Unpublished doctoral dissertation. University of Greenwich, Greenwich, UK.

Houston, T. (1997), 'Sentence processing in Spanish as a second language: a study of word order and background knowledge', in A. T. Pérez-Leroux and W. R. Glass (eds), *Contemporary Perspectives on the Acquisition of Spanish Vol. 2: Production, Processing and Comprehension*. Somerville: Cascadilla Press, pp. 123–34.

Hyams, N., Ntelitheos, D., and Manorohanta, C. (2006), 'Acquisition of the Malagasy voicing system: implications for the adult grammar'. *Natural Language and Linguistic Theory*, 24, 1049–92.

Kirby, S. (2010), 'Passives in first language acquisition: what causes the delay?'. *University of Pennsylvania Working Papers in Linguistics*, 16, 108–17.

Laval, C. (2013), 'The age factor on the primary, secondary and cumulative transfer-of-training effects on processing instruction on the acquisition of French as a second language', in J. F. Lee and A. G. Benati (eds), *Individual Differences and Processing Instruction*. London: Equinox, pp. 105–30.

Lee, J. F. (1987), 'Morphological factors influencing pronominal reference assignment by learners of Spanish', in T. A. Morgan, J. F. Lee, and B. VanPatten (eds), *Language and Language Use: Studies in Spanish*. Landham, MD: University Press of America, pp. 221–32.

— (2013), 'Foci and general findings of research on processing instruction: moving beyond limitations', in J. F. Lee and A. G. Benati (eds), *Individual Differences and Processing Instruction*. London: Equinox, pp. 19–46.

Lee, J. F. and Benati, A. G. (2009), *Research and Perspectives on Processing Instruction*. Berlin: Mouton de Gruyter.

Lee, J. F. and Malovrh, P. A. (2009), 'Linguistic and non-linguistic factors affecting OVS processing of accusative and dative case pronouns by advanced L2 learners of Spanish', in J. Collentine et al. (eds), *Selected Proceedings of the 11th Hispanic Linguistic Symposium*. Somerville, MA: Cascadilla Proceedings Project, pp. 105–16.

LoCoco, V. (1987), 'Learner comprehension of oral and written sentences in German and Spanish: the importance of word order', in B. VanPatten, T. R. Dvorak and

J. F. Lee (eds), *Foreign Language Learning: A Research Perspective*. Rowley, MA: Newbury House, pp. 119–29.

MacWhinney, B. and Bates, E. (eds) (2009), *The Crosslinguistic Study of Sentence Processing*. Cambridge: Cambridge University Press.

Malovrh, P. (2006), 'L2 sentence processing of Spanish OVS word order and direct object pronouns: an analysis of contextual constraints', in N. Sagarra and A. J. Toribio (eds), *Selected Proceedings of the 9th Hispanic Linguistics Symposium*. Somerville, MA: Cascadilla Press, pp. 169–79.

Malovrh, P. and Lee, J. F. (2010), 'Connections between processing, production and placement: acquiring object pronouns in Spanish as a second language', in B. VanPatten and J. Jegerski (eds), *Research in Second Language Processing and Parsing*. John Benjamins: Amsterdam, pp. 231–35.

— (2013), *The Developmental Dimension in Instructed Second Language Learning: The L2 Acquisition of Object Pronouns In Spanish*. London: Bloomsbury.

Qin, J. (2008), 'The effect of processing instruction and dictogloss tasks on the acquisition of the English passive voice'. *Language Teaching Research*, 12, 61–82.

Sanz, C. (1997), 'Experimental tasks in SLA research: amount of production, modality, memory, and production processes', in A. T. Pérez-Leroux and W. R. Glass (eds), *Contemporary Perspectives on the Acquisition of Spanish: Vol. 2 Production, Processing and Comprehension*. Somerville, MA: Cascadilla Press, pp. 41–56.

Slobin, D. (1966), 'Grammatical transformations in childhood and adulthood', *Journal of Verbal Learning and Verbal Behavior*, 5, 219–27.

Smith, M. and VanPatten, B. (2013), 'Instructed SLA as parameter setting: evidence form earliest-stage leaners of Japanese as L2', in A. Benati, C. Laval and M. J. Arche (eds), *The Grammar Dimension in Instructed Second Language Learning*. London: Bloomsbury, pp. 000–000.

Uludag, O. and VanPatten, B. (2012), 'The comparative effects of processing instruction and dictogloss on the acquisition of the English passive by speakers of Turkish'. *International Review of Applied Linguistics in Language Teaching*, 50, 189–212.

VanPatten, B. (1984), 'Learners' comprehension of clitic pronouns: more evidence for a word order strategy'. *Hispanic Linguistics*, 1, 57–67.

— (1996), *Input Processing and Grammar Instruction: Theory and Research*. Norwood, NJ: Ablex.

— (2004), 'Input processing in second language acquisition', in B. VanPatten (ed.), *Processing Instruction: Theory, Research and Commentary*. Mahwah, NJ: Erlbaum, pp. 5–31.

— (2007), 'Input processing in adult second language acquisition', in B. VanPatten and J. Williams (eds), *Theories in Second Language Acquisition: An Introduction*. Mahwah, NJ: Erlbaum, pp. 115–35.

VanPatten, B. and Borst, S. (2012a), 'The roles of explicit information and grammatical sensitivity in processing instruction: nominative-accusative case marking and word order in German L2'. *Foreign Language Annals*, 45, 92–109.

— (2012b), 'The roles of explicit information and grammatical sensitivity in the processing of clitic object pronouns and word order in L2 Spanish'. *Hispania*, 95, 270–84.

VanPatten, B. and Cadierno, T. (1993), 'Explicit instruction and input processing'. *Studies in Second Language Acquisition*, 15, 225–43.

VanPatten, B. and Fernández, C. (2004), 'The long-term effects of processing instruction', in B. VanPatten (ed.). *Processing Instruction: Theory, Research, and Commentary*. Mahwah, NJ: Erlbaum, pp. 273–89.

VanPatten, B. and Houston, T. (1998), 'Contextual effects in processing L2 input sentences'. *Spanish Applied Linguistics*, 2, 53–70.

VanPatten, B. and Price, J. (2012), 'What does explanation do for the language learner? An experiment in processing instruction with the causative *faire*'. *The French Review*, 86, 96–107.

VanPatten, B. and Wong, W. (2004), 'Processing instruction and the French causative: a replication', in B. VanPatten (ed.), *Processing Instruction: Theory, Research, and Commentary*. Mahwah, NJ: Erlbaum, pp. 97–117.

VanPatten, B., Collopy, E., Price, J., Borst, S., and Qualin, A. (2013), 'Explicit information, grammatice sensitivity, and the First-Noun Principle: a cross-linguistic study in processing instruction'. *The Modern Language Journal*, 97, 504–25.

Wong, W. (2010), 'Exploring the effects of discourse-level structured input activities with French causative', in A. G. Benati and J. F. Lee (eds), *Processing Instruction and Discourse*. London: Continuum, pp. 198–216.

8

Coproduction of Language Forms and Its Effects on L2 Learning

Hossein Nassaji and Jun Tian
University of Victoria, Canada

This study examined the role that collaborative output activities in L2 classroom learning. The focus was on learning English phrasal verbs, a subgroup of English vocabulary that has been shown to be difficult for L2 learners to master. Thirty-nine low-intermediate ESL students from three intact classes were randomly assigned to an experimental group (two classes) and one comparison group (one class). The comparison group received input-based instruction only with no opportunities for subsequent output. The experimental group first received input-based instruction and then performed output-based tasks either collaboratively or individually. The results showed that learners who received input and then performed output tasks developed knowledge of the target phrasal verbs significantly more than those who received the same input but did not have opportunities for output. Collaborative tasks also improved the task performance in terms of the accurate production of output and also led to more improved knowledge of the phrasal verbs than the individual output, though in the latter case, the difference was not statistically significant. The implications of the findings will be discussed.

Introduction

Learning a second language (L2) involves both exposure to input and opportunities for output. Although some researchers in the past (e.g. Dulay et al. 1982; Krashen 1981, 1985) argued that SLA is mainly driven by comprehensible input and that output does not play an essential role, many L2 researchers now support the idea that, to learn an L2 successfully, L2 learners also need opportunities to produce output (e.g. de Bot 1996; DeKeyser 2007; Ellis 2008; Skehan 1998; Swain 1993, 1995; Swain 2005). Swain, for example, has argued that output not only contributes to SLA, but its contribution is independent of the contribution made by input. In this respect, it has also been suggested that activities that require learners to work together and produce language forms collaboratively are particularly useful for language learning (Swain and Lapkin 2001, 2002). Such activities are considered beneficial because they provide learners with both output opportunities and also opportunities for peer feedback and scaffolding (Kowal and Swain 1994; Swain 2005; Swain and Lapkin 1995).

Argument for the role of output grew out of the findings of a number of studies in French immersion programmes in Canada, which have shown that although French immersion students were exposed to many hours of comprehensible input, their language performance was still inaccurate with respect to certain grammatical aspects of the L2 (e.g. Harley and Swain 1984; Lapkin et al. 1991). This has been taken to be due to the fact that the learners were not provided with enough opportunities for language production. Therefore, it has been suggested that in order for learners to be both accurate and fluent in their L2, they need to have opportunities for both meaningful input and output. Swain (1985), in particular, has argued for opportunities for *pushed output*, that is, output that pushes learners beyond their current level of interlanguage performance.

A number of benefits have been suggested for the role of output in language acquisition (de Bot 1996; DeKeyser 1997; Skehan 1998). Swain has argued that output forces learners to move from semantic processing used in comprehension to syntactic processing needed for production (e.g. Swain 1985, 1993). Output also helps learners notice a gap between their interlanguage knowledge and the target language available in input. When learners need to produce output, they may find that they have incomplete or partial knowledge of the target language forms (Swain 1993; Swain and Lapkin 2001). They may then try to search their existing linguistic knowledge to find solutions to the problem. If they work out a solution, they consolidate their existing knowledge. If they cannot find a solution, they may pay closer attention to relevant input. Output also provides learners with an opportunity to try out their hypothesized knowledge of the language (Swain 2005). When learners producing output, they can assess its suitability through the feedback they receive from others. In addition, output plays a role in automatizing and proceduralizing the cognitive processes involved in language production and, therefore, enhances fluency by turning declarative knowledge (i.e. knowledge about the language) into procedural knowledge (i.e. ability to use that knowledge in spontaneous discourse) (de Bot1996). Finally, output also triggers more input that the learner can use to further develop their language knowledge.

There are currently a number of studies that have examined the role of output and its various functions in L2 learning. These studies have suggested that output might facilitate L2 acquisition. For example, in a series of studies, Izumi and his colleagues examined the effects of output on noticing certain grammatical forms (Izumi 2002, 2003a, 2003b; Izumi and Bigelow 2000; Izumi et al. 1999) and provided some empirical evidence for the positive effects of output on SLA. Izumi (2002) investigated the effects of output on the learning of English relativization among adult English-as-a-second language (ESL) learners. The results demonstrated that output facilitated the learning of English relativization by showing that the learners who were engaged in output outperformed those who were exposed to input only. Izumi et al. (1999) examined the noticing function of output among ESL learners when learning the same target structure. Their findings showed that the group that had produced output not only showed an increased rate of noticing of the target form in the input but also achieved more significant gains of the knowledge of the target form on the production test following the treatment. Izumi and Bigelow (2000) replicated the study by switching the order of the two output tasks and changing the target form to past hypothetical conditional. Output was found to have no significant effects on the acquisition of the past hypothetical conditional. However, opportunities for output were found to have some positive effects on learners' accurate use of the target structure in the second reconstruction task. Swain and Lapkin (1995) examined the noticing function of output among French L2 learners. In their study, a group of grade 8 French immersion students thought aloud while they were writing an essay. LREs (defined as any segment in which the learner talked about language) were identified. An analysis of their think-aloud and LREs showed many instances where learners consciously noticed a gap in their language knowledge while producing output. The researchers also found that the act of writing triggered cognitive processes, such as searches for relevant lexical and grammatical forms. These processes, the researchers argued, might play a role in L2 learning.

Collaborative output

In recent years, arguments have also been made for the benefits of activities that encourage learners to produce output collaboratively. It is suggested that these activities are beneficial because when learners attempt to produce language through collaboration, they will not only produce output, but they will get help from their peers when trying to make their meaning precise (Kowal and Swain 1994; Swain and Lapkin 2002; Swain 2005). Collaborative output will also provide learners with opportunities to reflect on language consciously and to talk about and debate language forms, which would raise their attention to the problematic forms. Swain and Lapkin (2002) noted that the joint activities, along with the act of producing the language itself, mediate language learning because when learners produce the language through collaboration, the language is used not only to convey meaning, but also to develop meaning; this would help them internalize language forms.

In several studies, Swain and her colleagues have attempted to examine the benefits of collaborative output (Kowal and Swain 1994; LaPierre 1994; Lapkin et al. 2002; Swain and Lapkin 2002). Kowal and Swain (1994), for example, examined the use of collaborative output tasks in promoting learners' awareness of language forms. Using a text reconstruction task (i.e. dictogloss) (Wajnryb 1990), the researchers collected data from intermediate and advanced French learners who worked collaboratively to reconstruct a reading text. Their results showed that the students noticed gaps between their existing language knowledge and the target language, drew their attention to connecting form and meaning and also received feedback from their peers as they worked together to reconstruct the text. In a study on collaborative output with two groups of French immersion students, Swain and Lapkin (2001) compared the effects of two collaborative output tasks: a dictogloss task in which students constructed a text that they had heard and a jigsaw task in which pairs of students created a written story based on a series of pictures. Although the researchers did not find any significant differences between the two types of tasks in terms of the overall degree of form-focusedness, operationalized in terms of the number of LREs, they found that the dictogloss task led to more accurate reproduction of the target forms than the jigsaw task. In another study using the same database, Lapkin and Swain (2000) examined the learners' use of pronominal verbs when carrying out the two tasks. In these analyses, they examined whether giving a mini-lesson before that task would affect learners' performance. The researchers found that the use of the mini-lesson had positive effects on the learners' use and accuracy of the pronominal verbs in their written output.

The present study

The purpose of the present study was to examine, through a pre-test–post-test classroom-based study, the role that production of language forms in the learning of English phrasal verbs, a subgroup of English verbs that have been shown to be difficult for L2 learners to master. The aim of the study was twofold: (a) to determine whether learners who were exposed to input and were engaged in output-based tasks showed greater increase in their knowledge of the target phrasal verbs than those who were exposed to input only and (b) whether performing the output tasks collaboratively (in pairs) versus individually had any differential effects on learners' task performance and learning.

Method

Participants

Participants were 39 adult ESL learners from three intact low-intermediate classes enrolled in an intensive adult ESL programme in a university context. They attended classes 5 days a week for 13 weeks, receiving 20 hours of instruction in each week. The number of learners in each class was 12, 13 and 14, respectively. The classes were classified as low-intermediate according to the learners' scores on a four-skill language placement test administered by the programme. All three classes were taught by the same teacher and followed the same instructional programme. The teaching approach of the teacher was communicative and included a combination of input- and output-based practices.

Of the 39 learners, 12 were male and 27 were female. Their ages ranged from 18 to 32, with an average of 22.9 years of age. They were from a variety of language backgrounds including Chinese (n = 9), Japanese (n = 14), Korean (n = 8), Portuguese (n = 2), Spanish (n = 5) and Turkish (n = 1). At the time of the study, the participants had been in Canada for 2–6 months. Twenty-three of them were new to the programme, and fourteen were continuing students who had completed one lower-level session of the 13-week programme before starting the current session. Eighteen of the participants had a university degree, three were current university students, two had finished college studies and sixteen had finished high school in their home countries.

Research design

The three classes were randomly assigned to an experimental output group (two classes, n = 26) and a comparison input group (one class, n = 13). The experimental output group (henceforth called +output group) received input-based instruction on the target phrasal verbs and performed two output-based tasks in addition to input either collaboratively or individually. The comparison group (henceforth called –*output group*) received the same input-based instruction, but did not have opportunities for subsequent output relevant to the target forms. The effects of the treatments on learning the target words were measured by means of a depth of lexical knowledge test administered before and after the treatments (see below for detail).

Target words

English phrasal verbs were selected as lexical target forms for the purpose of the study (n = 16) (see Appendix 1). Teaching phrasal verbs effectively has long been a concern for ESL/EFL instructors. Phrasal verbs consist of different combinations of verbs and particles, each usually with several meanings. In some cases, the accompanying particle completely changes the meaning of the verb (e.g. *hang out* and *catch up with*), resulting in a figurative meaning. These meanings are often not transparent or obvious from an analysis of its parts. Thus, although extensively used by native speakers (Celce-Murcia and Larsen-Freeman 1999), L2 learners often find these verbs very challenging and difficult to learn (Dagut and Laufer 1985; Yan and Yoshinori 2004).

Treatments

The treatments took place in two cycles over a period of 2 weeks.

Input-based treatment: In each of the 2 weeks during which the treatments were implemented, the learners of the +output and the –output groups received input-based instruction on eight of sixteen target phrasal verbs. The input-based treatment consisted of two components: an input-based presentation component and an input-based practice component. The input-based presentation component involved familiarizing the learners with the target phrasal verbs and providing them with some initial input as to the meanings of the sixteen phrasal verbs. For this purpose, in each of the 2 weeks, learners each received a text (a written dialogue, consisting of 168 or 183 words). Each text contained half of the phrasal verbs. The teacher read the text at a normal pace twice and briefly explained the meanings of the target phrasal verbs. Such dialogues were constructed by the teacher and were typically used as part of the regular class activities. Following the presentation stage, the learners completed an input-based word recognition activity, which was a definition-matching task. The learners were given a handout including two columns. The left column listed the target phrasal verbs presented in the previous text, and the right column contained their definitions in a random order. The learners were asked to work in pairs and match the phrasal verbs with their appropriate definitions. The teacher checked the answers afterwards and explained the meanings of the phrasal verbs if needed. During this activity, the learners were not involved in any production activity, nor were required to produce any of the target phrasal verbs during the exercise.

Output-based treatment: After completing the input activities, the learners in the +output group were given opportunities to produce the phrasal verbs by completing four output tasks, two in each week. The output tasks were two reconstruction cloze tasks and two reconstruction editing tasks. Each of the four tasks was based on a short text (written dialogue) different from one another and from the ones they had been exposed to at the input-based presentation stage. Each dialogue included four of the eight target phrasal verbs, and every learner did all the four tasks. Two of the tasks were completed collaboratively and two individually. The order of the working conditions was counterbalanced in the 2 weeks to eliminate task order effects. That is, half of the learners completed the tasks individually in the first week and worked collaboratively in the second week, and half collaboratively in the first week and individually in the second week. The order of the dialogue editing and the dialogue cloze tasks was also counterbalanced for the same reason of eliminating task order effects. That is, half of the learners completed the editing task before the cloze task in the first week and completed the editing task after the cloze task in the second week. The other half did the opposite.

The procedure for the output-based activity followed the dictogloss procedure (Wajnryb 1990), a technique that has been frequently used in studies on output, particularly those on collaborative output (Kowal and Swain 1994; Swain and Lapkin 1995, 2001). For that purpose, the learners listened to a dialogue read by the teacher twice and jotted down notes related to the content while the teacher was reading it. When reading the dialogue, the teacher did not provide the meaning of the words or provide any explanation of what was happening in the text. Then, the learners received the same dialogue in the form of either a cloze task or an editing task. In the case of the cloze task, the dialogue contained 12 missing sections, 4 of which were the target phrasal verbs. The others were distracters and were about information not related to the target phrasal verbs. The learners were asked to reproduce the missing sections as closely as possible to the original dialogue. For the editing task, the learners received the same dialogue, but this time with ten erroneous sections to be edited. Four of the sections were related to the target phrasal verbs, and the others were unrelated. The learners were asked to identify and correct the errors.

When the +output group performed the output tasks, the −output group were involved in their routine classroom activities. The amount of time spent on input-based presentation and input practice in all three classes was almost the same: about 45 minutes each. The amount of time spent on the output tasks for the +output group was about 30 minutes in each cycle. While learners were performing the output tasks collaboratively, the interaction of each pair was audio-recorded, using a digital mini-disk recorder. The recorded collaborations were then transcribed and analysed.

Testing

Before and after the treatments, the learners' knowledge of the target phrasal verbs was assessed using a depth of vocabulary knowledge test. The test was the Vocabulary Knowledge Scale (VKS), a five-point-scale self-report test developed by Paribakht and Wesche (1993, 1996). An example of a test item is given in Appendix 2. The VKS measures L2 learners' lexical knowledge on a continuum from no knowledge of the target word to the ability to grammatically produce the target word in a sentence. The measure has been assumed to assess learners' depth of lexical knowledge by measuring not only the learners' knowledge of the meaning of the words but also of how to use the words accurately and appropriately in contexts (Hu and Nassaji 2012; Nassaji 2003, 2004; Nassaji and Hu 2012; Wesche and Paribakht 1996).

Pre-test: Before the treatment in each week, the students received a pre-test on the target phrasal verbs in the form of the VKS. Each pre-test included 12 phrasal verbs, 8 of which were the target phrasal verbs, and the other 4 were distracters. The 12 items were presented in a random order in the test.

Post-test: Four days after the treatment in each week, learners' degree of vocabulary knowledge was again tested, using the VKS, to determine whether there was any increase in the learners' knowledge of the target phrasal verbs. The post-test included the same eight target phrasal verbs, but the four distracters were different from those in the pre-test. The 12 items were presented in a different random order from the pre-test.

Data analysis and results

Our first research question concerned whether learners who were exposed to input and had opportunities for output showed greater increase in their knowledge of the target phrasal verbs than those who were exposed to input only. To address this question, we calculated the frequencies and percentages of each of the five VKS knowledge levels for each target word in the pre- and post-tests. Then following Paribakht and Wesche (1993) and Wesche and Paribakht (1996), we collapsed the five levels of the VKS into two categories of 'known' and 'unknown' with levels 1 and 2 representing 'unknown' and levels 3, 4 and 5 representing 'known' phrasal verbs. The frequency and percentage of these combined data were also calculated.

As mentioned before, the number of the learners in the +output group was 26 and the number of target words was 16. This resulted in 416 cases of VKS responses ($26 \times 16 = 416$). However, one student was absent in one of the two pre-tests, and five were absent in one of the two treatment periods. Therefore, these learners' pre- and post-test scores for 8 of the 16 target words were excluded from analysis. This reduced the response cases to 368 ($416–6 \times 8 = 368$). The number of the learners in the –output group was 13, so the VKS responses were 208 ($13 \times 16 = 208$). The total responses in both the pre- and post-tests were 576 ($368 + 208 = 576$).

First, the analyses examined the learners' performance on the pre-tests for both the +output and the –output groups. The results of these analyses are presented in Table 8.1 and Figure 8.1. Section A of the table shows the frequency and percentages of the learners' responses to each of the five levels of the VKS, and Section B shows the summary (i.e. the combined levels). The results showed that in the pre-tests, the majority of the learners' responses to the VKS in both groups represented level 1 and level 2 of the vocabulary knowledge test (level 1 = 18.2% in the +output group, 19.2% in the –output group; level 2 = 55.7% in the +output group, 59.1% in the –output group). Thus, altogether 73.9% of the words were unknown to the +output group, and 78.4% of them were unknown

Table 8.1 VKS Pre-test scores of the +Output and –Output groups

(A) VKS knowledge levels	+Output group		–Output group	
	n	%	*n*	%
1	67	18.2	40	19.2
2	205	55.7	123	59.1
3	27	7.3	19	9.1
4	36	9.8	9	4.3
5	33	9.0	17	8.2
Total	368	100.0	208	100.0
	p = ns		*p* = ns	
(B) Summary				
Unknown	272	73.9	163	78.4
Known	96	26.1	45	21.6
Total	368	100.0	208	100.0
	p = ns		*p* = ns	

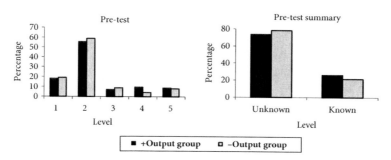

Figure 8.1 VKS Pre-test scores of the +Output and –Output groups.

to the –output group before the treatment. Chi-square analyses revealed no statistically significant difference between the two groups, suggesting that the +output and –output groups were similar in terms of their prior lexical knowledge of the target phrasal verbs.

We then analysed the performance of the two groups after the treatment in the post-tests. Table 8.2 and Figure 8.2 show the results of these analyses. As the table shows, the +output group exhibited higher percentages of the knowledge levels 3, 4, and 5 and lower percentages of levels 1 and 2 than the –output group. These results suggest that the +output group outperformed the –output group after

Table 8.2 VKS post-test scores of the +Output and −Output groups

(A) VKS knowledge levels	+Output group		−Output group	
	n	*%*	*n*	*%*
1	9	2.4^{-a}	13	6.3^{a}
2	180	48.9^{-a}	130	62.5^{a}
3	54	14.7	27	13.0
4	42	11.4	15	7.2
5	83	22.6^{a}	23	11.1^{-a}
Total	368	100.0	368	100.0

$$\chi^2\,(4, N = 576) = 21.78, p. < .001$$

(B) Summary				
Unknown	189	51.4	143	68.8
Known	179	48.6	65	31.3
Total	368	100.0	208	100.0

$$\chi^2\,(1, N = 576) = 16.46, p. < .001$$

Note. ^{a} indicates a standard residual equal to or higher than 2, and $^{-a}$ indicates a standard residual equal to or lower than −2.

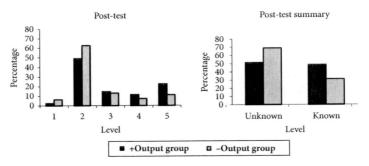

Figure 8.2 VKS post-test scores of the +Output and −Output groups.

the treatment. If we compare the results of Tables 8.1 and 8.2, an improvement in the knowledge of the target phrasal verbs can be observed in both the +output and the −output groups after the treatment. However, the improvement is much greater for the +output group than for the −output group. In the +output group, there is an increase in the percentages of the knowledge levels 3, 4 and 5. Level 3 has increased from 7.3% to 14.7%, level 4 from 9.8% to 11.4% and level 5 from 9.0% to 22.6%. In the −output group, there is also an increase in the percentages of the knowledge levels 3, 4 and 5. However, the increase is much less. Level 3 has increased from 9.1% to 13.0%, level 4 from 4.3% to 7.2% and level 5 from 8.2% to 11.1%. A chi-square test was used to compare the gain of knowledge in the two groups, and it revealed a statistically significant difference between the two groups [χ^2 (4, $N = 576$) = 21.78, $p. < .001$], suggesting that the +output group increased their lexical knowledge significantly more than the −output group.

We also calculated the standardized residual for each of the frequencies of the five VKS knowledge levels to see what knowledge level(s) contributed significantly to the difference between the two groups. A residual greater than 2.0 was taken to indicate a significantly higher frequency, and a residual smaller than −2.0 was considered to indicate a significantly lower frequency. These residuals are represented by superscript 'a' or '−a' in Table 8.2, respectively. As can be seen, +output group showed significantly lower percentages of levels 1 and 2 (which represent no knowledge of the target phrasal verbs) and a significantly higher percentage of level 5 (which represents productive knowledge of the phrasal verbs) than those in the −output group.

The combined data (second B of Table 8.2) further confirmed these findings by showing an overall higher percentage of unknown phrasal verbs for the −output group than for the +output group (68.8% vs. 51.4%), and the difference was statistically significant [χ^2 (1, $N = 576$) = 16.46, $p. < .001$].

We then examined whether the learners in the + output group benefited more from the output opportunities when they performed the output tasks in the collaborative condition than when they performed them in the individual condition. To this end, we first examined and compared the learners' success in completing the tasks in the two conditions (Research Question 2) and then their actual gains of knowledge of the target phrasal verbs (Research Question 3). To determine how successfully the learners completed the tasks, we examined the learners' production of each of the target phrasal verbs during the output tasks in both collaborative and individual conditions and coded their performance as either successful or unsuccessful. In the cloze tasks, learners' production was coded as successful if the learners correctly supplied the target phrasal verb in entirety in terms of both their meaning and grammatical accuracy. If the learners did not provide the phrasal verb in its entirety, their production was coded as unsuccessful (spelling errors were not considered). In the editing task, the learners' response was coded as successful if they not only spotted the erroneous section related to the target phrasal verb, but also corrected the error. Otherwise, the performance was coded as unsuccessful.

Table 8.3 Task-related output success in individual and collaborative conditions

	Unsuccessful output		Successful output	
	n	%	n	%
Individual	90	48.9%	94	51.1%
Collaborative	45	24.5%	139	75.5%
Total	135	36.7%	233	63.3%
	$\chi^2 (1, N = 368) = 23.69, p. < .0001$			

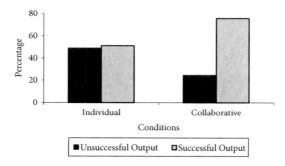

Figure 8.3 Output success for the output tasks in collaborative and individual conditions.

Table 8.3 shows a cross-tabulation of the learners' success in the collaborative and individual conditions (displayed graphically in Figure 8.3). As the table shows, when the learners completed the output tasks collaboratively, they produced more instances of accurate target phrasal verbs (75.5%) as compared to when they completed the tasks individually (51.1%). A two-way chi-square analysis revealed a statistically significant difference between the two conditions in the frequencies of the successful and unsuccessful output [χ^2 (1, $N = 368$) $= 23.69, p. < .0001$], suggesting that when the learners performed the tasks collaboratively, they produced significantly more correct instances of the phrasal verbs than when they performed the tasks individually.

Next, we examined whether collaborative and individual output had any differential effects on the learners' gain of knowledge of the target phrasal verbs. To this end, we first analysed and compared the learners' performance on the pre-tests in both the collaborative and individual conditions. The results of these analyses are shown in Table 8.4 and Figure 8.4. The majority of the

Table 8.4 VKS pre-test scores of +output group in collaborative and individual conditions

(A) VKS knowledge levels	Collaborative		Individual	
	n	%	*n*	%
1	37	20.1	30	16.3
2	100	54.3	105	57.1
3	15	8.2	12	6.5
4	18	9.8	18	9.8
5	14	7.6	19	10.3
Total	184	100.0	184	100.0
	p = ns		*p* = ns	
(B) Summary				
Unknown	137	74.5	135	73.4
Known	47	25.5	49	26.6
Total	184	100.0	184	100.0
	p = ns		*p* = ns	

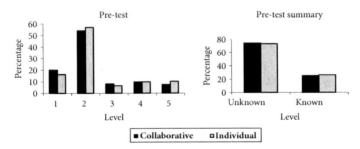

Figure 8.4 VKS pre-test scores of the +Output group in collaborative and individual conditions.

learners' responses to the VKS in both conditions represented levels 1 and 2. The results of the combined categories are represented in Section B of the table (unknown = 74.5% in the collaborative condition, 73.4% in the individual condition). That is, most learners were not familiar with the target phrasal verbs used in both conditions before the treatment. The chi-square analyses revealed no statistically significant difference between the two groups, suggesting that the learners' prior lexical knowledge of the target phrasal verbs was similar in both conditions.

We then examined the post-test performance of the learners in the two output conditions. The analyses are shown in Table 8.5 and Figure 8.5. As the table shows, the distribution of the five knowledge levels is very similar in both collaborative and individual conditions. The highest percentage of the knowledge level in both conditions is level 2 (47.3% in the collaborative condition and 50.5% in the individual condition), followed by level 5 (21.7% in the collaborative condition and 23.4% in the individual condition), then followed by levels 3 and 4, with the lowest level as level 1. But if we examine the improvement in the learners' knowledge of the target phrasal verbs in both conditions by comparing the results of Tables 8.4 and 8.5, we can see that the improvement is slightly higher for the collaborative condition than for the individual condition in each of the VKS knowledge levels 3, 4 and 5, which represented known knowledge. In the collaborative condition, there is an increase in the percentages of knowledge levels 3, 4 and 5. Level 3 has increased from 8.2% to 16.8%, level 4 from 9.8% to 12.0% and level 5 from 7.6% to 21.7%. In the individual condition, there is also an increase in the percentages of the knowledge levels 3, 4 and 5. But the increase is slightly lower. Level 3 has increased from 6.5% to 12.5%, level 4 from 9.8% to 10.9% and level 5 from 10.3% to 23.4%. Thus, overall the collaborative output has led to higher increases of levels 3, 4 and 5 of the VKS (representing known

Table 8.5 VKS post-test scores of the +Output group in collaborative and individual conditions

(A) VKS knowledge levels	Collaborative		Individual	
	n	%	*n*	%
1	4	2.2	5	2.7
2	87	47.3	93	50.5
3	31	16.8	23	12.5
4	22	12.0	20	10.9
5	40	21.7	43	23.4
Total	184	100.0	184	100.0
	p = ns		p = ns	
(B) Summary				
Unknown	91	49.5	98	53.3
Known	93	50.5	86	46.7
Total	184	100.0	184	100.0
	p = ns		p = ns	

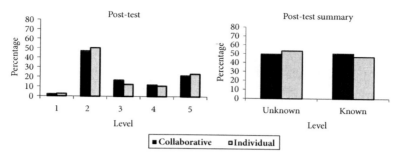

Figure 8.5 VKS post-test scores of the +output groups in the collaborative and individual conditions.

knowledge) and higher decreases in levels 1 and 2 (representing no knowledge) from the pre-test to the post-test than the individual output (see Section B of Table 8.5 and Figure 8.5 for the post-test summary). But the chi-square tests showed that the differences were not statistically significant.

Discussion and conclusion

The purpose of this study was to examine the role of output in learning English phrasal verbs. The study also examined whether producing output collaboratively subsequent to input had any differential effects on learning the target words in comparison to producing output individually.

The first question concerned whether learners who were involved in producing output in addition to receiving input showed greater increase in their knowledge of the target verbs than those who received input only. The answer to this question was affirmative. The results clearly showed that learners who received input and then performed output tasks developed knowledge of the target phrasal verbs significantly more than those who received the same input but did not have opportunities for output. A closer examination of the significant difference in the knowledge levels of the target words between the +output group and the –output group revealed that the opportunity for output not only familiarized more learners with the target phrasal verbs but also facilitated the learning of such words to an extent that more learners could produce semantically and syntactically correct sentences using the target words, as revealed by the VKS tests. The conscious reflection on the target words during output activities seemed to encourage learners to become more aware of these language forms. These findings suggest a facilitative role for output in learning L2 lexical forms, particularly L2 phrasal verbs. Theoretically, the findings contribute to the debate over the role of input and output in L2 acquisition (DeKeyser and Sokalski 1996; Krashen 1985; Swain 2005; VanPatten 2002), suggesting that output may not only contribute importantly to L2 development (Izumi 2002, 2003b; Izumi and Bigelow 2000), but may also provide learning opportunities beyond those provided by input.

The findings also showed that collaborative tasks that entailed co-production of language improved task performance in terms of the accurate production of output. These findings are consistent with Nabei's (1996) and Lapkin et al.'s (2002) studies, which found evidence for L2 learners' progress in their accurate use of the target forms when they worked on output tasks collaboratively. In addition, a comparison of the learners' pre-test and post-test scores also showed that the collaborative output led to more improved knowledge of the phrasal verbs than the individual output. However, the difference was not statistically significant.

One reason for this non-significant result could be related to our small sample size. In statistics, there is always a relationship between the number of the learners in the study and the probability of getting significant findings (Nassaji 2012). The second reason could be related to the quality of the interaction during collaboration. Although there was collaboration, the quality may not have been rich enough to contribute to significant gains of knowledge. This interpretation has important implications for collaborative work in L2 classrooms and confirms the suggestions by many L2 researchers that collaborative learning does not always guarantee increased gain of knowledge (Johnson and Johnson 1994; Nassaji and Swain 2000; Nassaji and Tian 2010; Storch 2001, 2002). Previous studies have shown that for collaborative work to be successful, it has to be able to lead to the kind of scaffolding needed for knowledge construction and language development (Nassaji and Swain 2000; Storch 2002). One way of ensuring this to happen is by carefully designing the group work so that it can generate adequate scaffolding. Another way to ensure effective collaboration is to train learners how to do so (Johnson and Johnson 1994). In the present study, although we attempted to make sure that the learners collaborate effectively by providing them with adequate instruction, we did not have an elaborate training session. We suggest that future research on collaborative output should employ a well-designed training session prior to the research so that learners know how to collaborate with peers when solving language-related problems together.

It should be noted that our study has other limitations that should be considered when interpreting its findings and their implications. First, as stated earlier, the study used a small sample size and also focused on a limited number of English phrasal verbs. These problems can limit the generalizability of the findings. Also, in this study, we analysed the data by grouping all the phrasal verbs together and did not conduct a word-by-word analysis. Given the fact that phrasal verbs may be different in terms of their semantic and syntactic structures, it is worthwhile to carry out further analyses looking at the learner's performance with respect to each of the individual phrasal verbs. Future research should also investigate the effectiveness of collaborative output for other linguistic forms. In this study, the focus was on phrasal verbs. Also there is a need to conduct similar studies with different student populations at different language proficiency levels. This study involved low-intermediate learners. As discussed earlier, many cases of interaction that occurred between learners were simple and brief. Since they were low-intermediate learners, the lack of quality negotiation might be due to the learners' limited linguistic competence to fully extend their discussion in the target language. Future research can examine the role of output in learning language forms among more advanced learners.

References

Celce-Murcia, M. and Larsen-Freeman, D. (1999), *The Grammar Book: An ESL/EFL Teacher's Course* (2nd edn). Boston, MA: Heinle & Heinle.

Dagut, M. and Laufer, B. (1985), 'Avoidance of phrasal verbs: A case for contrastive analysis'. *Studies in Second Language Acquisition*, 7, 73–9.

de Bot, K. (1996), 'The psycholinguistics of the output hypothesis'. *Language Learning*, 46, 529–55.

DeKeyser, R. (1997), 'Beyond explicit rule learning: Automatizing second language morphosyntax'. *Studies in Second Language Acquisition*, 19, 195–221.

— (2007), 'Situating the concept of practice', in R. DeKeyser (ed.), *Practicing in a Second Language: Perspectives from Applied Linguistics and Cognitive Psychology*. New York: Cambridge University Press, pp. 1–18.

DeKeyser, R. and Sokalski, K. (1996), 'The differential role of comprehension and production practice'. *Language Learning*, 46, 613–42.

Dulay, H., Burt, M., and Krashen, S. (1982), *Language Two*. New York: Oxford University Press.

Ellis, R. (2008), *The Study of Second Language Acquisition* (2nd edn). Oxford: Oxford University Press.

Harley, B. and Swain, M. (1984), 'The interlanguage of immersion students and its implications for second language teaching', in A. Davies, C. Criper, and A. P. R. Howatt (eds), *Interlanguage*. Edinburgh, Scotland: Edinburgh University Press, pp. 291–311.

Hu, H. M. and Nassaji, H. (2012), 'Ease of inferencing, learner inferential strategies, and their relationship with the retention of word meanings inferred from context'. *Canadian Modern Language Review/La Revue canadienne des langues vivantes*, 68, 54–77.

Izumi, S. (2002), 'Output, input enhancement and the noticing hypothesis: An experimental study on ESL relativization'. *Studies in Second Language Acquisition*, 24, 541–77.

— (2003a), 'Comprehension and production processes in second language learning: In search of the psycholinguistic rationale of the output hypothesis'. *Applied Linguistics*, 24, 168–96.

— (2003b), 'Processing difficulty in comprehension and production of relative clauses by learners of English as a second language'. *Language Learning*, 53, 285–323.

Izumi, S. and Bigelow, M. (2000), 'Does output promote noticing and second language acquisition?'. *TESOL Quarterly*, 34, 239–78.

Izumi, S., Bigelow, M., Fujiwara, M., and Fearnow, S. (1999), 'Testing the output hypothesis: Effects of output on noticing and second language acquisition'. *Studies in Second Language Acquisition*, 21, 421–52.

Johnson, D. W. and Johnson, R. J. (1994), *Learning Together and Alone: Cooperative, Competitive, and Individualistic Learning* (4th edn). Englewood Cliffs, NJ: Prentice Hall.

Kowal, M. and Swain, M. (1994), 'Using collaborative language production tasks to promote students' language awareness'. *Language Awareness*, 3, 73–93.

Krashen, S. (1981), *Second Language Acquisition and Second Language Learning*. Oxford: Oxford University Press.

— (1985), *The Input Hypothesis: Issues and Implications*. Oxford: Pergamon Press.

LaPierre, D. (1994), 'Language output in a cooperative learning setting: Determining its effects on second language learning'. Unpublished MA thesis, OISE, University of Toronto, Toronto.

Lapkin, S., Hart, D., and Swain, M. (1991), 'Early and middle french immersion programs – french-language outcomes'. *Canadian Modern Language Review*, 48, 11–40.

Lapkin, S. and Swain, M. (2000), 'Task outcomes: A focus on immersion students' use of pronominal verbs in their writing'. *Canadian Journal of Applied Linguistics*, 3, 7–22.

Lapkin, S., Swain, M., and Smith, M. (2002), 'Reformulation and the learning of french pronominal verbs in a canadian french immersion context'. *Modern Language Journal*, 86, 485–507.

Nabei, T. (1996), 'Dictogloss: Is it an effective language learning task?'. *Working Papers in Educational Linguistics*, 12, 59–74.

Nassaji, H. (2003), 'L2 vocabulary learning from context: Strategies, knowledge sources, and their relationship with success in L2 lexical inferencing'. *TESOL Quarterly*, 37, 645–70.

— (2004), 'The relationship between depth of vocabulary knowledge and l2 learners' lexical inferencing strategy use and success'. *Canadian Modern Language Review*, 61, 107–34.

— (2012), 'Statistical significance tests and result generalizability: Issues, misconceptions and a case for replication', in G. Porte (ed), *Replication Research in Applied Linguistics and Second Language Research*. Cambridge: Cambridge University Press, pp. 92–115.

Nassaji, H. and Hu, H. M. (2012), 'The relationship between task-induced involvement load and learning new words from context'. *International Review of Applied Linguistics in Language Teaching*, 50, 69–86.

Nassaji, H. and Swain, M. (2000), 'Vygotskian perspective on corrective feedback in L2: The effect of random versus negotiated help on the learning of English articles'. *Language Awareness*, 9, 34–51.

Nassaji, H. and Tian, J. (2010), 'Collaborative and individual output tasks and their effects on learning English phrasal verbs'. *Language Teaching Research*, 14, 397–419.

Paribakht, S. and Wesche, M. (1993), 'Reading comprehension and second language development in a comprehension-based ESL program'. *TESL Canada Journal*, 11, 9–29.

Skehan, P. (1998), *A Cognitive Approach to Language Learning*. Oxford: Oxford University Press.

Storch, N. (2001), 'How collaborative is pair work? ESL tertiary students composing in pairs'. *Language Teaching Research*, 5, 29–53.

— (2002), 'Relationships formed in dyadic interaction and opportunity for learning'. *International Journal of Educational Research*, 37, 305–22.

Swain, M. (1985), 'Communicative competence: Some rules of comprehensible input and comprehensible output in its development', in S. Gass and C. Madden (eds), *Input in Second Language Acquisition*. Rowley, MA: Newbury House, pp. 235–53.

— (1993), 'The output hypothesis: Just speaking and writing aren't enough'. *Canadian Modern Language Review*, 50, 158–64.

— (1995), 'Three functions of output in second language learning', in H. G. Widdowson, G. Cook, and B. Seidlhofer (eds), *Principle and Practice in Applied Linguistics: Studies in Honour of H. G. Widdowson*. Oxford: Oxford University Press, pp. 125–44.

— (2005), 'The output hypothesis: Theory and research', in E. Hinkel (ed), *Handbook on Research in Second Language Teaching and Learning*. Mahwah, NJ: Lawrence Erlbaum Associates, pp. 471–83.

Swain, M. and Lapkin, S. (1995), 'Problems in output and the cognitive-processes they generate: A step towards second language-learning'. *Applied Linguistics*, 16, 371–91.

— (2001), 'Focus on form through collaborative dialogue: Exploring task effects', in M. Bygate, P. Skehan, and M. Swain (eds), *Researching Pedagogic Tasks: Second Language Learning, Teaching and Testing*. Harlow: Pearson Education, pp. 99–118.

— (2002), 'Talking it through: Two french immersion learners' response to reformulation'. *International Journal of Educational Research*, 37, 285–304.

VanPatten, B. (2002), 'Processing instruction: An update'. *Language Learning*, 52, 755–803.

Wajnryb, R. (1990), *Grammar Dictation*. Oxford: Oxford University Press.

Wesche, M. and Paribakht, S. (1996), 'Assessing second language vocabulary knowledge: Depth versus breadth'. *Canadian Modern Language Review*, 53, 13–40.

Yan, L. and Yoshinori, J. F. (2004), 'Avoidance of phrasal verbs: The case of chinese learners of English'. *Language Learning*, 54, 193–226.

Appendix 1

The 16 Phrasal Verbs Used in This Study

1. move on
2. pay off
3. blow away
4. be into something
5. get behind
6. hang out
7. catch up
8. take off
9. run into
10. ask out
11. freak out
12. kick out
13. work out
14. get along
15. break up
16. grow up

Appendix 2

VKS Elicitation Scale Self-Report Categories
Directions: Choose one answer for sentences 1–3. If you answer number 5, please answer number 4 as well.

Hang out

1. I don't remember having seen this word before.
2. I have seen this word before, but I don't know what it means.
3. I have seen this word before, and I think it means _____ (synonym or translation)
4. I know this word. It means _____ (synonym or translation).
5. I can use this word in a sentence: (write a sentence) _____

_____

_____.

9

Raising Language Awareness for Learning and Teaching L3 Grammar

Tanja Angelovska and Angela Hahn
University of Munich (LMU)

Abstract:

As the consciousness about certain grammar forms and rules often relies on learners' prior language knowledge, among many other factors, there is a need for exploring the roles of language awareness in the process of L3 grammar learning.

The aim of our empirical study is to illustrate ways of successful language awareness raising in one-to-one (teacher-learner) language reflection sessions (LRSs) conducted over a period of 5 months in a face-to-face setting. The aim of the language reflection sessions is to help learners become aware of particular language problems they had encountered during the L3 writing. To achieve this, we analyse the performance of the language teacher when identifying concrete instances where opportunities to raise language awareness were met and/or missed and by looking at L3 learners' ways of reflecting on grammar.

We base our empirical analyses on two types of data: text writing from the L3 learners and corresponding language reflection sessions in which learners reflect on their language used in the written texts.

Our results show clear evidence that L3 learners were able to recognize and make conscious use of cross-linguistic similarities and differences as seen through their meta-linguistic comments, a crucial component of a successful discovery-based method of intelligent guessing (MIG). Implications are provided for the teaching and learning of L3 grammar in one-to-one tutoring. The implications are transferrable to other L3 grammar instruction contexts.

Introduction

Our interest is the teacher's raising language awareness for learners of L3 (third language, i.e., second foreign language) grammar[1] during language reflection sessions (LRSs). We focus on the teachers' tools and learners' work with their own interlanguage in the process of acquiring L3 grammar.

A lot of thinking has been done concerning grammar teaching in recent years, and suggestions have been offered ranging from propositions to abandon it along the lines of CLT, to dedicating a very small amount of the curriculum to grammar (Pica 2000) or to focusing on the teaching of grammar (Nassaji 2000). Many researchers have been trying to find solutions to how grammar should be taught with one main aim in mind: teach – so that grammar can be learnt (Benati 2013). It is beyond the scope of this study to discuss all the differing opinions in terms of grammar teaching approaches. We aim to present a theoretical review and a component analysis of our proposed MIG.

Background and motivation

Background for the MIG

We acknowledge the importance of three grammar teaching approaches developed within the SLA field upon which we base our MIG: Ellis and Gaies's 'Grammar Discovery Approach' (1998), Pienemann and Keßler's 'Interlanguage Approach' (2011) and 'Language Awareness Raising' Approach.

Ellis and Gaies (1998)'s **grammar-discovery approach** focuses on teaching explicit knowledge (i.e. knowledge about grammar) by providing learners with appropriate input illustrating the grammatical feature. Ideally, learners analyse their own output and discover how the feature/rule works by communicating about the grammar. His approach (Ellis and Gaies 1998) includes the following steps:

1. Exposure to input: learners are provided with the correct input to process for meaning
2. Focus on the target grammatical feature: listening for a second time, with the aim of noticing

3. Understand the rule: using the data to arrive at how the rule works
4. Error-identification task: checking whether the learner has understood the rule
5. Practice: using the correct grammatical structure, that is, production of output

In Ellis's approach, noticing (2) is the prerequisite for understanding (3) to take place. According to Schmidt (1990), **noticing** refers to any conscious registration of a form, but not necessarily with any meaning attached to it, and it is an essential requirement for an acquisition to happen (Swain 1998: 66).

The core elements of the Pienemann and Keßler's 'Interlanguage Approach' are the trajectories of interlanguage development. The interlanguage approach proposes predictable paths for all learners of a foreign language. Keßler and Plesser claim that 'if the teacher knows about the current state of interlanguage development of the learners s/he is in position to support each learner in the EFL classroom according to her/his individual state of the target language' (2011: 43). To compensate for the difficulties associated with determining whether learners are ready to acquire a certain grammatical feature or not, we propose that on the one hand, raising language awareness of L3 grammar may speed up the process of becoming 'ready' and on the other hand, it may help the learner to become 'aware to acquire', that is, being prepared to acquire.

As the L3 learners's prior languages play an important role in the learning of the target L3 grammar, terms which are important for the discussion of our results are **consciousness raising** (CR) and **language awareness** (LA), often used interchangeably, that is, even to define one another and hence can be said to be inherently compatible. Language awareness is understood here as 'a mental attribute which develops through paying motivated attention to language in use' (Bolitho et al. 2003: 251).

Another close term to LA is the term **meta-linguistic awareness** (MLA), defined by Thomas (1988: 531) as 'an individual's ability to focus attention on language as an object in and of itself, to reflect upon language, and to evaluate it'. Another concept important for the current study is **cross-linguistic awareness** (CLA), which we define as 'a mental ability which develops through focusing attention on and reflecting upon language(s) in use and through establishing similarities and differences among the languages in one's multilingual mind' using Bolitho et al.'s and Thomas's definitions of LA and MLA.

When attempting to figure out how an L3 language works, the learner has to exploit the available linguistic relationships between her/his prior languages or s/he is 'curious about grammatical relationships they have observed between the target language and their own language' (Seliger 1983: 181). Ó Laoire, Burke and Haslam (2000: 53) point out that there is evidence that learners 'consciously or subconsciously draw on various sources of previous language learning in all subsequent language learning'. In a number of studies, L3 learners whose L1 is typologically unrelated to the L2 and/or L3 tended to transfer knowledge from their L2 (Hufeisen 1991; Cenoz 2001; Angelovska and Hahn 2012). Such results clearly call for changes in the L3 teaching pedagogies of all domains.

In this line, the number of empirical studies dealing with the teaching and learning processes of L3 grammar is rather limited (with the exception of Kemp 2011). The call for an inclusion of 'entdeckendes Lernen [learning through discovery] by raising the students' learning awareness' emerged in the 1990s (Chamot and O'Malley 1994: 388). This was reinforced in 2008 by Jessner's suggestion 'to develop strategies for solving problems resulting from the variety of languages' (Jessner 2008: 45).

It is our aim to fill this gap without working on the target language in isolation, but by drawing learners' attention to features of their languages' repertoire through MIG, which builds upon existing SLA approaches by combining (e.g. exposure to learner's own output) and modifying elements from them (e.g. the 'error identification task' by Ellis and Gaies 1998) and adding new components specific for the process of L3 grammar learning.

The MIG

Under the MIG, we understand a process of a parallel series of challenging and understanding how the target language functions by discovering gaps in one's own output through interlanguage monitoring. The language teacher and the L3 learner engage themselves in an inductive guessing language play with clearly defined three-fold roles: the teacher having the role of a detector, setter of challenges and hint-giver; and the learner, of a thinker, decision-maker and responder. The attempt is to raise LA by exploiting all the means available, such as contrastive elements in L1, L2 and L3. The MIG stages are:

1. Exposing the learner to his/her own output: learners are provided with their raw output and challenged to find gaps
2. Focusing on the target grammatical feature: strengthening associations and divergences across learner's languages

3. Understanding the rule: using the data to understand how the rule works
4. Further challenging: checking whether learners have understood the rule
5. Decision-making: confirming the discovered rule by strengthening the learner's CLA and/or by providing explicit information

Research questions

The aim of this study is two-fold. First, we aim at analysing the way in which third-language learners reflect on L3 grammar learning through their meta-linguistic comments. Second, we analyse teacher's approaches when identifying concrete instances where opportunities to raise language awareness were met and/or missed. The research goals of this study are framed in the following questions:

(Q1): How do L3 learners at all proficiency levels discover gaps in L3 grammar knowledge?
The sub questions:

– Do L3 learners recognize and make conscious use of cross-linguistic similarities and differences?
– What kind of meta-linguistic comments do L3 learners express when reflecting on their L3 grammar?

(Q2): How does the teacher meet or miss opportunities to raise learner's awareness for L3 grammar?
The sub questions:

– Which concrete instances ('success stories' and 'failed attempts') can be traced in the process of raising awareness?
– What are the components of MIG?

Method

Participants

We report data from 13 L3 learners (see appendices, Table 9.1) of English, aged 20–25 years, with various L1s, at different L3 proficiency levels, according to the Common European Framework of Reference for Languages (http://www.coe.int/t/dg4/linguistic/Cadre1_en.asp), and a constant variable of L2 German acquired before their target L3 English. They all differ in two variables: the type of their L1s (five speakers with L1 Russian, three with L1 Polish and the remaining five with L1 Bulgarian, Croatian, Ukrainian, French and Portuguese) and the L3 proficiency level (three students at A2 level: TN, SA, TD; four at B1 level: NI, LK, MP, AM; five at B2: PV, MK, OC, WS; and one learner at C1 level: SB). German has been the dominant language for all of them, and they study at a German university. The recruiting took place at the University Language Centre where they have learnt English. Participants were tested for their English level by using the Oxford Quick Placement Test (QPT). The testing for their English level was necessary in order to:

a. be provided with learning materials tailored to their level and
b. have a representative sample of learners at various proficiency levels to analyse the effects of the MIG.

Data collection

Thirteen L3 learners underwent individual sessions which lasted approximately 30 minutes. The data elicitation took 5 months. The language reflection sessions were conducted by a German female language coach, who was studying English Linguistics in order to become a teacher. The teacher had the task of fostering L3 grammar learning by raising language awareness interactively. The grammar aspects were carefully chosen according to the needs of each learner and based on the learner's previously submitted written assignment.

The prerequisite for taking part in the LRS was to have previously written and submitted a text in L3 English. Learners were allowed to freely choose what they were going to write about. All 13 written assignments underwent a double correction and plagiarism check to ensure the validity of the data. Learners' produced texts were taken as interlanguage analysis material for the LRS. This is in line with the introspective research method 'Stimulated Recall' approach which accesses participants' reflections on mental processes (Mackey and Gass 2005).

The average number of words per written assignment was 306 (ranging from 142 to 533 words per assignment). Table 9.1 shows the number of words the L3 learners wrote in their written assignments, their L1 languages and their L3 levels. The researchers acted only as facilitators by carefully choosing the L3 grammar aspects that the language teacher was supposed to focus on during the LRS. The choice was based on a thorough analysis which included a look at cross-linguistic transfer phenomena and interlanguage developmental features. For detailed procedure of this analysis (see Angelovska and Hahn 2012).

Data analysis procedure

The 13 sessions (390 minutes) were transcribed, coded and analysed using the software MaxQda. The qualitative data analysis in this study applies to the interpretation of the language reflection texts. Before analysing the data, it was made interpretable, that is, analysable by its conversion from spoken files to texts. In this procedure, the following three processes were undertaken: transcription of the LRSs, coding and categorizing of the transcribed texts used for data analysis. We coded the data by assigning to words, passages and/or longer paragraphs patterns which characterize the essence of the coded part. After the second cycle of coding which also grouped the multiple components of the same data bits, data was arranged systematically. This process of codifying data was two-cycled and done by two researchers, so that our data could be categorized. (For more information on qualitative data analysis, see Miles and Huberman 1994; Flick 2009). As far as credibility of our data is concerned, we followed some of the strategies mentioned in Flick 2009: 383–400) to increase the credibility:

- data was coded, analysed and interpreted by two researchers
- peer-debriefing with other colleagues not involved in the research was included in order to disclose blind spots
- we included an analysis of the negative cases as well in the sense of analytic induction

Results

Learners' profiles

In the following, we present the profiles of each of the 13 learners. We determine success by the outcome of the language reflection session, that is, if the L3 learner finds about their own cross-linguistic transfer as judged by their meta-linguistic comments and/or explanation of rules or self-interpretation about the functioning of the language.

Student SA (with L1 Croatian and at L3 level A2) experiences difficulties in the L3 use due to the transfer of both L1 and L2 during her L3 production, as she reported. She constantly activates (even 'online' during the language reflection session) her L2. However, this learner is aware of her L2 activation and reports of having activated German very often when speaking as well as when writing in L3 English. Student SA is also aware of the L1 grammar rules and the fact that Croatian does not have any articles but one determines the gender from the nouns by the word ending. She is a very ambitious student who tends to be a perfectionist by reporting that she is very often aware of her 'mistakes' and tends to correct her own output, which is a sign of a very high level of self-monitoring.

Student TD with L1 Russian at L3 proficiency level A2 has seven occurrences of awareness of transfer of L1 grammar rules into her L3 English. Based on her self-reports during the LRS, she has dealt intensively with comparing her three available 'grammars' and has even established some similarities between them (Transcript 1).

> TD: erm ich ich ich hab einfach so so aehnlichkeit festgestellt. in grammatik. im russischen und englischen. <LNru> x </LNru>, <LNeng> she </LNeng>, sie also sie

Transcript 1. Self-report by student TD regarding L1 and L3 grammar similarities

On another occasion, student TD informs her teacher of the differences she has realized regarding morphological word building rules in L1 versus her L2 and L3 languages. When searching for the correct preposition, she realizes that the same kind of preposition is used in German. On another occasion, she explains (Transcript 2) that in her L1, one can verbalize the noun in order to express the action of having a lunch with a verb (Russian verb: пообедать, substantive: обед). Regarding success or failure in raising language awareness, this learner is only provided with explicit information on three occasions during the LRS, which proves unhelpful to her. What is helpful to her is a warning (about having a pronoun) with explicit information and a question given by the teacher ('What kind of a park is it?'). The learner then proves able to deliver the correct answer 'a noun preceded by a definite article, that is, "the park".

> TD: ja erm also bei uns ist das nicht so i have, sondern diese li len oder lunch oder mittagessen wird als ein verb gemacht.

Transcript 2. Self-report by student TD

Student TN with L1 Ukrainian at L3 level A2 displays successful language awareness raising in four cases. She compares grammatical features with other languages four times. Repetition of the word containing the mistake by the teacher did not help her in raising awareness. She proves rather successful when the teacher uses a warning followed by explicit information about a certain grammar aspect. On two occasions, she also expresses grammatical awareness about parts of speech.

Student NI with L1 Russian at L3 proficiency level B1 expresses grammatical awareness about the parts of speech, and she is very aware of the grammar rules regarding word-order rules of the L2 and L1, which she transfers into her L3. Similarly, this learner is aware of the grammar properties of her L1 Russian and as a consequence, she thinks that this difference causes problems in her L2 (and L3, since she does not have a basis on which to make cross-linguistic associations that may be helpful).

Student AM with L2 Russian at L3 proficiency level B1 displays grammatical awareness of the infinitive in English and its difference to her L1 Russian. Regarding the awareness of the L2 influence on her L3, she says that she is referring back to her L2 when having to produce in L3 (translation from her L2 into her L3). On one occasion, this learner self-corrects herself while reading her 'erroneous' sentence, that is, she shows proof of 'interlanguage monitoring'. However, interventions on the side of the teacher are successful only when presented in the form of a paralinguistic sign, that is, sighing and showing hesitance. This 'warning' makes the learner think and come up with the correct answer, which concerns the use of the collocation 'to have an influence on' (Transcript 3).

> AM: but nowadays, English influences it.
> Int.: mhm. yeah.
> AM: or HAS an influence on it.
> Int.: on it. exactly.
> AM: @
> Int.: so, can you write it erm down here?
> AM: okay.
> Int.: because erm that's actually that's wonderful, you discovered your own mistake.@

Transcript 3. MIG with student AM

Student MP, with L1 Polish at L3 proficiency level B1, displays awareness of the uncontrolled activation of her first language whenever she tries to produce something in L3 English. When retelling her experiences of learning English to her teacher in L2 German, she uses the L3 word 'pronunciation' at the end of her sentence, although that part of the conversation is in German. On the other hand, she also shows knowledge of the verb tense system in her L1 Polish as well as about the non-existence of articles and the attention to word endings as 'signs' of gender. On six occasions, she shows that she is aware of her L1 activation in L3 production. When the teacher provides her with explicit information only, she is not able to raise her language awareness. Neither raising intonation of the 'erroneous' part nor the teacher's attempts to guess the problem help her develop awareness. But when the teacher asks her to compare the particular sentence with her L1 and to provide a translation from her L1, student MP begins to trace differences and realize what she needs.

Student LK with L1 Russian at English B1 proficiency level shows awareness of word-order rules in her L1. She reports that she is also quite aware of her L2 influence on her L3, of its activation and her thinking in L2 for all of the time and of no need to rely on her L1. On two occasions, she even activates her L2 online while interacting with the teacher, which is a confirmation for what she has reported herself. Student LK reports of translating texts from L1 into L2 and then from L2 into L3 when being given writing task in L3 English, which is contradictory in terms of her as reporting 'not having to rely on her L1'. However, the translation strategy she uses might be a specific strategy common for multilingual learners. Regarding her success stories, on two occasions, when the teacher sets a question wanting her to make a guess about detecting whether 'something is wrong', the teacher supports her by giving explicit direction about which part of the sentence is problematic and by explicit information about what would not go, but the teacher does not reveal the correct choice. Learner LK realizes because of being given the clue 'third person', meaning she needs a verb in the present simple in the if-sentence (Transcript 4).

> Int.: and if you look at that sentence, erm can you detect something in this?
> LK6: @@
> Int.: the if-sentence. let's only look at the if-sentence.
> LK6: on the end mh erm (a comma)?
> Int.: mmh no.
> LK6: comma.
> Int.: er i'm i'm not rea er i'm looking at the verb.
> LK6: if would lie er @
> Int.: mhmh, no. if and would never go together. that's erm erm
> LK6: if

Int.: look at the verb.

LK6: one person

Int.: one person is? what is that? erm it's

LK6: third person

Int.: yeah.

LK6: er singular, lies.

Int.: mhm, exactly.

Transcript 4. MIG with student LK

Student MK with L1 Russian and L3 level B2 is very successful in using the introduced MIG to realize what kind of correct grammatical item she needs. Hence, the teacher just asks a question about 'what type of word is it? if you look at <to work>?', student MK realizes that – as 'work' is a verb-, she needs the adverb 'diligently' and not the adjective 'diligent'. Another useful intelligent guessing is the teacher's question 'Int.: (is that) can you think of anything else how you might construct that sentence?' upon which the learner provides a correct construction using the correct preposition. Similarly, the request to reformulate the sentence results in correct language production.

   Student WS, with L1 Polish and L3 English at B2 proficiency level, displays grammatical awareness of how her languages function and differ in their constructions. When asked to give a translation into her L1, she realizes that she has used a noun in her L3 corresponding sentence instead of an adjective (which would have been correct). A request to translate the produced L3 sentence into her L2 helps her to analyse the similarities in her two sentences (the translated one in her L2 and the L3 produced one) and realize that the word order of both is identical, that is, German. Later, the confirmation that this approach works for her is given by her self-realization while reading her own L3 produced text aloud. At the end of the sentence she stops saying 'NO' and the teacher gives her a warning. She is able to detect the correct word order immediately, which means that the 'translation request' with a follow-up analysis proves beneficial for her.

   Student ST with L1 Bulgarian at English proficiency level B2 is aware of L1 influence in her L3 production, and in her case, an intelligent approach is unsuccessful although it contains a lot hints, questions, translation requests and warnings. There is also no trace of any grammatical awareness during the LRS, except a statement about the non-existence of articles in her L1 and awareness of a literal translation of an idiom from her L1 into her L3 English. However, she displays a good deal of semantic meta-linguistic awareness.

Student PV, with L1 Portuguese at L3 proficiency level B2, is distinct from all other learners being especially aware of the activation of the other languages in L3 grammar production. She activates her L2, German on 15 occasions and also expresses clearly that she is very well aware of and concerned about her 'multiple interferences' from all the languages at her disposal. On one occasion, she makes a phonological comparison between L2 German and L1 Portuguese. Otherwise, no success stories of awareness-raising can be traced based on the data we have from this student.

Student OC, with L1 Polish at B2 English proficiency level, is a student for whom MIG does not really work. She gives the impression of being in a hurry and approving everything the teacher explains through explicit information confirming that she has understood.

Student SB, with L1 French and the only student with the highest L3 proficiency level of C1, reports an awareness of her thinking in L2 and activating both her L1 and L2. When reflecting on her L3, she proves to be quick in realizing the gaps she is supposed to re-fill in her output and displays grammatical awareness of parts of speech. The request to associate a particular item with her L2 German does not prove really successful; however, when asked to translate another sentence into her L1 French, she realizes herself that the L3 English sentence is actually a literal translation from her L1, in which case the MIG with a translation-request component (transcript 5) proves very helpful to her. On other occasion, when she uses a singular instead of a plural noun, she is only given a warning with a direction that a word might be erroneous and she realizes where the 'gap' is. An open question in the form of whether she has any idea of what might be wrong in the particular sentence helps her to sharpen her grammatical awareness and come to the item she was supposed to 'notice' (Transcript 6). In eight cases, the MIG proves effective for this learner.

> Int.: erm how would you say it in French?
> SB: <LNfr> pour cette raison. @ c'est pourquoi. </LNfr>
> Int.:o:kay.
> SB: <LNde> also </LNde>, exactly translated from French. @

Transcript 5. MIG with a translation-request component

SB: <reading> erm concerning my education, i studied 1 year in <un> x </un>, in France, in a preparation class in order to prepare the (entry) <un> xxxx </un> course known as (institute) of politics studies. the core areas er are <un> xxx </un> politics, society and history and languages, however, my interest for other countries and everything which are related to it like the differences in <un> xxxx </un>, in the language, the culture, the values et cetera convinced me to study abroad. </reading>

> Int.: mhm. i'd like to look at this sentence as well. erm if you er look at the sentence,
>   any idea that there something might not be correct?
> SB: (8) which IS related?
> Int.: mhm. and why?
> SB: because everything is singular.

Transcript 6. MIG with an open question component

(B) Meta-linguistic comments in L3 grammar learning

In the process of raising language awareness and reflecting on L3 grammar, L3 learners make several types of grammatical meta-comments. The following of them were most frequent: awareness of word building rules, awareness of lack of articles in the L1, contrasting with other languages, awareness of word order and awareness of parts of speech. The sum of all occurrences is 50. Eight of the students make such meta-linguistic comments of various types with specific functions. Student NI proves to have made most of the comments: 11 occurrences of grammatical meta-linguistic awareness in total.

The following learners' meta-linguistic comments are traced: explicit deficit statement followed by an example, explicit deficit statement, example trial followed by an explicit deficit statement, search for alternatives and a reference to other languages. In order to understand how learners come to making meta-linguistic comments, one inevitably has to pay attention to how they are 'pushed' to give signs that their language awareness is 'on guard'. For this purpose, it is interesting to see first, how learners reflect on their interlanguage by monitoring it, and second, how they fail to show traces that their language awareness is working for them in the process of L3 grammar learning.

(B) Success stories versus failed language-awareness raising attempts

Our examination of all 13 learners and the material, of 6 hours of language reflection sessions, reveals instances where language awareness raising for learning L3 grammar has both been successful and instances where attempts to raise learner's awareness for learning L3 grammar have failed. Quantitative data reveals that there are 32 instances of success stories achieved by 9 L3 learners and 12 instances of failed attempts to raise language awareness emerging among

6 L3 learners. Clearly, some of the learners have displayed both successful and failed attempts.

Our qualitative analyses of the 'success stories' reveals that the following steps were taken by the teacher: detecting whether the learner knows which grammar aspect needs to be looked at through challenging the learner to guess, responding to first, second and third guessing trials by the learner, giving hints on which grammar aspect to focus on, pointing out, requesting an explanation and agreeing or disagreeing. The steps taken by the learner range from thinking, processing, guessing by reconstructing knowledge or self-reflection, translating or making cross-linguistic associations, testing the decisions made to decision-making. The way of being confronted with a challenge to the final decision made by the learner is accompanied by interlanguage monitoring, that is, the way in which the learner makes use of their individual interlanguage knowledge of the prior languages.

One example of the observed steps of a successful MIG sequence from our data entails the following steps:

1. The teacher begins with a 'detective' question making the student think whether there is something peculiar in the sentence. The student is laughing.
2. The teacher gives a specification/hint about which part of the sentence the learner should concentrate on. Student guesses (by asking whether a comma is missing).
3. The teacher responds to the guess. Learner gives a second try (a wrong one).
4. The teacher gives a third specification/hint narrowing the possible choices of the 'erroneous' part of the sentence. The learner reconstructs the 'if- sentence' again in a wrong way.
5. The teacher explains to her that the try she made is not possible at all. Learner sticks to the 'if' part thinking further.
6. The teacher intervenes by giving her a concrete help with pointing out the erroneous word of the sentence, which is the 'verb'. In the meantime, the learner realizes that the sentence deals with one person only.
7. The teacher goes on further with asking about the meaning of the one person. Learner confirms her realization by stating it is the third person.
8. The teacher agrees. Learner delivers the correct answer that the verb should be 'lies' (third-person singular).
9. The teacher confirms the correct answer.

Our analysis reveals that the failed attempts in raising language awareness happen due to teacher's quick reaction in immediately explaining what kind of a grammatical error the learner is dealing with or revealing to the learner the correct grammar choice. Another problem which hinders language awareness raising is the teacher's use of complex terminology (e.g. 'negation' and 'auxiliary verb') without having checked whether the learner understands the terms. Hence, we conclude that language awareness raising cannot happen if an opportunity is not given to the learner to discover the erroneous parts themselves.

(B) The components of MIG

We present our complete list with teacher-initiated hints that appeared to be helpful in applying MIG for L3 grammar learning and teaching, such as challenging questions, teacher-initiated requests for cross-linguistic comparisons, paralinguistic warnings and giving information through focusing the learner's attention on the grammatical element in question.

(a) Challenging questions (guessing and detecting)
- And if you look at that sentence, erm can you detect something in this?
- One person is . . .? What is that?
- Erm if you er look at the sentence, any idea that something might not be correct there?
- Okay, you hesitated with your voice here while reading the sentence, you stumbled across that sentence. Why?
- *Überlegen Sie, ob der so korrekt ist, oder ob da vielleicht was nicht ganz stimmt*/Think about whether this is correct like this or whether there might be something which is not correct.

(b) Teacher-initiated requests for cross-linguistic comparisons
- Request to reformulate (e.g. Can you think of anything else how you might construct that sentence?)
- Request to translate in one of the prior languages:
  o *Wenn Sie den Satz auf Deutsch formulieren würden, wie würde er dann heißen?*/If you express the same sentence in German, what would it be?
  o Can you translate that sentence into German, please?
  o How would you express that sentence in Russian?
- Request to contrast a particular L3 feature/occurrence with the L1 or L2 rule:
  o Would this rule be the same in your first language?

- o *Also siehst du da Ähnlichkeiten/Unterscheide zum Deutschen?*/So, can you see any similarities/differences with German?
- o *Sagt man es genauso in deiner Muttersprache?*/Would you say it like this in your first language, too?

(c) Paralinguistic warnings
- Silence, in the case when the learner was either hesitating or going into the wrong direction
- Paralinguistic warning sign of hesitation ('erm', 'hm' etc.)
- Repetition of a part of the sentence containing the problem (e.g. 'mhm hang on a second. er if we look at er the erm the second sentence')
- Repetition of the word containing the grammatical problem
- Warning expressions (e.g. be careful)
- Warning with a concrete hint of what to focus on (e.g. '*Sie müssen mal aufpassen, wenn Sie sich mal des Verb anschauen?*/You have to be careful, have a look at the verb?')
- Rising intonation, used to highlight the 'erroneous' word and to make the learner notice it

(d) Informing through focusing
- Giving directions to what to focus on ('look at the verb'; '*aber schau'n Sie sich vielleicht mal die Satzstellung an*'/Maybe you could have a look at the word order)
- Giving explicit information (e.g. *Das ist ein bestimmter Park, also brauchen wir was?*/It's a special/particular park, so what do we need?).

Discussion

(Q1): How do L3 learners at all proficiency levels discover gaps in L3 grammar knowledge?

Our first research question deals with finding the most successful way for L3 learners across proficiency levels in raising language awareness. The analyses of our transcribed data included tracing associations between the instances of 'success stories'/'failed attempts' and proficiency level of the L3 learner and observing the components of the IG approach which proved successful for raising language awareness. Thus, an analysis of the cases in which L3 learners are able to recognize and make conscious use of cross-linguistic similarities and differences and an analysis of their meta-linguistic comments was needed.

About 32 instances of success stories were classified as cases of MIG. These occurred at all four levels of the 13 learners: at A2 level, we have 5 cases of MIG among 2 learners; at B1 level, 6 cases of MIG among 3 learners; at B2 level, we have 8 cases among 3 learners and 13 cases for the one C1 learner. Clearly, MIG has an interesting effect rising from the lower to the higher proficiency level as observed by the number of instances.

The majority of learners (n = 10) have displayed grammatical awareness (31 instances) about word-building rules, lack of articles in the L1, word order and/or parts of speech. Our explanation of this result is that they were reflecting on their writing, in which skill grammatical problems are most obvious. In addition, the focus given by the teacher was a very influential one. The three learners (PV, OC and MK) who did not express any instances of grammatical awareness all share one L3 proficiency level (B2). The distribution of the number of instances of displayed grammatical awareness across language levels reveals the following: at level A2, there are 12 instances; at B1, there are 15 instances; at B2, 4 instances; and at C1, 1 instance. Hence, regarding grammatical awareness across levels, our results show that it has the form of an inverted-U shape. This can be explained by the limited grammar resources available to the lower level A2 and by the increased knowledge of grammar at the higher proficiency levels B2 and C1 and the expanded focus from grammar onto other lexical and stylistics devices.

Regarding the cross-linguistic comparisons of L3 learners, we have found that learners (n = 7) are not only aware of their L1 influence on their L3, but also of the influence of their L2. Moreover, we have obtained results of 13 occurrences, where 7 L3 learners contrast a particular grammar feature with other languages and instances, whereas other learners make references to their prior languages (n = 4), searching for alternatives from their prior languages (n = 4) and comparing the same feature with the identical feature of their prior languages (n = 4).

One of the most valuable results in our data is the analysis of the cross-linguistic connections and their position within the MIG. We have found that L3 learners with a high level of grammatical awareness made cross-linguistic connections right after the teacher initiated an interaction, that is, learners started their guessing procedure by finding out cross-linguistic associations across their available languages. In those cases where cross-linguistic connections and comparisons are a component of the process of guessing and discovering, it is always the case that the learner's expressed CLA is confirmed by the teacher in the end.

(Q2): How does the teacher meet or miss opportunities to raise learner's awareness for L3 grammar?

The role of the teacher is one of the most influential in MIG not in the sense of constructing the learning process as teacher-centred, but in the sense of initiating the L3 grammar learning process by providing a correct direction for the discovery process and by giving appropriate hints during the challenging. This ranges from guessing, detecting, initiating cross-linguistic comparisons, paralinguistic warning to informing through focusing.

In the whole process of 'intelligent guessing' in the entire data, the teacher's L1 (i.e. learners' L2) German was consistently and carefully used to raise L3 language awareness. With the use of the L2, which is in this case the *lingua franca* for the teacher and the learners, the practical obstacle of using L1 (which the teacher does not know) in teaching the target language is solved. On the other hand, through the teacher-initiated L2 requests for cross-linguistic comparisons, the teacher compensates for the fact that she is unlikely to be able to refer to all the various L1s that her students speak. Furthermore, within MIG, both the teacher and the learner exchange roles in that the teacher is being taught about a certain grammar aspect of the learner's L1 and the learner has gained the opportunity to inform the teacher about the L1 and ideally to compare cross-linguistically as a result.

A discussion of the success stories or the tools used is not productive if it is not accompanied by listing the reasons and giving useful suggestions of what could have been done differently. The missed opportunities range from the use of complex linguistic terminology the learner was not familiar with, direct flooding of the learner with theoretically explicit information to not being given any opportunity to discover language. On some occasions, the failed attempts were due to the use of unclear language, inappropriate terminology or incomplete explanations by the teacher. Even when the teacher started with a correct challenge requesting the learner to refer to her prior languages, but missed the opportunity to react appropriately to the given translation by 'pushing' the learner to find the cross-linguistic associations on their own, the attempt to raise CLA was not successful. A suitable example is the following: after responding to the teacher's request to give a sentence translation into German, the learner was confronted with the teacher's statement that the translated sentence was a 'literal translation from German'. Clearly, the learner could not do anything further with such a statement. Moreover, we do not have any proof that the learner really understood the parallel between the two statements, the original one and the literal translation of the erroneous interlanguage statement.

Conclusion

It was not long ago when Bono stated that 'gaining access to the mental processes and representations involved in cross-linguistic comparison remains a considerable challenge for researchers' (Bono 2011: 26). Through the introspection approach in this study, we have obtained clear evidence for students' language awareness regarding their cross-linguistic consultation when reflecting on L3 grammar. Several types of grammatical language awareness accompanied the cross-linguistic consultation.

Based on our analyses and observations of the teacher's approaches, we identified concrete instances where opportunities to raise language awareness were met and/or missed. The MIG proved to be successful in all its 32 identified instances occurring at all four represented L3 proficiency levels. The components of the MIG are different for the teacher and the learner. The teacher's role is to detect whether the learner knows which grammar aspect needs to be looked at through challenging to guess, to respond to first, second and third guessing trials by the learner, to give hints, to point out, to request for an explanation and to agree and/or disagree. These roles were realized through teacher-initiated hints, such as challenging questions, requests for cross-linguistic comparisons, paralinguistic warnings and determining the learner' focus.

The benefits of the MIG for our learners were numerous: students were made to think, to reconstruct existing knowledge, build upon, reflect on and make decisions based on previously tested cross-linguistic comparisons. Their insights grew, as they were explaining German or L1 grammar rules to their teacher. Hence, being asked to instruct the teacher on this by drawing similarities and finding differences gave them confidence to continue with the grammar learning process and a sense of empowerment (cf. Horst et al. 2010 for similar results found in a bilingual cross-linguistic awareness pedagogy).

Limitations and future directions

In every research design, some limitations are inherently involved. One of them is that we did not measure whether any particular kind of attempt taken by the teacher to raise language awareness would have any outcome on the L3 grammar learning.

We acknowledge the small sample size in our study ($n = 13$), but we did compensate for this limitation with the rich amount of data (we analysed transcriptions of 390 minutes and text productions of 3975 words).

We showed that the ability to link existing knowledge (in this case grammar knowledge of prior languages) is just one of the most important features of effective teaching approaches. Although this view of building upon existing knowledge has been neglected in language teaching in a way that many previous generations of teachers were instructed not to refer to the first language, it is now clear through our results that such a linkage is not detrimental in all cases. Making links to the learner's prior languages can only enrich the learning context. We hope that this direction will find its way into future third-language-learning environments. However, we are aware that this can happen only if teachers are made familiar with the goals of raising language awareness for L3 grammar.

We gained an understanding of aspects we need to consider in our further research. In this study, we only looked at the way L3 learners reflect on their interlanguage grammar. However, we are aware that we have to investigate the exact processing of the L3 grammar in the next phase by keeping learners' level and background languages constant within a more controlled experimental setting.

Acknowledgements

We would like to thank the participants from the Language Centre at the Ludwig Maximilians University of Munich in Germany. We are also grateful to the teacher (who wishes to remain anonymous) for her willingness to support this research and to the student research assistant, Caroline Klein, for transcribing one part of the research data.

Note

1 The teacher had the choice to decide on which grammatical aspects to focus on during the language reflection session due to the fact that learners had different needs. Since this study is not an experimental, but rather an empirical, we have decided to keep many options open for the teacher who was in charge of conducting the language reflection session.

References

Angelovska, T. and Hahn, A. (2012), 'Written L3 (English): transfer phenomena of L2 (German) lexical and syntactical properties', in D. Gabrys-Barker (ed), *Crosslinguistic Influences in Multilingual Language Acquisition*. Heidelberg: Springer, pp. 23–40.

Benati, A. (2013), *Issues in Second Language Teaching*. London: Equinox.

Bolitho, R., Carter, R., Hughes, R., Ivanic, R., Masuhara, H., and Tomlinson, B. (2003), 'Ten questions about language awareness'. *English Language Teaching Journal*, 49, (4), 251–9.

Bono, M. (2011), 'Crosslinguistic interaction and metalinguistic awareness in third language acquisition', in G. De Angelis and J.-M. Dewaele (eds), *New Trends in Crosslinguistic Influence and Multilingualism Research*. Bristol: Multilingual Matters, pp. 25–52.

Cenoz, J. (2001), 'The effect of linguistic distance, L2 status and age on crosslinguistic influence in third language acquisition', in J. Cenoz, B. Hufeisen, and U. Jessner (eds), *Crosslinguistic Influence in Third Language Acquisition*. Clevedon: Multilingual Matters, pp. 8–20.

Chamot, A. and O'Malley J. (1994), 'Language learner and learning strategies', in N. Ellis (ed), *Implicit and Explicit Learning of Languages*. London: Academic Press, pp. 371–92.

Ellis, R. and Gaies, S. (1998), *Impact Grammar*. Hong Kong: Longman.

Flick, U. (2009), *An Introduction to Qualitative Research* (4th edn). London/Thousand Oaks, CA/Dehli: Sage.

Horst, M., White, J., and Bell, P. (2010), 'First and second language knowledge in the language classroom'. *International Journal of Bilingualism*, 14, (3), 331–49.

Hufeisen, B. (1991), *English as First and German as Second Foreign Language. Empirical Investigation of Foreign Language Interaction*. Frankfurt: Peter Lang.

Jessner, U. (2008), 'Teaching third languages: findings, trends and challenges'. *Language Teaching*, 41, (1), 15–56.

Kemp, C. (2011), 'Strategic processing in grammar learning: do multilinguals use more strategies'. *International Journal of Multilingualism*, 4, 241–61.

Keßler, J.-U. and Plesser, A. (2011), *Teaching English Grammar. Standard Wissen Lehramt Englisch*. Paderborn: Schöningh/UTB.

Miles, M. and Huberman, A. (1994), *Qualitative Data Analysis: An Expanded Source Book* (2nd edn). Thousand Oaks, CA: Sage.

Mackey, A. and Gass, S. M. (2005), *Second Language Research: Methodology and Design*. Mahwah, NJ: Lawrence Erlbaum Associates.

Nassaji, H. (2000), 'Towards integrating form-focused instruction and communicative interaction in L2 classroom: some pedagogical possibilities'. *The Modern Language Journal*, 84, (2), 241–50.

Ó Laoire, M., Burke, M., and Haslam, M. (2000), 'From L2 to L3/4: an investigation of learners' metalinguistic awareness and learner strategies', *Teangeolas (Dublin)*, 38/39, 52–8.

Pica, T. (2000), 'Tradition and transition in English language teaching methodology'. *System*, 28, 1–18.

Pienemann, M. and Keßler, J.-U. (eds.) (2011), *Studying Processabilty Theory. An Introductory Textbook*. Amsterdam: John Benjamins.

Schmidt, R. (1990), 'The role of consciousness in second language learning'. *Applied Linguistics*, 11, 129–58.

— (1993), 'Awareness and second language acquisition'. *Annual Review of Applied Linguistics*, 13, 206–26.

Seliger, H. W. (1983), 'The language learner as linguist: of metaphors and realities'. *Applied Linguistics*, 4, (3), 178–91.

Spada, N. and Lightbown, P. M. (1993), 'Instruction and the development of questions in the L2 classroom'. *Studies in Second Language Acquisition*, 14, 205–21.

Swain, M. (1998), 'Focus on form through conscious reflection', in C. Doughty and J. Williams (eds), *Focus on Form in Classroom Second Language Acquisition*. Cambridge: Cambridge University Press, pp. 64–82.

Thomas, J. (1988), 'The role played by metalinguistic awareness in second- and third-language learning'. *Journal of Multilingual and Multicultural Development*, 9, 235–46.

Appendix

Table 9.1 L3 participants with L1s, L3 levels and number of words of written assignments

Student	L1	L3 level	Total number of words per learner
SA	Croatian	A2	174
TD	Russian	A2	533
TN	Ukrainian	A2	203
NI	Russian	B1	348
AM	Russian	B1	142
MP	Polish	B1	178
LK	Russian	B1	275
MK	Russian	B2	365
WS	Polish	B2	291
ST	Bulgarian	B2	386
PV	Portuguese	B2	239
OC	Polish	B2	331
SB	French	C1	510

Author Index

Subject Index